Charles Welch, John Wolfe Barry

History of the Tower Bridge and of Other Bridges Over the Thames

Charles Welch, John Wolfe Barry

History of the Tower Bridge and of Other Bridges Over the Thames

ISBN/EAN: 9783744650045

Printed in Europe, USA, Canada, Australia, Japan

Cover: Foto ©ninafisch / pixelio.de

More available books at **www.hansebooks.com**

HISTORY

OF

The Tower Bridge

AND OF OTHER BRIDGES OVER THE THAMES BUILT
BY THE CORPORATION OF LONDON.

Including an account of the Bridge House Trust
from the Twelfth Century, based on the Records of the
Bridge House Estates Committee.

BY

CHARLES WELCH, F.S.A.,

LIBRARIAN TO THE CORPORATION OF LONDON.

With a description of the Tower Bridge by

J. WOLFE BARRY, C.B., M. INST. C.E.,

ENGINEER OF THE BRIDGE.

And an Introduction by

THE REV. CANON BENHAM, B.D., F.S.A.

PREPARED UNDER THE DIRECTION OF THE BRIDGE HOUSE ESTATES COMMITTEE
AND ALBERT J. ALTMAN, CHAIRMAN.

LONDON
SMITH, ELDER AND CO.,
1894.

BRIDGE HOUSE ESTATES COMMITTEE.

Sir ALBERT JOSEPH ALTMAN, *Chairman.*

ALDERMEN.

Sir WILLIAM LAWRENCE, Knt.
Sir FRANCIS WYATT TRUSCOTT, Knt.
Sir JOSEPH SAVORY, Bart., M.P.

Sir JOSEPH RENALS, Knt.
Lt.-Col. HORATIO DAVID DAVIES.
ALFRED JAMES NEWTON, Esq.

FRANK GREEN, Esq.

COMMONERS.

PEARSE MORRISON, Esq.
WILLIAM HENRY PANNELL, Esq., F.C.A.,
  F.S.S.
JAMES GALLAHER, Esq., F.R.A.S.
DANIEL GREENAWAY, Esq.
DANIEL ROBERT DALE, Esq., F.R.I.B.A.
FREDERICK PRAT ALLISTON, Esq.
WILLIAM HENRY WILLIAMSON, Esq.
EDWARD COUCHMAN BREDELL, Esq.
DAVID BURNETT, Esq., F.S.I.
WILLIAM THORNBURGH BROWN, Esq., Dep.
RICHARD CLARENCE HALSE, Esq., Deputy.
GEORGE JOSEPH WOODMAN, Esq.
SIDNEY MATTHEWS, Esq.
ALFRED THOMAS LAYTON, Esq., J.P.
ROBERT HARGREAVES ROGERS, Esq., Dep.

JOHN JAMES BADDELEY, Esq.
GEORGE HARRIS HAYWOOD, Esq., Dep.
CHARLES DEW MILLER, Esq.
WILLIAM ALFRED PLUNKETT, Esq.
HORACE BROOKS MARSHALL, Esq., J.P.,
  F.R.G.S.
JOHN BERTRAM, Esq., Deputy.
WILLIAM HENRY LIVERSIDGE, Esq.
JAMES LEWIS DOWLING, Esq., Deputy.
THOMAS REYNOLDS BOSE, Esq.
JAMES NORRIS PIMM, Esq., Deputy.
HENRY HODSOLL HEATH, Esq., J.P., Dep.
GEORGE BERRIDGE, Esq.
JAMES GEORGE WHITE, Esq., Deputy.
JOHN THOMAS BEDFORD, Esq., Deputy.
ALFRED PURSSELL, Esq.

ARTHUR BYRNE HUDSON, Esq., F.S.I. *(late Chairman).*

JOHN ALEXANDER BRAND, Esq.,
Comptroller of the City of London and of the Bridge House Estates.

J. WOLFE BARRY, Esq., C.B., M.Inst.C.E.,
Engineer of the Tower Bridge.

CONTENTS.

PAGE

LIST OF ILLUSTRATIONS.

LONDON BRIDGE, THE BRIDGE

:, AND THE TOWER OF LONDON.

in the time of Elizabeth.

Introduction.

A SHORT REVIEW OF THE PUBLIC WORK ACCOMPLISHED BY THE
CORPORATION OF LONDON.

BY THE

REV. CANON BENHAM, B.D., F.S.A.

I AM not proposing to write the history of the Corporation of the City
of London; whoever undertakes to do so will have a noble as well as
most interesting theme. A Blue Book issued in October last year by
the Corporation, and prepared for the Royal Commission on the Amalga-
mation of the City and County of London, is full of valuable information
gathered from many sources, and to it I am greatly indebted for the matters
mentioned in the following sketch. The greatest of our kings, probably the
very noblest king in the whole history of the world, Alfred the Great, gave
London its first municipal governor in the person of his son in law Ethelred
in the year 886. That the city had been an important one for many
centuries is attested not only by the ancient annalists, but by the Roman
remains which even still are from time to time brought to light in public
works. It had not, as yet, attained the status of the Royal City of England:
that title would then be claimed by Winchester. But even already London
probably stood first as a commercial city; it grew in prestige; the great
struggle between the English and the Danes—so disastrous whilst it lasted,
but terminating at length to the advantage of both—was marked by the
steady growth of London's supremacy.

When England fell under the Norman yoke, and for a while it
seemed as if English liberty was dead, it was London which took the
lead in the movement which ended in the victory of English law and

independence. The Charter of the Conqueror to the City is a memorial of this. Green, the historian of the English people, points to the election of Stephen as the date which proves beyond all others the supremacy which London had by that time gained over all English cities. "It was in the Revolution which seated Stephen on the throne that London first assumed that constitutional position which it has retained for so many centuries since. The struggles of the great City against Cnut, her capitulation with William, the charters she wrested from the Conqueror and his son, are enough to prove her importance at an earlier date than this; but with her part in the Revolution begins that peculiar individual influence which she was to exercise on our national history" (*Old London*, pp. 261-2). The brilliant historian goes on to show how the action of the citizens put an end to anarchy on that occasion, and how entirely they were moved by patriotic and religious motives, and in so doing left a permanent stamp for good on the very fabric of the English constitution. The compact between king and people became a part of constitutional law, and the responsibility of the Crown for the execution of that pact was recognised from that day forward for ever. There were, indeed, acts and movements in those confused days how could it be otherwise? which were incoherent and blundering, but they all expressed the right of a nation to good government, and were the means of establishing peace and freedom.

The Blue Book to which I have already made reference discusses the question of the establishment of the mayoralty, the substitution of a form of government fashioned after a French model for the office of "portreeve," and says that, "although the City's Commune was recognised by King John in the absence of his brother Richard in 1191, there is reason for believing that the City had its Mayor some years before this." The earliest mention of a mayor in a formal document is said to occur in a writ of Henry II. The precedent established on the accession of Stephen was followed at other great crises of our national history. The thoughtful student of history learns how important was the part played by the Londoners in extorting from King John the Great Charter, in putting an end to the disastrous Wars of the Roses, in the Grand Remonstrance and in the Bill of Rights. It would be a great omission from any sketch of City history were we not to make mention of the "Five Members" of Charles I's Parliament, and of the struggle of Wilkes and Brass Crosby with the House of Commons on behalf of the City liberties in 1771. It is, in fact, quite true to say that in all these cases the citizens of London took a leading part, a part worthy of the first City of the Kingdom.

But in the following pages I shall confine myself to events and incidents of the present century. Some of the cases to which I am about to refer are matters wherein the City was rather the expresser of public opinion than a leader of it. But such a function is a very important one, and, when worthily discharged, reflects honour upon the whole nation. There lie before me the proof sheets of Mr. Welch's book on the medals issued by the Corporation from 1831 to the present time, in commemoration of events which have taken place in London. A few, a very few, of these events might be made the subject of cavil, such for instance as the enthusiastic reception of the Emperor Louis Napoleon in 1855. But no one who remembers it will question that the enthusiasm was thoroughly that of the English nation. The Crimean war was in progress; the two nations, so often fighting against each other, had fought side by side on the deadly fields of the Alma and Inkerman, and the hope had gone forth, as a glance at any contemporary newspaper will show, that ill-feeling and jealousy between France and England could never be again. And the King of Sardinia was welcomed the same year because he had joined the Anglo-French alliance against Russia. There was equal enthusiasm on the French side. And it was a good, a righteous enthusiasm, even the hope, which we may still cherish, that the nations may live in peace, and love as brethren. The medal which commemorates the utterance of that hope will never be a thing for the City of London to be ashamed of. And so with the similar ones, the reception of the Sultan, of the Shah, of the Russian Czar; in every case it was the yearning of the nations that the long-deferred prophecy might be fulfilled, that the swords might be beaten into instruments of peaceful labour, and that wars might cease.

And a few of the medals relate to events in home history, which also were at the time gladdening all hearts. Some of the hopes have, by the inscrutable Providence of the Most High, been blighted so far as we, in our limited vision, have been able to see. Such was that attending the reception in the City of the late lamented Duke of Clarence. But loyalty and generosity of spirit can never be forgotten; it all brings forth good fruit, though not always in the manner we had anticipated.

The best history of public opinion for the last fifty years is the series of *Punch*. To turn over Tenniel's cartoons week by week, is to see what English people were, for the time being, thinking and believing, just as the social caricatures tell us better than any book of fashion how ladies dressed and what was the shape of their bonnets. Even so these medals commemorate for all days to come what were the excitements from time to time which moved and strengthened and brought honour to the English nation. In some cases results which might have seemed ephemeral were not so. I believe keen political observers are agreed that the action of the City of London in its warm and genuine reception of the present German Emperor has provoked a corresponding cordial affection on the other side. It is impossible now, after more than twenty years have passed, to recall without a glow of delight and enthusiasm the spectacle presented by London on the day of the public thanksgiving for the recovery of the Prince of Wales, "this solemn ceremonial and perhaps unparalleled manifestation," as Mr. Gladstone called it. It was a joy which entered into the very heart of the whole nation.

It will be interesting to enumerate the medals in their chronological order

> Opening of London Bridge, 1831.
> Passing of the Reform Bill, 1832.
> Foundation of the City of London School, 1834.
> Visit of Queen Victoria to Guildhall, 1837.
> Opening of the Coal Exchange, 1849.
> Reception of the Emperor and Empress of the French, 1855.
> Reception of the King of Sardinia, 1855.
> Entrance of the Princess Alexandra into London, 1863.
> Reception of the Sultan of Turkey, 1867.
> Thanksgiving for the Recovery of the Prince of Wales, 1872.
> Reception of the Shah, 1873.
> Reception of the Emperor of Russia, 1874.
> Removal of Temple Bar, 1878.
> Reception of the King of the Hellenes, 1880.
> Dedication of Epping Forest by the Queen, 1882.
> Opening of the New City of London School, 1882.
> Opening of the New Council Chamber, 1884.
> Admission of Prince Albert Victor to the Freedom of the City, 1885.
> Colonial and Indian Reception, 1886.

> The Queen's Jubilee [Visit of the Queen to Mansion House, Reception of many
>   Royal Guests at the Guildhall], 1887.
> Seven Hundredth Anniversary of the Mayoralty, 1889.
> Reception of the Emperor of Germany, 1891.
> Marriage of the Duke and Duchess of York, 1893.
> Reception of the King and Queen of Denmark, 1893.

The object of the present paper is to speak of subjects connected with
our municipal history, and therefore I pass by without further remark
what I may call the national commemorations of the medals, and pass on
to those which belong to London. Even the first, that which commemorates
the opening of London Bridge, I pass by with a very few words, because
it will be dealt with in a future page by a writer who has gathered with
admirable skill a great amount of information. The history of London
Bridge, from the days of Olaf downwards, may be called with absolute truth
a series of romances.

The next item in the list claims one glance, though that is one which
belongs chiefly to our general history as a nation. There are but few persons comparatively who remember the enthusiasm in London over the passing
of the Reform Bill in 1832. The City showed itself, as ever, eager for the
rights, for the elevation and advancement of the people. During the progress
of the great struggle the excitement had risen to fever height, almost to that
of civil war. The tension was now over, and there was a profound sense of
relief. A magnificent festival was held at the Guildhall to give Lords Grey
and Althorp the Freedom of the City in a gold box, and London went
half wild in its desire to do honour to the men who were held to be national
benefactors. Lord John Russell, who brought in the Bill, became Member
for the City in 1841, and remained so until his elevation to the peerage.

If any differences of opinion exist as to that subject, there will be none
as to the next, the foundation of the City of London School in 1834.
Now this school, like those of St. Paul's and Merchant Taylors, as well as
many other noble foundations, owes its existence to a London citizen. The
founder of the school before us, John Carpenter, was the Common Clerk in
the days of Henry V. He wrote a treatise on the laws and customs of the
City of London, which is still preserved among the archives of the
Corporation, and still regarded as of the highest value and authority. It
was originally called *Liber Albus*, but this name was afterwards transferred

to a transcript made in the reign of Queen Elizabeth, and the original was then named *Liber Niger.* Carpenter was one of the executors of Sir R. Whittington, who died in 1423, having been Lord Mayor four times; and one of the many important trusts which he carried out was the foundation of the Guildhall Library. The only portion, however, which concerns us here, is the fact that (in the words of Stow) "he gave tenements to the Citye for the finding and bringing up of foure poore men's children, with meat, drinke, apparell, learning at schooles in the Universities, etc., untill they be preferred, and then others in their places for ever." The property was situated in Thames Street, Bridge Street, Houndsditch, and Tottenham Court Road. The rental, originally very small, gradually increased; but in 1633 amounted to only £49 13s. 4d. After various schemes had been framed for extending the advantages of the bequest, the Court of Common Council decided in 1832 that four boys, from the age of eight to sixteen, sons of freemen of London, should be nominated from time to time by the Lord Mayor, and sent to the Skinners' Grammar School at Tonbridge, on leaving which each boy should receive £100, to be applied to his advancement in life. Still it was felt that the benefit might be still further extended, and in 1834 the Corporation obtained an Act of Parliament for leave to discontinue Honey Lane Market in Milk Street, and to erect on its site a school "for the religious and virtuous education of boys and for instructing them in the higher branches of literature and all other useful learning." The sum of £900 a year was to be devoted to the school and charged upon the Carpenter Estates, and a building was erected at a cost of nearly £20,000, the first stone being laid by Lord Brougham on the 21st October, 1835. The school was completed and opened for work on the 2nd February, 1837, when upwards of 400 pupils assembled. From the first it was a brilliant success; the City Companies and private individuals gave scholarships, exhibitions, prizes. The prizes annually awarded are worth £120, the scholarships tenable at the school reach a total of £300 a year, and those available at the Universities more than £1,150.

Still educational ideas advanced; the buildings were considered too confined and therefore unsuitable, while the site was increasingly valuable for building purposes, and thus it was that, the Court of Common Council having granted a site of an acre and a half on the Thames

Embankment, valued at £95,000, the present school was built and was opened by the Prince of Wales, December 12, 1882. In the speech of the Lord Mayor on that occasion, it was shown that the Corporation had added to the proceeds of the Carpenter Estates no less than £217,000, to which the Livery Companies and private individuals had made further munificent contributions.

This seems the fitting place for reference to other great educational efforts made by the Corporation of late years, and when we speak of education, though giving the word a wide sense, it is strictly accurate. Education does not cease when we get out of our teens. Every wise and thoughtful man will be ready to agree with the great Bishop Lightfoot, who said, in his very last days, that he had tried to be a learner all his life; Sir Andrew Clark repeated the sentiment in a speech at the Mansion House on behalf of the Hospital Fund.

We take first of all the Guildhall School of Music. It is one of three great institutions in London for the study of the Art of Music, the other two being the Royal Academy and the Royal College of Music. The Guildhall School began in a small way, but has now grown into an important institution, and under the principalship of a conductor and teacher second to none in the musical world, Sir Joseph Barnby, it bids fair to have a yet more brilliant success. The buildings on the Thames Embankment were erected, at a cost of £25,930, by the Corporation, which also contributes about £1,100 a year to their maintenance. There are between three and four thousand pupils on the register, and the teaching staff is in the highest state of efficiency.

The Freemen's Orphan School, at Brixton, was founded by the Corporation in 1850, and over £5,000 a year is still expended upon it. Altogether £162,422 have been given to it.

The great encouragement given to Technical Education began with the guilds. The Turners' Company claim to have led the way, being closely followed by the Clothworkers and Drapers. Then the Goldsmiths, Fishmongers, Mercers, and others joined in, subscribing largely from their funds. The Corporation, as a body, took up the work, and the City and Guilds of London Institute is the result. Technical classes are organised, and technological examinations are held simultaneously at various centres in connexion with the headquarters of the Institute at South Kensington and Finsbury, on the same plan as the Science and Art Department examinations. The sum of £14,702 has been expended on this work by the Corporation.

The history of the City Library is one of the most interesting in our City annals. It is the subject of a monograph of sixty-eight pages by the present Librarian, a work from which I take most of these few notes about it. Such a Library existed in 1425 (temp. Henry VI), for there is a grant of "the New House or Library' that year to the executors of Richard Whittington and Wm. Bury, to be in their custody, and one of these executors, John Carpenter, some of whose other good deeds have already been mentioned, worthily fulfilled his trust, and bequeathed valuable books of his own. All went well with the Library, and there are pleasant notes about it from time to time which Mr. Welch has gathered together, until the evil days of Protector Somerset. That rapacious scoundrel sent to "borrow" the books, promising to return them shortly, and they were carried away in three "carriers" and never returned.* The Corporation were negotiating with him to allow them to carry out some improvements in the City, and were afraid to say him nay. Probably many of the valuable MSS. and ancient books have found their way into private libraries. The building being of no further use was turned into a cloth market.

And there was no more City Library until 1824. On the 8th of April in that year, Mr. Richard Lambert Jones moved and carried in the Court of Common Council the appointment of a Committee, to consider how " a Library of all matters relating to this City, the Borough of Southwark, and the County of Middlesex " might be formed. On the report of that Committee it was done, the purchases at first being confined to books relating to the manners, customs, laws, privileges and history of the City of London and the neighbouring localities. " The condition of the book market," says Mr. Welch, " was then favourable for the procural of old and scarce London books, private collectors being fewer than at present, and our American rivals not being then in the field." So the books were bought and catalogued by Mr. Upcott, of the London Institution, and the Library was

---

* This was the same patriot who, having built himself the mansion known as Somerset House, proposed to remove all the buildings eastward of it as far as St. Paul's Churchyard, in order to make himself a grand park.

opened with 1,700 volumes in June, 1828. Before the end of the following year the number had increased to 2,800, to which were added 2,100 prints and drawings. In 1840 there were 10,000 volumes. From that time the Library has steadily increased, both in the number and importance of its books, and the extent to which they have been used by the public. It would be impossible to enumerate here the splendid additions which have been made to the Library since its formation. Sir David Salomons and his brother Philip gave a magnificent collection of Hebrew works, illustrating not only the religion of the Jews, but their history and general condition in the world. Mr. J. R. Daniel Tyssen gave an interesting collection (comprising 1,000 volumes) of Nonconformist writings, and in 1863 the valuable library belonging to the Dutch Church in Austin Friars was presented to the Corporation. Three or four years later the Library Committee proposed to the several Wards and Parishes that they should deposit their records in the Library, not only for safe custody, but also to make archives of so much importance more available for historical research, and several have been so deposited. It is not possible to refer to these records without bearing testimony to the splendid service which Dr. Edwin Freshfield has rendered to London history by his reprints, and his other publications, teaching the value of these manuscripts.

Of course such large accretions rendered new buildings necessary, and in 1869 a motion was carried by Dr. Sedgwick Saunders, in the Court of Common Council, for the erection of a new Library and Museum at a cost, exclusive of fittings, of £25,000. The formal public opening of the new Library by Lord Selborne, then Lord Chancellor, took place on the 5th of November, 1872, and it was thrown open for the admission of readers in the following March. That the work was appreciated was shown by the fact that the yearly attendance of readers rose from 14,316 in 1868, the last year of the old buildings, to 173,559 in 1874, the first complete year of the new. Since then splendid additions have been made to the Library; the Clockmakers', Shipwrights', Fanmakers', Gardeners' and Parish Clerks' Companies having made valuable donations. The Catalogue is an excellent piece of work, and has served as a model in various libraries; the Library has 68,369 volumes and 38,075 pamphlets. Some of these are very rare, early printed plays and pageants connected with the City, works referring to the history and archæology of London, and a priceless collection of engravings illustrating its topography and architecture. In the adjacent Museum may be seen a deed of conveyance with Shakespeare's autograph upon it, which the Corporation bought at a public sale for £147. Muniment rooms are provided for the City archives, which extend in an unbroken series from the Conquest to the present day, and the Museum is equally rich in London antiquities. It contains the whole of the remarkable "find" discovered in excavating for the Royal Exchange, supplemented by others, hardly less interesting, made in digging for the foundations of the many large buildings since erected within, and several found beyond, the City boundaries, including pavements of tesseræ, a group of Deæ Matres found in Crutched Friars, a fluted marble sarcophagus from Clapton, etc. Of later date are a large collection of mediæval pilgrims' tokens, and the fine Beaufoy collection of tavern and tradesmen's tokens; signboards, the most interesting of which is the carved and painted Boar's Head from the tavern in Eastcheap where Prince Henry and Sir John Falstaff played their wild revels: the parish syringe of the days before fire-engines were invented, and hundreds of other relics of old London.

These buildings involved an outlay of £100,000 from the City's cash. £1,000 is granted each year for the purchase and binding of books, and for other expenses £5,000 a year. In 1893 the total number of persons visiting the library, reading room, and museum, amounted to no less than 300,445. The museum is open daily from ten to five, the library from ten to nine. The arrangements to facilitate the work of readers are admirable, and the courtesy offered them above all praise.

In 1886 the Guildhall Art Gallery was opened. It contains a great number of pictures and works of art belonging to the Corporation, amongst which is a munificent gift of paintings presented last year by Sir John Gilbert. In addition to these a loan exhibition of pictures was held in 1890, when the Gallery was enlarged, and it was visited by 109,383 persons. A second was held in 1892, to which over 240,000 persons came; and a third during this present year, at which the number of visitors has exceeded 300,000. The whole expense is borne by the Corporation, amounting during the past six years and a half to £7,650.

To all these noble educational institutions we have to add yet another, namely, the Gresham College. Its Committee consists of twenty-four members appointed in equal numbers by the Corporation and the Mercers' Company, and its history is this: Sir Thomas Gresham by his will, dated 1575, devised one moiety of the Royal Exchange to the Mayor and Commonalty of London, and the other moiety to the Mercers' Company on trust for the City of London, to provide lectures in Divinity, Astronomy, Music, Geometry, Law, Physic, and Rhetoric; and he also devised his mansion in Bishopsgate Street to be the residence of the Lecturers. This house was sold in the reign of George III, and Gresham College was built in Gresham Street with the proceeds. There is a large lecture hall capable of holding 600 persons, as well as a library. The lecturers are some of the most eminent men in England in their respective subjects, and not unfrequently the hall is not large enough to contain the crowds who seek to attend the lectures. The writer of these lines has frequently attended the Divinity lectures of Professor Bevan and found people unable to get in, and those of Dr. Bridge on Music are obliged to be given at the City of London School, so great are the numbers of people attending. Twice since Gresham's will came into operation the Royal Exchange has been burnt down, and on the Gresham trustees has devolved the duty of managing the cost of re-building. That the funds at their disposal have been most wisely applied will be evident to anyone who will carefully look into the accounts.

We turn to another of these commemorations, that of the dedication of Epping Forest by Queen Victoria in 1882. This medal at once suggests thoughts on a most interesting and important subject, namely, that of the recreation grounds of the London people. No apology will be needed for following out this subject with some care. When London meant the City and the parts immediately adjacent, when Islington and Hoxton were hamlets approached by lanes, and Chelsea was a far-off village, to and from which the carriers' carts lumbered along over unpaved roads two or three times a week—and unless you had a horse of your own or walked you had to go by them—in those days the rural retreat of the citizens was the Moor, between Cripplegate and Bishopsgate, the site of the present Finsbury. There, sometimes, the Lord

Mayor and Corporation went hunting,* the apprentices practised their
archery and in winter-time skated, their skates being made of shank
bones of animals, and their speed accelerated with iron-pointed poles
which they carried in their hands. It was a wild and desolate-looking
spot : the pools of standing water, dotted over with reeds, formed,
except in dry weather, a most dismal swamp, so that Shakespeare talks
of the "melancholy of Moorditch" as a gruesome simile. People were
sometimes drowned, and fever and plague found here their most congenial
preserves. Lord Mayor Falconer, in 1414, made some progress in
draining this district, and he constructed causeways through it, that
passengers to the northern suburbs might at least go dryshod. People
had begun to realise that fever and pestilence came not by chance, but
through bad drainage and bad water. They needed to learn the lesson,
for the 14th century was one of almost continuous plague, and two-thirds
of the whole nation died. In Charterhouse Square, 50,000 persons
were buried in 1349, who had died of the Black Death. Murrain, which
swept off geese from the village green and bees from cottagers' gardens,
destroyed the greater part of the live stock of the nation. The air was
tainted with rotten carcases, dogs and ravens which fed upon them died,
and birds on the wing dropped dead as they flew through the poisoned air.
Even in the days of James I the Moor is described as a "most noysome
and offensive place, being a general laystall." Consequently, in 1606, fresh
efforts were made to render the place decent. Between Cripplegate
on one side and Bishopsgate on the other lay the district which was now
known as Moorfields, and there were three divisions of these. "Upper"
Moorfields was on the site of Finsbury Square, "Lower" of Finsbury
Circus, and "Middle" on the ground now occupied by South Street
and Cross Street. To the north of the Upper Moorfields was a great
mound, consisting of hundreds of cartloads of bones which the Protector
Somerset had caused to be removed hither from the vaults of Old
Saint Paul's and covered over with a layer of earth. It was called the
Bonehill, and the name still survives as Bunhill. At a later date a windmill
was set up on this hill, and the name Windmill Street, which has only
recently been altered to Tabernacle Street, is a memento of it. The

---

* The site of the Dogkennel, near where South Place Chapel is now, was discernible as late as 1732.

three Moorfields were in different hands. Upper and Middle were ecclesiastical property, belonging to the Dean and Chapter of St. Paul's, but were in the occupation of the Corporation of London, and used partly as a recreation ground, partly as meadow land. Laundresses used to come and hang out their linen to dry. Lower Moorfields belonged to the family of Fiennes, and it is from them, and not from the "Fen," that the name Finsbury is derived. The family dwindled down to two maiden sisters, and they, in the reign of Queen Elizabeth, gave their land to the City authorities in trust for the use of the citizens. Trees were planted and it was laid out in walks. This then was the first London Park, and very much the citizens appear to have prized it. There and in the Upper Fields were musters of militia, cudgel players, peripatetic vendors of sweets. And not only respectable citizens, but the riffraff came, for health, for amusement, for gambling, for pocket-picking. At a time when Aldersgate Street was inhabited by peers, when the Duke of Norfolk lived in Thames Street, and Prince Rupert and the Spanish Ambassador in Barbican, and there was no West End, and people went snipe shooting in St. Martin's-in-the-Fields, Moorfields was the St. James's Park and Hyde Park of Court and City, noisy with the throng of pleasure seekers. Sam Pepys and his wife came with hundreds of citizens and walked on Sundays at noon and evening. And sometimes there was a wrestling match; sometimes apprentices met to discuss their grievances who does not remember Mr. Sim Tappertit? and workmen gathered to discuss the fall of wages and the rise in food prices. In fact, we recognise the anticipation of the Marble Arch meetings. Under the trees were stalls of second-hand booksellers, and on lines stretched from limb to limb halfpenny ballads fluttered in the breeze. Men with telescopes at eventide invited you to have a look at the moon. The great attraction was the whipping a thief at the cart's tail, and the Moor was the favourite spot chosen for this interesting spectacle. Now and then there was a hanging. And amid thimble-riggers' tables, gingerbread stalls, Punch and Judy, merryandrews, stages for grinning matches, jugglers, might be seen grave ambassadors walking with noblemen and talking affairs of State.

The great fire of 1666 produced a marked change in the condition of these fields. The burnt-out citizens came here by hundreds and took up their habitation, at first in tents, afterwards in wooden shanties. Pepys tells how he came the next spring and found "new houses of two stories," new streets and shops. These were mostly on the eastern side. They became permanent dwellings, and thus the area of the open ground was considerably diminished. But the "Park," as I have called the Lower Moorfields, now Finsbury Circus, remained open. No one will doubt now, probably, that the governing body would have done well to have left it so. The first encroachment on this open ground was, also indirectly, owing to the great fire. Bedlam Hospital, originally founded as a religious priory by a sheriff of London, had shared the general fate and been dissolved by Henry VIII, who gave it to the City of London as a hospital for lunatics. Its exact site was on the present Liverpool Street, between the underground railway and the Great Eastern Hotel. The fire having, as we have seen, driven the population more thickly into the neighbourhood, and the hospital requiring more space, the Corporation decided on removing it to the south side of Moorfields, and it was done in 1676. The frontage reached from Finsbury Pavement to Blomfield Street. This was the first encroachment on the open land of the recreation ground, and so far as the lower fields were concerned it was the only one till 1812. I have before me a paper dictated by a lady still living, a hundred and one years old, with a goodly number of healthy great-grandchildren in their teens, who, in her childhood of seven years old, was taken into these fields. These are her words: "Moorfields were fields then. It was a large space divided into four by wooden railings with broad footpaths between, which were a favourite resort of nursemaids and children. My nurse used to take me there to see the cows milked. On one side was Bedlam. It was a long range of buildings, and I used to be amused by watching the poor lunatics come to the windows. There were some good houses regarded as decidedly superior where Finsbury Square is; we had friends living there whom we used to visit. The City Road had only scattered houses along it, with large intervals between. The Artillery ground was not enclosed." Now, I have some interesting and striking proofs of the accuracy of these recollections. For first, in Horwood's great atlas of London (1794), a copy of which is in the Guildhall Library, there are the "four portions," and the wide footpaths, and the wooden rails. Then in Mr. Wheatley's recently published "London Past and Present," he adduces abundant evidence of the "amusement" which the little child was taught by her nurse to seek after, in witnessing the antics of the poor patients. Steele, twice in the *Tatler*, tells of the entertainment which he found in this spectacle for London sight-seers who put themselves under his guidance. Even Cowper in one of his letters writes: "In those days, when Bedlam was open to the cruel curiosity of holiday ramblers, I have been a visitor there. Though a boy, I was not altogether insensible to the misery of the poor captives, nor destitute of feeling for them. But the madness of some of them had such a humorous air, and displayed itself in so many humorous freaks, that it was impossible not to be entertained, at the same time that I was angry with myself for being so."

And further, this lady is exactly correct in what she remembers about Finsbury Square and the City Road, as we shall now show. The opening of the City Road in 1761 is, of course, a record of the growth of North London, the previous road to Islington being the narrow and tortuous John Street. One old volume before me pronounces the newly formed City Road the finest street in London. I have already said that the Upper Moorfields belonged to the Dean and Chapter, but had been leased to the Corporation. The lease ran out in 1768 and was renewed for ninty-nine years, and it was after this renewal that the Corporation proceeded to build upon the ground, and thus arose Finsbury Square, begun in 1777 and completed in 1791, and the streets between it and the Circus were built at the same time. It is somewhat amusing to read in Boswell's "Johnson" how Miss Burney expressed her disgust that "these very beautiful new buildings" should be erected there, *not* because the City could ill afford to lose its open grounds, but because they were between Bedlam and St. Luke's, which was enough of itself to drive people into madness.

The lower fields still formed the park of the City, but the cacoethes of building presently prevailed here as well. Bedlam was removed to its present site in St. George's Fields in 1815, but the old site received fresh buildings, and not only so, but the London Institution and the rest of the Circus houses before long closed in the recreation ground which had seen so much of the amusements and recreations of the citizens. So ended the City park, as we may call it. The West End parks, full of interest as their several histories are, do not enter within our present scope. The happy and now well-known phrase, "The lungs of London," was invented by Lord Chatham.

Many years passed before the loss was in anywise supplied of "lungs" for the City. The population grew all round it, and open spaces grew more and more scarce. There is a great deal of real pathos, when we think of our modern opportunities, in reading of the outings of our predecessors of a century ago. The well-to-do John Gilpin celebrating his wedding-day by an excursion to Edmonton, his first country holiday for twenty years, seems to belong to a different state of existence. When omnibuses and short stages came into use, we get the signs of the change in writings like Dickens's early "Sketches," the descriptions of the tea gardens, and similar places of amusement in the suburbs. An excursion to the seaside was rare even to well-to-do people before the days of railways.

Victoria Park was formed under the authority of an Act of Parliament passed in 1842. The remainder of a Crown lease in St. James's was sold to the Duke of Sutherland for £72,000, and with the proceeds 265 acres were bought. The Metropolitan Board of Works gave £24,000 for twenty-four additional acres, and the purchase has, it is said, perceptibly lengthened average life in north-east London. We must content ourselves with barely enumerating the steps taken by the Corporation in acquiring open spaces. First came Bunhill Fields, an historic spot of great interest, a part originally of the Moor on which I have already said so much. It was at first set apart for the burial of the victims of the great Plague of 1665, but was not used for that purpose. Some Nonconformists who objected to the Church of England Liturgy acquired it, and it became recognized as "the Campo Santo of the Dissenters," to use Dean Stanley's phrase. Some of the most conspicuous names in English literature will be found inscribed on its tombs, notably those of John Bunyan, Daniel Defoe, Isaac Watts. It was closed in 1832, after 123,000 burials had taken place in it, and then lay for many years neglected. In 1867 a Committee appointed by the Corporation laid out £3,000 upon it, arranged the tombstones and planted trees, and in 1869 it was opened to the public. A plan of the ground and record of every name and inscription is preserved at Guildhall.

West Ham Park for Eastern London and "London over the border" consists of seventy-seven acres, and was purchased for £14,000: £4,000 was raised by public subscription and the Corporation found the rest. It was opened by the Lord Mayor in 1874, and is one of the most beautiful parks in England, possessing some rare trees planted by Dr. Fothergill in the end of the last century. The cost of maintaining this park is entirely defrayed by the Corporation of London.

But even this was but a small acquisition compared with that of Epping Forest. This is not the place to recount the historical and legendary lore so thickly clustering round the famous forest, ranging from Boadicea and King Harold to Dick Turpin and Barnaby Rudge. Suffice it to say that it was in ancient times known as the Great Forest of Essex, as marked a feature of the county as were the Andredesweald and the New Forest of Sussex and Hampshire. Unlike the last named, Epping grew smaller each century as the population near London increased. At one time it covered the greater part of the county, reaching as far east as Colchester. When this was partially cleared the name changed into a double, Hainault and Waltham Forests, two portions of the same great labyrinth, divided by the river Roding. Both have again become smaller, Hainault the more so, and within the last two centuries Waltham has been re-named Epping Forest. It is curious to trace some of the epochs which mark the diminishing of this great forest. In the days of the Norman kings it was strictly preserved to the Crown, in those of King John the northern part, all north of Dunmow, was disafforested, and in those of Edward I it was still further diminished. In 1640, by a Royal Commission, a perambulation of the forests in general having been ordered, the extent of Hainault and Epping combined was estimated at 60,000 acres, of which 48,000 were private property, and the rest unenclosed wastes and woods. Hainault was disafforested in 1851, and was subsequently enclosed. Epping was in somewhat different condition. The Crown rights had not been so clearly defined as in Hainault, and a most complicated system of ownership prevailed. The soil of the open waste belonged to seventeen different lords of the manors, but certain rights of pasturage existed all over the tract, and rights of wood cutting (said to have been granted by Queen Elizabeth) were claimed, with certain restrictions, by the inhabitants of particular parts, just as is the case in the New Forest at present. Unfortunately, after the disafforesting of Hainault the Crown rights over Epping, such as they were, were sold to the lords of the manor for £18,000, and it became a fixed idea of the possessors that they were now entitled to enclose against all comers. Ten years after Hainault had been disafforested the open land had dwindled from 6,000 acres to 3,000, and the alarm was naturally taken that beautiful Epping too would be enclosed and built over and so lost to the community at large. It was this alarm which led to the appointment of the Open Spaces Committee in 1863, when it was found that in the manor of Loughton alone an enormous enclosure of about 1,500 acres had been effected, and this in the heart of the wildest and most lovely portion of the forest. The grabber had won the consent of the influential neighbours by the distribution among them of three or four hundred acres. But the poor were up in arms. They declared that their rights had been infringed, that hitherto they had been allowed to get their winter fuel by lopping the trees, and to find employment not only by supplying their own needs, but by selling to their richer neighbours. Thus there was a declaration of war; bands were organized who pulled down the fences, and some influential members of the Corporation of London aided and abetted. The result was the appointment of a commission to enquire into the contending rights, but before this had even received the royal assent the Corporation of London took the matter up, and they did it on two grounds. In the first place there was a tradition that certain rights of hunting in the forest had been granted to them by royal charter, and though the existence of no such charter could be found there were entries in the Corporation archives which seemed to imply it. But further there was a very definite possession, namely that of the City of London Cemetery, of which they had purchased the site. This gave them a foothold, and they used it to resist the land-encroachers. A strenuous and determined litigation ensued, which resulted in a powerful and lucid judgment of Sir George Jessel, delivered November, 1874. The lords of the manors, who had combined as defendants, were adjudged to have acted illegally, and all enclosures made since the 14th August, 1851, were condemned. But the difficulties were not yet ended. There were many who had bought land in good faith and built upon it; and it was impossible to pull down houses and whole streets. The Corporation was willing to leave these, but claimed back land which remained in its natural condition, or which had been taken up for agricultural purposes. Meanwhile the Epping Forest Commission delivered its report, not altogether in agreement with this, for it recommended that enclosures should be retained by the owners and remain enclosed on payment of an annual rent-charge. This led to further difficulties and fresh litigation, which was happily terminated by the appointment of Sir A. [now Lord] Hobhouse as arbitrator. He completed his very difficult task in 1882. Five or six hundred acres were restored to the public; no one was wronged. The Crown appoints the ranger, the Corporation of London are appointed conservators, to keep the Forest unenclosed, and to preserve, as far as possible, its natural features. The total cost of the acquisition to the Corporation was £291,087. Queen Victoria graciously opened it, and dedicated it to the use of the people on the 6th of May, 1882. The Forest consists of 5,374 acres, to which Wanstead Park (182 acres) has since been added. The Corporation thus secured a priceless boon to the Londoners, especially of the East End; on Whitsun Monday last many thousands of persons visited it.

Burnham Beeches, a spot of lovely woodland scenery, and with timber almost unique in its beauty and majesty, was acquired by the Corporation in 1888, at a cost of £10,241. It is not far from the Slough station on the Great Western Railway, and is attractive, not only by its glorious scenery, but by the many interesting places in the vicinity. Beautiful Dropmore, and Stoke Poges, with its sweet and peaceful churchyard, the burial-place of the poet Gray, are within the day's excursion to Burnham.

Coulsdon Common with Riddlesdown and Kenley are an equal boon to the South Londoners. Though the wood scenery cannot be compared with Burnham, there is a magnificent sweep of landscape from the hills, equal probably to any in England. There are 347 acres, and the Corporation paid for them £7,157. Highgate Wood and Queen's Park, Kilburn, were acquired for £5,343, and £500 was also paid towards the purchase of West Wickham Common, a place dear to artists, and the scenery of which furnished the subject of at least one of the pictures of our greatest living artist. In the recent Loan Collection at the Guildhall is Sir

J. E. Millais's picture of "The Proscribed Royalist." I have good reason for saying that he took his tree and ferns from West Wickham Common.

To all these let us not forget to mention the laying out and planting of St. Paul's Churchyard, with the supply of the drinking fountains, at a cost of £5,606. Anyone looking in at any hour on a summer's day at the men, women and children resting there and feeding the pigeons, will feel that the money has been well bestowed. I will only mention further the contributions made by the Corporation to the preservation of Banstead and Mitcham Commons and the purchase of Shiplake Island.

We pass on to glance at the vast public improvements which have been made in London during the century. Of one most important class I say nothing, because they deservedly have a chapter of their own in this volume by a most competent hand, I mean the bridges and the approaches to them. Nor can we enumerate the magnificent but costly works of setting back houses and widening thoroughfares. Sir Walter Scott, speaking of the imperceptible gradations by which national and political changes are wrought, finely says, "Like those who drift down the stream of a deep and smooth river, we are not aware of the progress we have made until we fix our eye on the now distant point from which we have drifted" (last chapter of "Waverley"). There are many streets which appear in Aggas's and Horwood's maps of London, which are familiar to us of the present day, and yet, except it be a church or public building, there is hardly a feature of the old remaining. As I look at the admirable and clear engravings in Charles Knight's excellent work on London, published fifty years ago, I sometimes fail to recognise the modern street bearing the same name, so wonderful is the improvement made. This indeed will apply to nearly all the streets in the City, but (only to speak of old streets, and altogether omitting those new ones which have been constructed as approaches to the bridges) I found in the accounts such items as these: Widening Billiter Lane, £3,560; Chancery Lane, £2,100; Coleman Street (corner of), £2,550; Dowgate Hill, £1,240; Farringdon New Street, £70,633; Fenchurch Street, £1,490; Fleet Street, £4,000; Giltspur Street, £8,834; Limehouse, £2,500; Long Lane, £9,349; Maiden Lane, Wood Street, £3,136; Mansion House Street, £30,000; Newgate Street, £2,000; Fetter Lane, £2,000; Old Jewry, £2,490; Upper Thames Street, £3,750; Watling Street, £3,133.

But these are small items in comparison with others, *e.g.*, Improvements in Moorfields and Bishopsgate, £16,500; improvements in the Strand (1811), £246,300; providing site for General Post Office (1815 and 1824), £80,000; Farringdon Street and removal of Fleet Market, £250,000; building new Coal Market and widening Thames Street and St. Mary-at-Hill, £111,518; forming New Cannon Street and improving Queen Street, £540,000.

Even these become small when we read of such items as "Holborn Valley Viaduct, £1,571,000." To this sum must be added three quarters of a million more for the purchase of houses and the formation of approaches. In the old maps, the highway from Drury Lane to Brook Street is "High Holborn," then to Farringdon Street comes "Holborn," after that "Holborn Hill." The present generation will remember well enough what a terror the said hill was to travellers before the Viaduct was made. The history of Holborn is a very curious and interesting subject. The accepted derivation has always been till lately the *Old* Bourne, but Mr. Waller has adduced evidence to disprove this. It is probably the *Hollow* Bourne, on account of its being situated in a deep declivity. The "Fleet" once ran up from the Thames to above Farringdon Street, over which a low stone bridge crossed on the site of the present Viaduct. Curiously, though London does not come into the Domesday Survey, there is mention of "Holebourne," where the Sheriff of Middlesex has two cottages for which he pays twenty pence a year, and "William the Chamberlain" has a vineyard for which he pays six shillings. The site of this vineyard is still marked by the name of Vine Street in Hatton Garden. Needless to say, the road along what is now a crowded thoroughfare was through fields, but it was one of the principal highways for the importation of corn, wood, wool and hides into London. Henry V gave directions for paving it as far as Holborn Bars (bottom of Gray's Inn Road). Many and many a sad procession has gone up this hill, for it was the road from Newgate to Tyburn, and up the same road, the same distance, Titus Oates went howling at the cart's tail, suffering one of the whippings to which Judge Jeffreys sentenced him. The Viaduct, which is a very fine specimen of engineering skill, was opened by Queen Victoria in 1869, and she passed along it again in an imposing procession, amid thousands of glad spectators, to return thanks at St. Paul's for her son's recovery on the 27th of February, 1872.

The arrangements for the food supply of the great City startle one by their vastness, even when the mere figures are written down. Thus:

Providing New Cattle Market at Copenhagen Fields, 1852-6, 1873-5-6-7	£504,842
London Central Meat, Poultry and Provision Market, 1862, 1881-2	£1,412,000
New Central General Market, 1876-92	£533,000
New Foreign Cattle Market, Deptford, 1870-90	£382,500
Enlargement of Billingsgate Market, 1872-80	£272,000
New Leadenhall Market and Approaches, 1880-8	£258,942

Smithfield (originally *Smooth* Field, "*campus planus re et nomine*") was a market for cattle, sheep, horses, hay, as far back as the days of Henry II. It was of course then clean outside the City. In 1615 the Corporation "reduced it to a fair and comely order," paved and drained it, and made roads through it with strong rails. This was the more needful because by this time Newgate, Cheapside, Leadenhall and Gracechurch Markets were become crowded. Smithfield horses were a byword for badness in Shakspeare's time, as appears from a passage hardly quotable in Henry IV. and Dryden writes

> "This town two bargains hath, not worth a farthing—
> A Smithfield horse and wife of Covent Garden."

Smithfield, too, has an evil memory in that it was the scene of the burnings for heresy in the days of religious persecution. The first victim in England was William Sautre, parish priest of St. Osyth, in London, burnt in 1401. In Queen Mary's reign 200 persons were burnt here. In the days of her father, Henry VIII, three Protestants were burnt for heresy, and three Roman Catholics were hanged, drawn and quartered at the same time for denying the King's supremacy. The stake stood opposite the gateway of St. Bartholomew the Great.

What an intolerable moral and physical nuisance Smithfield Cattle Market became is abundantly testified by contemporary literature. The caricatures of Leech and Doyle in *Punch*, laughable as they are, are yet fierce in their satire. What can be more exquisitely funny than the fifth page of *Punch's Almanack* for 1850, where every figure is a study, though there are hundreds of figures in the page; everybody must laugh and yet it is all a tragedy together. There is a policeman charging a supercilious-looking ox which has just tossed two men into the air: a cockney is tumbling off his horse, which is entangled amid a drove of pigs; another ox has poked its head into a carriage full of ladies: another, having sent an unfortunate man headlong into an open sewer, is rushing at a little boy who has tumbled down in front of it, whilst his mother with an armful of babies is in full flight, and an omnibus conductor is holding the door open for an unfortunate female to step out into the path of the angry beast. It is clear that she will be tossed at once. All this and very much more Doyle has contrived to get into a page. And readers of *Oliver Twist* will remember with what a powerful pen Dickens has described the same scene.

With some trouble the Corporation procured the necessary Act of Parliament, thirty acres were bought for a new market in what was then known as Copenhagen Fields, and on June 11, 1855, Smithfield ceased to be a live cattle market.

Now let us put together a tabulated statement of the moneys which have been expended by the Corporation for public improvements and for charitable or national purposes since the year 1760, the year in which Blackfriars Bridge was built. They will best be seen by a simple classification under half-a-dozen heads.

1. *Public Improvements.*—Under this head we place new bridges, sanitation, markets and roads, £10,523,350.
2. *Open spaces acquired and freed.*—Of these we have already spoken in detail, £341,522.
3. *Dwellings for labouring poor,* £105,806.
4. *Charitable purposes* (1781-1892). These include *(a)* asylums, almshouses, cathedrals, churches and chapels, hospitals, dispensaries, infirmaries, sufferers by fire, schools, *(b)* naval and military charities, foreign sufferers, home and colonial sufferers, £925,018.

E

5. *Public purposes.* Royalty and nobility, ministers of the Crown, military and naval, philanthropists and other public men, public exhibitions, Arctic and other expeditions, £154,108.

Total, £12,049,805.

Other matters crowd upon us as we once more look round upon the work of the great municipality. The thought and labour and money spent upon the sanitary welfare of the City have at least made it probably the healthiest capital in the world. The medical officers of the port have manifested a diligence beyond power of telling in watching vessels which arrive when epidemics have been doing deadly work in foreign countries. When last year cholera was devastating Hamburg and other continental coast-towns, Dr. Collingridge and his assistants were literally ceaselessly at work visiting, isolating and disinfecting the plague-stricken ships. The Corporation procured a section in the Public Health Act of 1872, which gave them full powers as the Sanitary Authority of the Port of London, and these powers were re-enacted and strengthened in the new Act of 1883; and in the Act of 1891 they were again re-enacted with considerable enlargements. The result has shown how thoroughly the trust thus given by the legislature has been justified. A pitched battle between the Corporation and the Metropolitan Board of Works on the subject of the drainage of London and the condition of the Thames led to the appointment of a Commission in July, 1882, which declared that the Corporation had entirely proved their case, and that the river below London was in a dangerous condition of pollution. This contention cost the Corporation over £20,000, but it had the effect of causing the Board of Works to construct their new works at Barking.

Yet more important has been the subject of the water supply of London. Here, too, has been not one fight, but a whole series, extending over many years, between the Corporation and private interests. The Water Bill of 1892 will, it is hoped, result in providing an adequate supply of pure water to the millions around us, and at a fair cost.

Just once more, before concluding, let us turn to the medal list, *Opening of the new Council Chamber.* I have done so not to speak of the beautiful chamber itself, which is well worth a visit, and worthy of the municipality of the greatest City in the world, but because I hold that the above tables prove very thoroughly for what noble and beneficent purposes the Council Chamber of the City of London has been used. But I go further and say, that any man who will visit it when the discussions are going on, or who will read them in the public press, will be fairly convinced that a patriotic, generous, unselfish spirit pervades the debates. There is a marked absence of personalities and bitterness, even during the warmest contests, and the citizens of London have good reason to be proud of the men that they send to represent them. And, when I add to all this, the noble works outside London which have been inaugurated here, and at the Mansion House, deeds of sympathy and brotherly feeling which have reached to every corner of the earth, words and acts which have kindled enthusiasm, pity, self-sacrifice, in a thousand centres, to follow in their wake; then I make bold to express my pride in the City of London, and to utter my conviction that there is no organisation within the whole Church of God which has done so much for the furtherance of religion, of civilisation, of the good of mankind, as the Corporation of London.

LONDON BRIDGE AND THE TOWER OF LONDON, ABOUT A.D. 1500.

From an illuminated MS. volume of Poems by Charles, Duke of Orleans.

(Brit. Mus., 16 F ii, xv.)

CHAPTER I.

The Story of London Bridge down to the Middle of the 18th Century.

> . . . . "When I behold ye forest of masts upon your river for trafic, and that more than miraculous bridge which is y^e *communis terminus* to join ye two banks of that river; your Royal Exchange for merchants, your halls for companies, your gates for defence, your markets for victuals, your aqueducts for water, your granaries for provision, your hospitals for ye poor, your Bridewells for ye idle, your chamber for orphans, and your churches for holy assemblies; I cannot deny them to be magnificent works, and your city to deserve ye name of an Augustious and majestical city; to cast into ye reckoning those of later addition, ye beautifying of your fields without, your pitching your Smithfield within, new gates, new water-works and ye like, which have been consecrated by you to ye days of his Majesty's happy reign; and I hope the cleansing of the river, which is *tanqua porta* to your city, will follow in good time." .
>
> *Sermon of ye Bishop of London [John King], at Paul's Cross, on ye 26 March, 1620, on behalf of ye Cathedral.*
>
> [4to., 1620, E. Griffin for E. Adams.]

§ 1. Preliminary.

WHETHER the Romans built a bridge across the Thames at London, or not, is a question which has been much debated among antiquaries. The negative view is strengthened, if not confirmed, by the fact that no remains of piers or abutments of the substantial character which might be looked for in Roman engineering work have been discovered on either side of the river.

The earliest London Bridge was built by our Saxon ancestors. The structure must have been a rude one, constructed probably of thick, rough-hewn timber planks placed upon piles, perhaps with movable platforms to allow the Saxon vessels to pass through it westward.

Snorro Sturleson, the Icelandic writer of the 13th century, in his account of the Battle of Southwark, which took place between the Danes and the Saxons in the year 1008, described the bridge over the river, then existing between the City and Southwark, as "so wide that if two carriages met they could pass each other." The Danes were at that time in possession of Southwark and also of the bridge, which they had strongly fortified. King Ethelred determined to attack the bridge by land, being assisted, as an ally, by Olaf, the Norwegian King and martyr, his former foe, who, with his ships, succeeded in destroying the bridge by uprooting the piles on which it was built. The memory of Ethelred's faithful ally is preserved in the City and environs of London by four churches which bear his name, viz., St. Olave Jewry, St. Olave Hart Street, St. Olave Silver Street, and St. Olave Tooley (i.e., St. Olave's) Street, Southwark.

London Bridge is thus referred to in the laws of Ethelred: "Whoever shall come to the bridge in a boat, in which there are fish, he himself being a dealer, shall pay one half-penny for toll, and if it be a larger vessel, one penny." As to the erection of the bridge there is much doubt and controversy. Stow attributes its foundation to the pious brothers of the Monastery of St. Mary Overies, on the Bankside, but this has been disputed by other writers. This first wooden bridge, however, though doubtless repaired after the attack upon it already described, was not fated to stand long. On the 16th November, 1091, a dreadful storm occurred in London, which overthrew more than 600 houses, and greatly damaged the tower of St. Mary-le-Bow, in Cheapside. The Thames being greatly swollen, the rush of the tide was so violent that London Bridge was entirely swept away, and the lands on each bank were submerged for a considerable distance.

Stow relates that on the 10th October, 1114, the river was so dried up, and there was such want of water, that between the Tower and the bridge, and even under it, "a great number of men, women and children did wade over, both on horse and foot," the water coming up to their knees.

In the reign of Stephen, A.D. 1136, a fire consumed the southern part of the City from Aldgate in the east to St. Paul's Cathedral in the west. London Bridge was also destroyed, but was soon again repaired, as Fitz-Stephen, writing between 1170 and 1182, speaks of it as affording a convenient standing-place for witnessing the citizens' water-tournaments. Stow informs us that the bridge was not only repaired but re-built of elm

timber, by Peter of Colechurch, in 1163. Most other writers, however, give
the date of its re-construction as 1176, when the first stone bridge over the
Thames was begun by that pious architect. Peter was a priest and chaplain
or curate of St. Mary-Colechurch, which curious edifice stood, before the
Great Fire of London, at the corner of Conyhoop Lane in the Poultry, and
was "built upon a vault above ground, so that men were forced to ascend
into it by certain steps." This church was famous as the place where
St. Thomas-à-Becket was baptized.

§ 2.   Origin of the Bridge House Trust; Control by the Corporation; Wardens or Keepers; Records; Seal and Mark.

The origin of the trust exercised by the Corporation of London with
regard to the bridge extends back probably to the early wooden bridges
which existed previous to the commencement of Peter of Colechurch's
stone bridge in 1176. More than half a century before this last event,
London Bridge was possessed of a goodly property, as, in 1122, the monks
of Bermondsey and the Church of St. George in Southwark received five
shillings (a very large sum for that period) as an annual rent out of the
bridge lands. None of the names of the benefactors to this old bridge have
come down to us, but its revenues must have been obtained from charitable
contributions and grants of tolls or taxes by the Saxon and early Norman
kings. This bridge found an early patron in William Rufus, who, in
1097, imposed a tax to furnish labourers for re-building it, for erecting his
palace at Westminster, and for constructing a wall round the Tower. To
defray the charges of the new bridge of Peter of Colechurch, liberal
contributors came forward, among them being Richard, Archbishop of
Canterbury (Becket's successor) in 1174, and Cardinal Hugo di Petraleone,
papal legate to this country in 1176; and the worthy priest himself, besides
designing and carrying out the entire work, is said to have built the chapel
from crypt to roof at his own costs and charges. Henry II also assisted
the work by the imposition of a tax on wool, which gave rise to the popular

tradition that London Bridge was built on woolpacks. In 1201, four years before the death of Peter of Colechurch, a letter was received by the Mayor and citizens of London from King John, recommending Isenbert of Xainctes as a new architect to finish the work. The King's letter also provided that the rents and profits of the houses to be built on the bridge should be devoted to its repair and maintenance. King John contributed in 1213 to the repair of London Bridge by appropriating to its use the "God's pence" taken of foreign merchants. In 1212, not long after the erection of the houses on the bridge, which were intended as a means of its support, they were swept away by a disastrous fire, which even threatened the destruction of the bridge itself, and threw a further burden upon its revenues. But a still worse fate awaited the Bridge House funds. Henry III. King John's successor, was no friend to the citizens of London, and in the 34th year of his reign, May 20th, 1249, he ordered his Treasurer, his Chamberlain and the Constable of the Tower to seize the City of London, the County of Middlesex, and London Bridge, and to pay their revenues into his exchequer. It was doubtless in consequence of this confiscation that the Brethren of the Chapel of St. Thomas on the bridge were compelled to solicit charitable donations for the maintenance and repair of the bridge. A grant of protection to the Brethren for this purpose was issued by the King in 1252 ; this provided them with a suitable reception in all churches and towns throughout the kingdom. How long Henry retained possession of the estates of the bridge is not known, but in 1265 he resumed its custody and revenues, and granted them for five years to the Hospital of St. Katherine. A further grant followed in 1269 to his consort, Queen Eleanor, for a term of six years. After the death of Henry III, in 1272, a long dispute arose between the Queen and the citizens with respect to her claim to the disposal of the bridge and its revenues. King Edward I appointed Commissioners of Inquiry, before whom the citizens complained that the keepers of the bridge appointed by the Queen "expended but little in the amending or sustaining of the said bridge, whence danger may easily arise, very much to the damage of the King and of the City." Very soon afterwards the Corporation appears to have regained possession. King Edward did his best to make amends for the injustice of his predecessor, and, in 1280, authorised a further appeal for the contributions of the benevolent. The document states "that the Bridge of London is in so ruinous condition that not only the sudden fall of the bridge, but also the destruction of innumerable people dwelling upon it, may suddenly be feared." A more reliable source of revenue was soon found necessary, and in the following year the King gave authority to the Mayor and citizens to take customs or toll from passengers using the bridge. Every man crossing "the water of Thames" from either side was to pay a farthing, and every horseman one penny, and the charge for every pack carried on a horse across the bridge was one halfpenny. Other grants for the support of this great public thoroughfare, described as "pontage for London," or "pontage patents," were made by King Edward I, who showed himself most solicitous for the commercial growth and prosperity of the City of London. Side by side with the royal grants and public contributions which emphasised the national character of the work, the stream of private benevolence continued to flow, and soon placed the finances of the bridge on a satisfactory footing. The long roll of private benefactions (a selection from which will be found in the Appendix), was contributed to by persons of all ranks, from the wealthy Godard, "late chaplain" of the bridge, who, in 1271, left a munificent bequest of more than 180 marks, to William King, who, two hundred years later, served the bridge in the humble capacity of labourer, and bequeathed a pittance of ten shillings.

The supreme control over the bridge was, as we have seen, vested in the Corporation of London, who exercised their authority in early times through the Court of Common Council, although the Court of Aldermen appear to have had some power over the Bridge House funds. Matters of great moment were decided directly by the Common Council. An instance of this occurred in 1390, when the wardens prayed allowance from the Common Council of £38 8s. 7½d., which William Leddrede, their renter (collector of rents), failed to account for; for which default he was sent to prison at the suit of the wardens. This sum was remitted by the Common Council, but only on the understanding that it should not be taken as a precedent, "but that the wardens of the bridge shall always answer and be chargeable for their servants." Matters of minor importance appear to have been deputed to a committee appointed annually by the Common Council to audit the accounts of the bridge. This committee consisted of two aldermen elected by the Court of Mayor and Aldermen, and four commoners elected by the Commonalty; but their number and the proportion of aldermen to commoners varied from time to time. In 1397 their names were John Walcote and Hugh Short, aldermen, and John Wakalee, John Lyngge, Richard Merlowe and Geoffrey Broke, commoners. Their election took place a few days before Michaelmas, and they met to examine the accounts on the "morrow of St. Michael." It was the duty of the Sergeant-at-Mace to summon them for this purpose, as well as to arrest fugitive tenants who refused to pay their rents. At a later time it was usual for the Lord Mayor to act as an *ex-officio* member of the committee. In 1298 the audit was directed to be held twice a year, viz., in the first week in Lent and at the beginning of autumn, but the Lenten audit had been discontinued in 1550. In 1547 two more aldermen were appointed auditors. At this, and probably from a much earlier, period, the audit included an examination not only of the bridge accounts, but also of those of the City.

The custody of London Bridge was naturally confided to the man who had devoted his life and fortune to its construction and support, and so we find Peter of Colechurch officiating as bridge-keeper or warden. On Peter's death, King John appointed "Brother Wasce, his almoner, and a certain other lawful man of London," keepers of the bridge, by a writ dated 18th September, 1205. From this document it also appears that the appointment of warden was then exercised by the King jointly with the Mayor of London. The office held by Peter of Colechurch is described as that of "proctor" in an undated deed by which he and his brethren of the bridge grant to Gilbert de Walton, carpenter, a house belonging to the bridge trust, in the parish of St. Dionys Backchurch, on lease at a yearly rent of ten shillings. Peter of Colechurch had a successor, or colleague, in the office of warden, in the person of Godard the chaplain, whose munificent bequest to the bridge has been already alluded to. The post was subsequently assigned to laymen, who were men of the highest position in the City, such as Michael Tovy, bridge-master during his mayoralty, in 1248, and John Sturgeon, who, in 1548, was elected Governor of the Merchant Adventurers' Company. Sturgeon had been elected out of ten candidates in the previous year. The wardens' duties were honourable, and doubtless profitable, but they entailed great responsibilities, as will be seen from the oath of the wardens in the Appendix. They had in their "warde" "all the goodes of the bridge, whether lands, rents, tenements, or commodities." Not only were they executive officers, but they were associated with the Mayor and Corporation as trustees of the bridge property. Bequests of lands, houses and money for the use of the bridge were made to them separately or in conjunction with the Mayor and Commonalty. They possessed large, if not absolute, powers of dealing with the bridge property, by sale or otherwise, for the profit of the trust.

There were two wardens or proctors who jointly filled the office, but, in some early grants, the trust is represented by only one of the wardens : and in one deed dealing with bridge property, the grantees are described as "Benedict Sypwrighte, of London, warden of the bridge of London, and the proctors of the said bridge, and the brothers and sisters there serving God." Their official title was subsequently Warden, but, among the citizens generally, they were known as Masters of the Bridge. The present title is that of Bridge-master.

From the earliest wardens' accounts of the year 1382, we learn that the salary of these officers was £10 each. In 1562 they received £26 13s. 4d. each, with a further allowance jointly of £4. In 1597 their principal salary was raised to £50 each yearly. At the audit of 1598 the wardens produced the magnificent surplus of £109 17s. 6¾d. on their accounts, in reward for which they were allowed the sum of £16 10s. 10½d., or fifteen per cent. upon their balance. The wardens, in 1434, received an indemnity from the Common Council for divers sums which they had advanced for the repair of the bridge. On the other hand, instances of unthrifty wardens occur ; in 1351 the wardens were removed, after ten years' service, for showing a deficit of £21 odd. The unfortunate wardens for the year 1440, Thomas Badby and Richard Lovelas, owed no less than £327 9s. 10d., the loss having arisen from many of the houses on the bridge being dilapidated and unlet. The wardens obtained the King's intercession on their behalf, and the Court of Aldermen compromised the matter by accepting 200 marks in full discharge of the debt.

The appointment of wardens was in the hands of the Mayor, Aldermen and Commonalty, although occasional pressure was used by the Crown on behalf of a *protégé*. The election was annual, and they held office from Michaelmas to Michaelmas. On 14th April, 1491, the Common Council ordered that "four men shall be named by the Mayor and Aldermen, whereof two to be elected wardens of the bridge by the Commonalty." The election still rests with the Commonalty or Livery; and takes place on Midsummer Day, at a Common Hall held for the election of Sheriffs, Chamberlain and other officers. An order of the Common Council, 8th October, 1556, provided that any vacancy occasioned by death or other cause should be filled at a Common Hall, to be summoned within three days of notification of such vacancy to the Lord Mayor. Another order (23rd September, 1467), which was not strictly acted upon, directed that the masters of the bridge should not be together in office more than two years, and that, on the retirement of one, the other should remain for a year, to instruct the new comer in his duties. Instances occur of their authority being superseded by the Corporation. From the accounts of June, 1414, it appears that Richard Osgood, one of the clerks of the chapel, had been removed from his position by the wardens for handing the keys of the Chapel, without the licence of his superiors, to one John Hert, a jeweller, by which "the same John, at daybreak and secretly, wholly unknown to the same wardens, chaplains, and clerks, was married by a strange priest." At the Mayor's instance the said Richard was restored to office, for reasons not stated. Again, in 1315, we learn that, at a Court of Husting, Henry de Gloucester and Anketyn de Gisors were newly elected and sworn wardens in the place of Thomas Prentice and John de Wymondeham, who were removed from the office. At a much later date (May 4th, 1744) the Committee for the Bridge House Lands found it necessary to censure Thomas Hyde, the senior bridge-master, and to reprimand Thomas Piddington, the junior. In 1354 John Le Benere and William Jordan, then wardens, were relieved by the Mayor and Aldermen from all "tallage touching the City, and from every office of the same City, while they were in office of keeping the bridge." About 1462 the accounts show an annual allowance of 20s. for the wardens' "clothing," that is, their official costume or livery: but in 1468 the auditors thought proper to curb a little extravagance by ordering the bridge-masters not to keep horses to ride on on the business of the bridge, but to hire them if necessary.

It is now time to say a few words about the Bridge House records,

FACSIMILE (REDUCED) OF THE BEGINNING OF THE WARDENS' ACCOUNTS FOR 1422–23.

which form, as will be seen, the chief source of our information concerning
the bridge. These were, in 1272, kept in the chamber of the Guildhall, as
we learn from the will of Isabella, the wife of Thomas le Juvene. They
were afterwards kept at the Chapel on the bridge, and, early in Elizabeth's
reign, were ordered to be removed from the Chapel to the Bridge House.
They are now, and have been for a great many years, lodged in a strong-room
in the Guildhall, under the custody of the Comptroller. The accounts were
all made in duplicate, one copy being delivered into the Chamberlain's office,
and the other being retained at the Bridge House. The principal series

FROM THE WARDENS' ACCOUNTS,
1480.

FROM THE WARDENS'
ACCOUNTS, 1489.

is that of the bridge-masters' accounts, which extend back as far as 1381.
From that year to 1405 they consist of seventeen parchment rolls, which
are followed by sixty volumes extending from 1405 to 1853. Two or three
of these are in duplicate, and one volume, containing the accounts
for the years 1445 to 1458, is missing. The accounts are beautifully kept,
as a glance at the illustration on page 35, taken from the statements of
the year 1422–23, will show. Initial letters and other ornaments of great
beauty are sparingly introduced. Illustrations of four of these are

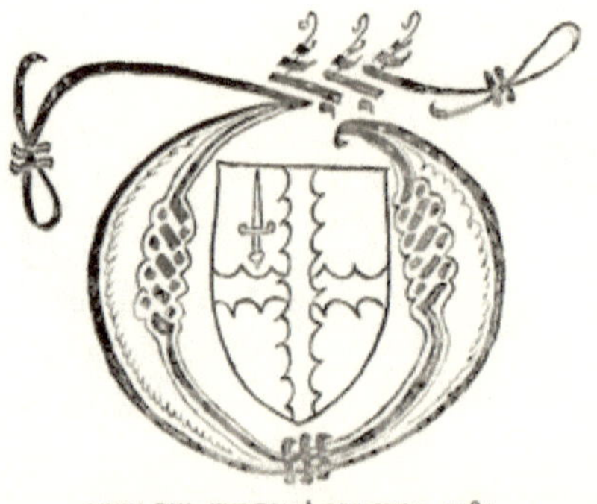

FROM THE WARDENS' ACCOUNTS, 1489.

here given, among them being an early representation of the City Arms, taken from the accounts for 1489. They were the work of John Normanville, clerk of the works, as appears from the sketch of a dragon holding a scroll, inscribed *Normanvyle fieri me fecit A° dni 1490*. There is another series of documents beginning at an earlier date. They consist of original charters, grants, deeds, leases and other official instruments from the end of the 13th century to the 17th century. These records, with their attached seals, possess great interest, apart from their connection with the Bridge House, on account of their early date and the importance of the persons whose "acts and deeds" they commemorate. Among the contracting parties are Henry Fitz Ailwyn, the first Mayor of London, a facsimile of whose seal, unfortunately broken, is given on page 38. Peter of Colechurch himself, Michael Tovey, and Godard, the priest, also appear, with other prominent citizens of the 13th and 14th centuries. The deeds are well preserved and are bound in volumes bearing the letters A to K, but are not arranged in chronological order. There are also two " bokes of evydences," containing transcripts of many

FROM THE WARDENS' ACCOUNTS, 1490.

of the deeds above-mentioned, as well as other extracts and memoranda relating to the Bridge House Trust. One of these, a small folio volume (which may be described as the "Small Register"), is evidently

referred to in the accounts for 1504–5, which record the payment to Thomas Symondes, stationer, of 3s. 4d. for binding the volume. The other is a larger and much finer volume, which will be referred to as the " Register of Deeds." It was presented by the wardens to the Common Council on the 6th September, 1515, and was stated to contain a transcript of all the evidences concerning the bridge. At the same time the wardens also produced three keys of a great chest kept in the Chapel, in which these evidences were deposited. The Court gave directions for one key to remain in the custody of the Mayor, the second to remain in the Chapel "fastenyd with a chayn to a lytell cloge of wode where-

SEAL OF HENRY FITZ AILWYN,
FIRST MAYOR OF LONDON.

uppon beea wretyn these wordes, 'The ijth keye of the chest in the Chapell of London Brigge,'" and the third key to be kept by the bridge-masters. This book also contains many beautiful initials, examples of which are annexed.

ORNAMENTED INITIAL LETTER FROM THE REGISTER OF DEEDS.
(Two-thirds of actual size.)

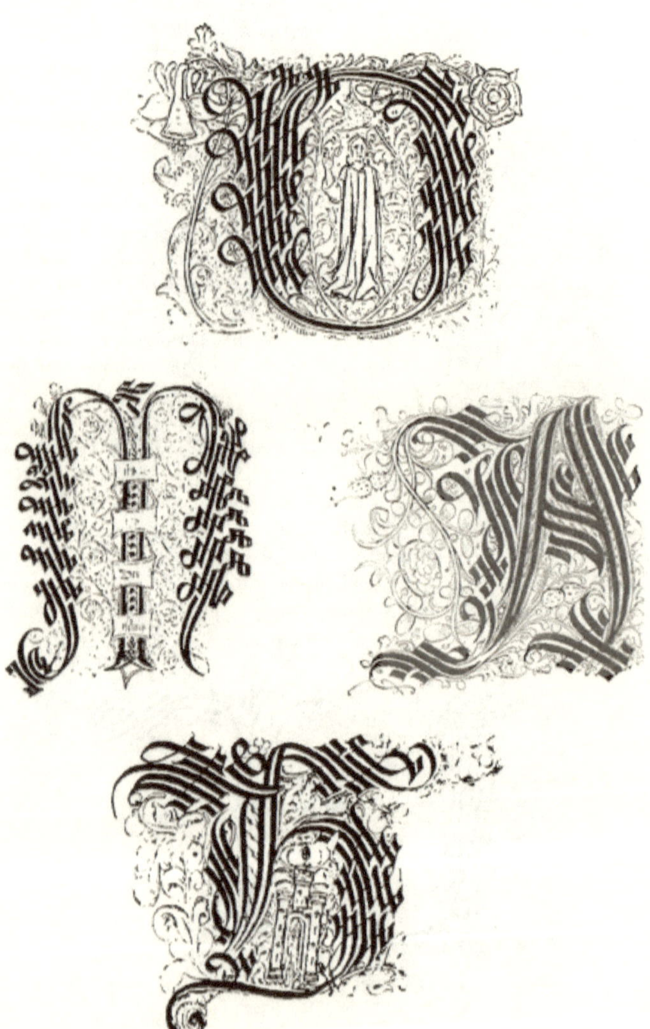

ORNAMENTED INITIAL LETTERS FROM THE REGISTER OF DEEDS.

(Two-thirds of actual size.)

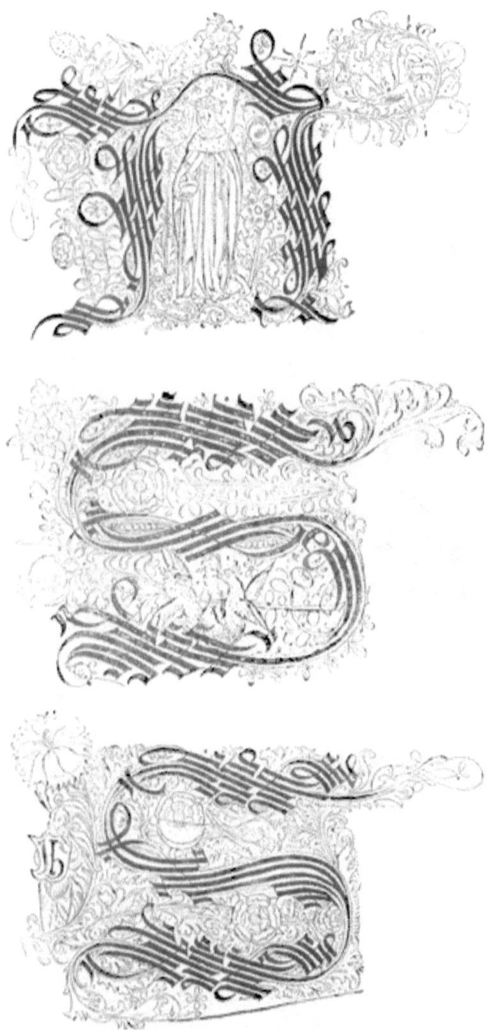

ORNAMENTED INITIAL LETTERS FROM THE REGISTER OF DEEDS.

(Two-thirds of actual size.)

Among the deeds preserved in book B is one containing the ancient seal of the Bridge House. This seal, which is here illustrated, is unfortunately imperfect, the top and the greater part of one side being broken away. Of an impression affixed to another deed only the extreme base remains, and no other copy is known to exist in any public or private collection. The seal is lozenge-shaped, and, in its complete form, appears to have measured 2¾ inches by 1½ inches. The obverse is inscribed [SIG] ILL : BEATI : THOME . . . . and bears the following device :— An arch of London Bridge, with a boat riding on the water below ; upon the bridge above St. Thomas of Canterbury is seated, holding in his left

OBVERSE.   REVERSE.

ANCIENT SEAL OF THE BRIDGE HOUSE.

hand a long upraised cross, his right hand being apparently lifted in an attitude of benediction. The workmanship closely corresponds with that of the old Mayoralty seal, as will be seen from the above illustration. The reverse is inscribed . . . [SEC]RETI : PONTIS : LOND . . . and bears a very interesting representation of the martyrdom of Thomas à Becket. The archbishop is kneeling before the altar, which is indicated by a lofty candlestick. His arms are raised, and his hands joined in a posture of resignation. Immediately facing him on the left are two knights, armed cap-à-pie in chain armour; each of whom is protected by a long pointed shield. The foremost knight is smiting the archbishop on the head with a sword, the other is striking with a sword his companion Grim, who is holding the cross. Above the knights is a star of five points.

No particulars of the date when this seal was first ordered can be found, but it must have been nearly co-eval with the foundation of the bridge, as a common seal would be necessary for conveyances of the bridge property. In 1539 Henry VIII issued a proclamation for abolishing all images of St. Thomas à Becket within his dominions. As regards the Bridge House the Common Council were not prompt to obey this injunction. On July 14th, 1542, it was "agreyd that the seale of the Brydgehouse shalbe chaunged forasmuche as the ymage of Thomas

OLD SEAL OF THE MAYORALTY
, Hen. III

NEW MAYORALTY SEAL, 1380.

Bekkett sumtyme Bysshop of Canterburie ys graven therein, and a newe to be made, and the same newe seale to be fyrst devysed by Mr. Hall, to whome the same olde seale ys nowe delyvered." In the case of the City seal more alacrity was shown. The Court made an order on 28th September, 1539, that the arms of the City should be substituted for the figure of St. Thomas (p. 43). Strangely enough, the saint was not dethroned from his seat on the Mayoralty seal, where he reigns, jointly with St. Paul, to this day. To exemplify the hold which the City's patron had upon the affections of Londoners, and to afford a comparative view of the treatment he received from the City engravers at various periods, we give illustrations of (1) the old Mayoralty seal, made in the reign of Henry III, with the figures of SS. Thomas and Paul; (2) the new Mayoralty seal, made in 1380, with a

similar but more elaborate device ; and (3) the old reverse of the City seal,
showing St. Thomas seated above London Bridge, with a view of the City
and its wall below ; replaced in 1539. Of the new Bridge House seal thus
ordered in 1542, no example has yet been found, but it may have been the
Bridge House "mark," although this, if ever used as a seal, is no longer
employed in sealing official documents, the City seal having been substituted
for that of the Bridge House for some time past.

Only two references to the Bridge House mark are to be found in the
records. The earlier is in the wardens' accounts for 1462-3, which record the
payment of 2s. 6d. for "one markyng iron for markyng the timber." Again,
on 15th August, 1561, 28s. was paid "unto a paynter for markyng the

REVERSE OF OLD CITY SEAL, REPLACED IN 1539 BY
THE CITY ARMS.

BRIDGE HOUSE
MARK.

STONES FOUND IN LONDON
BRIDGE IN 1758.

lether buckettes with the housse marke." The origin of the mark has not
been ascertained. It appears to have existed in a somewhat rudimentary
form at the beginning of the 16th century, as will be seen from two
stones (*see* illustration) which were removed from the bridge when the
houses upon it were being pulled down in 1758. One bears the
inscription "Anno dñi 1509," followed by a mark in the shape of a cross
charged with a small saltire. The other stone, dated 1514, bears two
marks which may, as some have suggested, represent the initials "R. A."
of Sir Robert Acherley, Lord Mayor in 1511. Some writers have attributed

an heraldic meaning to the mark as now used, being doubtless led to this opinion from its employment as a device by the borough of Southwark. Mr. Philip Norman, in his interesting work, "London Signs and Inscriptions," suggests that the device may originally have been a merchant's mark. It is somewhat disappointing that the careful search of the Bridge House records, instituted for the purpose of this work, has not yielded more information to solve the problem.

§ 3.   The Bridge Finances.

We now proceed to examine more in detail the way in which this vast trust was managed by the wardens and their subordinate officials.

In earlier times, as we have seen, there was often great difficulty in meeting the current expenses of the bridge, especially when any unforeseen calamity occurred. Such a misfortune befell the wardens for the year 1540, when they lost a large number of quitrents paid by many of the greater Abbeys and Priories which were dissolved by a statute of 1539. The City estates also lost some profitable rents, and it was considered advisable to expend 24s. 2d. out of the Bridge House funds, as the "costes of the one-halfe of a dynner made at Brooke's House in Fletstrete unto the Councell of the Coarte of thaugmentacyons and for a rewarde gyven unto them to be goode concernynge the quitrentes latlye payde unto the chambre and the Brighous by the suppressyd houses." Whether the "dinner" and "reward" had a beneficial effect or not does not appear, but about sixteen years later a portion of the Bridge House funds was wisely invested in the purchase of monastic lands from the Crown.

In a rental prepared in 1358 by the wardens, Richard Bacon and John de Hatfeld, the bridge property is described as situate in London, Southwark, Hatcham, Camberwell, Lewisham and Stratford. The number of shops on the bridge is said to be 138, and the amount of their rents £160 4s. 0d.; this includes a mansion in the stone gate and a house in the same building occupied by John Bedell, keeper of the gate. A copy of this return will be found in the Appendix. A detailed enumeration of the bridge tenements, dated 1460, divides them into six sections, with the rental of each separately indicated, thus: "The beginning at the east of the bridge," £60 10s. 8d.; "The beginning at the west side of the bridge," £54 19s. 8d.; "The middle of the east of the bridge," £19 8s.; "The middle of the west of the bridge," £24 7s. 4d.; "The end of the east side of the bridge," £19 13s. 4d.; "The end of the west side of the bridge," £26 3s. 4d. In a rental for the year 1601-2, the yearly revenue derived from houses on the bridge is £472 11s. 8d., and the total rent of the estates £1,546 16s.

Defaulting tenants were summoned before the Mayor and Aldermen; thus in the twenty-sixth year of Edward I (1298) Robert le Trayer and Stephen Pykeman, citizens of London, were summoned for arrears of rent from a house called "le Hales," amounting to the large sum of £60 4s. 10d. Among the property belonging to the bridge from a very early period was Stocks Market, which was occupied by butchers and fishmongers, who rented their stalls of the Bridge House. Over these stalls were thirty-eight "cupboards" for the drapers, which produced, in 1382, a rent of £32 18s. 8d. The payments were made "to groomes of the Chamber of Guildhall for keeping of the hucksters by the stocks." On 1st November, 1319, William Sperlyng, of West Ham, was convicted of exposing for sale two beef carcases, putrid and poisonous, and was adjudged to stand in the pillory and the said carcases burnt beneath him. The market place, being situated in the middle of the City on the site of the present Mansion House, was usually smartened up on occasions of festivity. The accounts for 1545-6 show a payment to plasterers for washing and colouring the Stocks against the coming of the Lord Admiral of France. The property disappears from the Bridge House accounts about the year 1564.

The earliest account (for 1381-2), an abstract of which is given in the Appendix, opens with a statement of arrears from the last account, of £22 1s. 3d. The total receipts amounted to £755 19s. 6d., and the total expenditure to £699 19s. 2¾d., leaving a balance in hand for the next year of £56 0s. 3¼d. These figures represent a large sum in those early times, and are further evidence of the importance of the trust exercised by the bridge wardens. As we have seen, these officers were personally responsible for the financial prosperity of their trust, and, on more than one occasion, a considerable time elapsed before they obtained their discharge for the annual accounts. A serious loss occurred in the year 1550-1, by two

successive falls in the value of silver money.
The entry given in the accounts under the
9th July shows that the wardens kept the
large sum of £404 in "schelyngs and
grottes" (shillings and groats) in their chest,
the loss by depreciation amounting to one-
fourth. On the 17th of August their stock
of shillings and groats was £76 9s. 3d.,
which was depreciated by one-third, besides
15s. 6d. in groats and pence, which diminished
in value to one-half.

The accounts were kept in Latin until
the year 1480. They appear to have been
presented at the audit in loose quires, which
were afterwards bound together in volumes.
In the account for 1525-6 is an entry "of
payment to Thomas Symondes, stationer, for
binding in boards 17 quires of parchment,
containing 17 accounts of the bridge works,
&c." The binding of these massive volumes
is decorated with a curious stamped border,
consisting of the royal arms, rose, pome-
granate, fleur-de-lis, and other emblems, including the elevation of a building, which
may perhaps be intended for the bridge
Chapel. The name of an earlier bookbinder
occurs on 13th December, 1421, when "3s. 4d.
was paid to Peter Bilton, bookbinder, for
binding a great paper."

At the yearly audit of the accounts the
auditors were provided with counters, which
were employed in a similar manner to those
used at the famous Exchequer table. The
auditors would probably sit on one side of

STAMPED BORDER OF LEATHER BINDING
OF BRIDGE HOUSE ACCOUNTS. EARLY
16TH CENTURY.

the table and the wardens on the other, and as the former read the items of the account the wardens had to produce their vouchers for the same, whereupon the auditors would call out *allocatur*, it is allowed, or *dis allocatur*, it is not allowed, as the case might be. As each item was allowed, an officer, probably the accountant, put down counters representing the amount upon a table or counter, having probably five columns ruled upon it, each column representing a numerical value of money, namely, hundreds, tens and units of pounds, shillings and pence. This somewhat cumbrous mode of auditing was in use at a very early date, and, as regards the Bridge House accounts, continued down into the 17th century. The counters or jettons used were of an ornamental character, and doubtless remained the perquisites of the officials, as the item for their purchase appears yearly in the accounts. At a later date purses were also regularly provided, but both purses and counters appear to have been discontinued about 1453. The wardens were assisted in these duties by an accountant, whose office, or house, was on the bridge. In 1414, twenty pence was paid for carriage of the bridge books from the house of the warden to that of the accountant for half a year and more.

Early in the 16th century the wardens began to lend money for public objects, and occasionally to borrow for the use of the bridge. In October, 1601, they advanced £50 for sending 1,000 men to Ostend; and in the following February, the sum of £500, "for the full accomplishing of the Cittye's stock of £1,000." £290 was lent to Christ's Hospital in 1604, and in 1608 £100 to provide armour for 250 soldiers sent to Ireland. During the Civil Wars the surplus became a deficit, and in 1648-9 the wardens were obliged to borrow £1,100 of certain persons at 7 per cent., a rate which fell to 6 per cent. in 1666-67.

An important source of revenue was the tolls for vehicles and the passage of ships. Certain persons were permitted to compound annually, as "bere-bruers," who, at the beginning of Edward IV.'s reign, paid 6s. 8d. yearly for every car; and the prioress of Hallywell (in Shoreditch), who paid 3s. 4d. for her cart for the same period. In 1460 a toll of 2d. was charged for a cart with unshod wheels and 2s. for one with iron bound wheels. In the same year the toll from five vessels passing through the bridge amounted to 10s. 2d. In 1463 this charge was reduced by the Mayor and Aldermen from 2s. to 6d. for each vessel, and a penalty of 3s. 4d. imposed upon the bridge-masters for refusing to draw the bridge. The tolls were in early times collected by one of the chapel clerks, who, in 1413, is described as "keeper of the carts and ships passing by the bridge." In Michaelmas, 1490, the tolls for carts and cars were leased to John Hasteler, haberdasher, for nine years, at the rent of £21 a year. Hasteler appears to have made a bad bargain, for the accounts of 1496-97 contain an allowance to him of 74s. 6d. towards his losses by carts of divers great persons, "by whose colour other mean folkes nothing wolde pay for their carriage over the said bridge, whereby the same John myght not raise his said ferme that yere." In 1506 the tolls remained in the hands of the wardens for default of a farmer, and had considerably decreased in amount. On the withdrawal of certain duties Hasteler was again induced to farm the tolls at the former rate. They were afterwards leased to Raynold Blake in 1527-28; to John Wood in 1529-30; to Thomas Mallidge in 1566-67 for £30; and to Thomas Horner in 1578-79, at the augmented rent of £55 13s. 4d.

A curious bequest was left in 1458 by William Strafford for the payment of £8 yearly to the Sheriffs of London on condition that they should take no toll for the carriage of the goods of citizens at the Great Gate of the bridge or at the drawbridge. The testator acted under a strange misapprehension, and a note appears in the register that the Sheriffs never had anything to do with the wheelage, which was collected by a City officer, and accounted for at the Bridge House. From a paper-covered toll-book in the Bridge House strong-room, it appears that the toll for every waggon, cart, dray, truck, etc., bound with iron and loaded, was 4d.; for every slug-wheeled carriage, charged as above and drawn by more than two horses, 2d.; the same loaded with coal, meal, flour, etc., 3d. Empty casks, packages, etc., were allowed to pass free on their return. The farming of the tolls was still maintained in 1758, when £40 was allowed to Thorpe, the lessee, for his loss through the destruction by fire of the temporary bridge. The average of a day's toll in 1777 was from £9 to £10, and the total receipts from this source for 1777-8 amounted to £3,006 17s.

With the increase of prosperity in the finances of the Bridge House trust, the claims of charity and public duty, both to the immediate vicinity and the City at large, were not ignored. Among the recipients were the hospitals for the sick and poor (especially the neighbouring one of St. Thomas's) and the churchwardens of St. George's, St. Olave's and St. Thomas's, Southwark, for their poor and for the maintenance of divine service. Literature was patronised in the person of William Smith, Rouge Dragon, who received £30 in July, 1609, for his "booke of armes." For some service to the City which is not explained, Sir John Fortescue received, under the Lord Mayor's warrant, in February, 1597, a silver-gilt cup costing £14 2s. 8d. Towards the great work of building the new Guildhall 100 marks was annually contributed from 1413 for six years, afterwards extended to nine. The old Guildhall is mentioned in the accounts for 1390-1, "divers victuals being bought there by the wardens on the day they rendered their account." The Lord Mayor was not forgotten, Sir Peter Probyn receiving in 1622 £40 "towards his postes and other ornaments of his house." This payment was continued in subsequent years. It was also customary at that period to pay £100 as a contribution to the Mayoralty banquet at Guildhall. We may conclude the list with a contribution which was probably

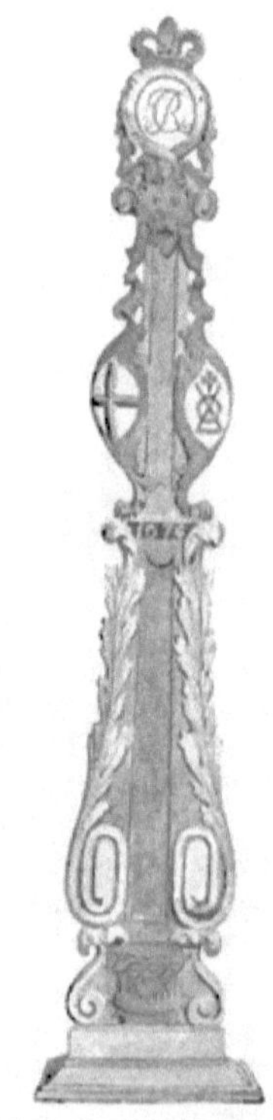

not of a voluntary character, viz., a gift of £10 to "the Lady Elizabeth," daughter of James I, in 1612, on her approaching marriage with the Elector Palatine.

Another non-optional payment was that levied in 1547 by "the collector of Walbrook ward towards a fifteenth and a-half gathered within the City at the King's [Edward VI] coming to coronation."

Towards the close of Elizabeth's reign a significant change in the governing authority of the bridge occurs, in the appointment of a standing committee to manage its affairs. The modern system of delegating powers of administration to committees affords a striking contrast to the ancient plan of entrusting large executive powers to individuals, a controlling authority being exercised by the governing body only in matters of great moment. The authority of the "master and wardens" in the guilds, and of the "rector and churchwardens" in the parishes, for example, was formerly much greater than at present, and similarly the office of bridge warden began from this time to decline rapidly in importance. As will be seen later, the granting of leases, which was formerly in the hands of the bridge-masters, was in 1528 taken by the Common Council into their own hands. In 1592 a further step was taken, and on 24th April a Committee of Aldermen and Commoners was appointed to let the Chamber and Bridge House lands. This committee was re-appointed on 15th November, 1609, when two Aldermen and three commoners were newly added to the committee of the same number then existing. The names of the old members were "Sir Henry Rowe and Sir John Swynarton, aldermen, and William Greenewell, merchaant taylor, William Tirverson, skynner, and Nicholas Leate, ironmonger"; the new members were "Sir Humphrey Weld and Sir William Romney, aldermen, and John Newman, grocer, Richard Wiche, skynner, and Lawrence Campe, draper." The new members of the committee were to remain in office till the next Common Council after Mid-summer-day, 1611.

Special committees were also occasionally appointed, as in 1698, when a committee was nominated "to inspect into the Bridge House revenues and accounts and the management of the estates belonging to the said bridge." The committee for letting the City and Bridge House lands continued, with enlarged numbers and increased duties, till 1818, when its functions were delegated to two committees, viz., the City Lands Committee and the Bridge House Estates Committee, by an order of Common Council dated 10th February in that year.

§ 4.   Officials and Workmen.

The staff of officials of the bridge was very large ; some had their offices on the bridge and others at the Bridge House. They were treated by the Corporation and the wardens with great consideration. Not only were gratuities allowed them during sickness, and medical and surgical attendance provided for their wants, but pensions were habitually granted to those who were incapacitated by old age or infirmities. At the end of the account for 1494-5 is an allowance by the auditors "to oon John Isaac, late servaunt and laborer unto the said bridge, in consideracion of his good and true service doon unto the same bridge by meny yeris past and nowe is fallen blynde and impotent, 6s. 8d." Towards the close of the 14th century the accounts record the payment of oblations at Christmas and Easter to the clerks and artisans engaged on the bridge, but on the 21st October, 1560, a payment of 10s. was made to the labourers "to the entent that they shall beg no offrynges at Christmas." Another officer, the Renter, has been already mentioned ; his election lay with the Court of Mayor and Aldermen, as appears from the appointment of Robert Watson to the office on 13th May, 1440. The Clerk of the Works was an important officer. He was granted a special reward of £6 13s. 4d. in 1407 for his diligence in superintending the works of the bridge. This fortunate recipient was John Normanville, who engrossed the wardens' accounts, and has revealed his identity by inscribing his name in one of the beautiful embellishments already alluded to (see page 39). The origin of the office of Comptroller of the Chamber and the Bridge dates from 1496, when an oath was devised for the appointment.

A list of the inferior officers and workmen, with their weekly stipends, is found in the earliest wardens' account, 1381-2. It includes (apart from the chapel staff) the clerk of the drawbridge 20d., six carpenters 22s., four masons 14s. 3d., two sawyers 7s., one mariner 2s. 6d., the cook and keeper of the dogs 22d., the carter 22d. (a week's provender for the horses 15d.), a boy 2s., one paviour 3s. 4d., one plasterer and his servant 4s. 6d., twenty-one tidemen working at the ram for six hours 32s.; the last mentioned were paid at the rate of 3d. each per tide, and 2d. was paid for drink to twenty-four of these men for one week. Other workmen were employed as necessity arose, as plumbers, plasterers, tilers, painters, smiths, etc. In 1405-6 the staff includes, beside the above, a keeper of the Bridge House and a man for keeping the carts passing over the bridge.

There was another important servant called the "shuteman," who had charge of the "shoute" (a kind of barge used for conveyance of timber and other building materials) and of the boats belonging to the bridge. On 23rd April, 1405, two new "ores" called sculls were purchased, and in 1414-15 four men were hired for two days and four nights at 9*d.* each for the carriage of elm in "le shoute" from Fulham to the Bridge House. Two years afterwards the shoute was docked for repairs at Deptford; John Patteslee, the shouteman, was also under repair, the wardens paying 20*d.* "for his aid to cure his finger wounded and broken in the work of the bridge." From the accounts of 1461 it appears that the wardens used to let out their boats and carts for hire, and in 1581 there were at least two shutemen (then called scavelmen), who received 2*s.* 4*d.* "to warne the Lords of the Council to dine with my Lord Mayor" at the audit feast. The conveyance of materials for the repair of the bridge seems to have been almost wholly by water. When horses were required they were hired of "hakenay men"; such an entry appears in the accounts under 8th April, 1424.

A curious glimpse at the workmen's commissariat is afforded by a report of the auditors in 1480. The auditors understanding that the water reeve warden of the carpentry of the bridges and divers of his fellowship carpenters and the masons keep "a comyns of bordemen" within the Bridge House, of which one is weekly steward and purveyor, and daily buys and dresses their meat, and spends the wood and fuel of the bridge for "sethyng and rostyng ther viteles"; and considering the cost that the City has been put to in time past by means of the same "comyns" expended in wood and fuel, it is ordered that from Sunday next following, being the 2nd September, that the said persons keep no commons in the Bridge House, but they are "to have loggyng within the place, suche as is convenyent for them to thentent, that they and everych of hem shalbe redy bothe by day and by night to helpe yf any jeparde and casuelte of hurte falle atte bridge or within the place, etc."

In 1498, urgent repairs to the drawbridge being necessary, 18*d.* was given to the workmen as a reward "to forbere theire noncions (luncheons) and slepe for the more spede of their works." Again, in 1500, the carpenters received 16s. 6d. for working night and day to repair "the full ruynous drawbridge and therof making sure for to be drawen alle redye for the Kinges berkis [barks] to have hadde passage." The zeal of the bridge servants was warranted by the kind attention shown to them by their masters. In 1547 two City surgeons, George Gyme and Robert Modesley, were paid 58s. 4d. "for healing of a great wound in the head of John Alerton, carpenter, hurt at the bridge by default of the old gin." Many similar entries follow, as well as of pensions to workmen on the sick list. William, the carpenter of the bridge, and three other servants were recipients of legacies under the will of Isabella la Juvene in 1272. At a still earlier period, Gilbert de Waltham, the bridge carpenter, was the lessee of Bridge House property under a grant made by Peter of Colechurch and his brethren of the bridge. Many entries occur from 1441 onwards of the purchase of shoes for carpenters working in the water (nine pair costing 3s. 4d. per pair in 1478), and of gloves for carpenters and masons, which cost, in 1553, 2d. a pair. On 4th March, 1423-24, Richard Beke and his fellow masons received for making windows in the Stone Gate and "that they should not go out of the house for dinner," 6½d. In 1430 these workmen are described as "fremasons." Among miscellaneous workmen mentioned are a diver, Thomas Wellinge, who was paid 4d. in 1553 for fetching up an ox, and Richard Man, a glazier, who received 16d. for glazing two panels in the chapel in 1407, and a rat taker, whose charge for "layeing bayte to kyll rattes," in 1564, amounted to 2s. 10d.

The relative importance of the various officials, as estimated at the beginning of the 18th century, is shown in the following valuation of appointments taken from "a list of the rooms and offices bought and sold in the City of London": "One clerk of the Bridge House, £1,250; two carpenters, £200 each; one mason, £200; one plasterer, £200; one pavier, £250; one plummer, £250; two porters, £100 each; one purveyor, £200; one shotsman, £200."

§ 5. The Bridge, its Structure and Repairs.

Stow relates that in 1209 the bridge was "finished by the worthy merchants of London, Serle, mercer," Mayor of London in 1214 and

1217-22, "William Almaine and Benedict Botewrite, principal masters of that work." The bridge thus completed consisted of a stone platform, erected somewhat westward of the former wooden bridge, and was 926 feet long and 40 feet in width, standing about 60 feet above the level of the water. It contained a drawbridge and nineteen broad-pointed arches, with massive piers varying from 25 feet to 34 feet in breadth, raised upon strong elm piles covered by thick planks bolted together. It is possible that the immense wooden sterlings attached to the piers did not form part of the original structure, but were added afterwards to keep the foundations of the piers from being undermined. The obstruction caused by these huge barriers, and the large number of piers, reduced the entire channel of the river from its normal breadth of 900 feet to a total waterway of 194 feet, or less than a fourth of the whole. Peter of Colechurch's work has, however, not been without defenders (even as regards these points) among architects in more recent times, who have urged that the narrowness of the arches tended to preserve the navigation of the river above the bridge.

The forces of natural decay, coupled with the continual danger caused by the violent impact of river and tide, rendered ceaseless vigilance necessary on the part of the wardens, for the prevention of accident to the structure itself and to the persons who passed over and under it. We can, however, scarcely hold the masters responsible for a peculiar mishap which occurred in 1278 to one Gilbert Clope, who was foolish enough to go to sleep while standing against the wall of the bridge, and overbalancing, through the lowness of the parapet, fell into the stream and was drowned. At the inquest duly held he was pronounced *non compos mentis*. A most ingenious method for raising funds for the reparation of the bridge was hit upon in 1298 by the Court of Aldermen. A dispute between two masons was argued before the Court, who decided, in the spirit of an eastern Cadi, that if either should again offend by abusive words, he would be required to contribute the sum of 100*s.* towards the fabric of London Bridge, the amount to be levied by the Chamberlain in case of refusal to pay. In like manner, Nicholas, a "Cornhuile" baker, was bound over, in 1301, to keep the peace on penalty of paying 20*s.* towards the same excellent object. Thus, at one stroke, the worthy aldermen hoped to safeguard the morals of the citizens and the interests of their bridge.

The accounts contain a few allusions to the mediæval machinery employed in the various repairs of the bridge. For driving the piles, strong "rams" were used, and somewhat amusing were the names by which the workmen distinguished these appliances. Thus we read, in the accounts of 1440, of the "great Gebet-ram," the "Lesser Rennyng ram," and the "Great rennyng Gebet." A large "rynnyng ram of bras" was brought from "the King's works at Portsmouth to the Bridge House" in 1496, the carriage amounting to 46s. 8d. Another ram is described as a "wilkyn." Wages were paid to navvies, if we may so term them, in 1462, for "drawing the Gebet ram in pylyng lez stadelles next the bridge," and for "holding of iron to direct le ram upon lez piles." In the time of Elizabeth, we find a piece of apparatus in operation which enjoyed the title of the "Beetle." Besides the ordinary materials for repair and construction, we may note references to elm timber. In 1415, the bridge-barge, or "shoute," is mentioned as fetching a load of this wood from Fulham to London; and a little later we note the purchase of an elm growing "next Trillemyllebroke," near the house of the bishop of Ely in Holborn. The topic is illumined with a ray of pathos by the entry under March, 1422-3, "to John Fuller, a poor carpenter who was hurt in cutting down elms for the bridge, 12d." In the following June a quantity of elm was bought for the piles. Other personages besides the wardens understood the value of this species of wood, for, in 1492, it was found advisable to give 20d. to one William Mower, "to forbere the taking of elmyn timber for the kyng, provided at Bekynham for the saied bridg werkes." For some years in the reign of Henry VII a recurring item in the annual accounts, which at first sight has a whimsical appearance, is a consignment of "oistershells," at 3d. per bushel. It is difficult to clear up the obscurity of this entry, but it may be conjectured that the shells were utilized in some form as building materials.

The history of the bridge is almost a narrative of repairs. Only four-score years had passed after its completion in 1209, when the structure was so decayed through want of repairs that men were afraid to pass over it. Thus early did the bridge gain a reputation for frailty. And, in the course of time, when the incessant need of mending the bridge had become proverbial, a song was composed, which became so popular that it has now attained the rank of a nursery rhyme.   The ditty is too long to be quoted at length, but the first, second and last stanzas run as follows :—

> " London Bridge is broken down,
>   Dance o'er my Lady Lee ;
> London Bridge is broken down,
>   With a gay lady.
>
> " How shall we build it up again ?
>   Dance o'er my Lady Lee ;
> How shall we build it up again ?
>   With a gay lady.
>
> " Build it up with stone so strong,
>   Dance o'er my Lady Lee ;
> Huzza! 'twill last for ages long,
>   With a gay lady."

In 1289 we learn from Stow that a subsidy was granted towards the restoration of the structure.   A hundred years subsequently the condition of the bridge engaged the attention of "a great collection or gathering of all archbishops, bishops and other ecclesiastical persons." Notwithstanding the counsels of this distinguished assembly, things went from bad to worse, for in 1424-5 our records tell how 4s. was "paid to Richard Carleton and his fellows" for mending the pavement and examining the arch of the bridge in the middle on the west side, opposite the seventh, eighth, ninth and tenth tenements.   At this spot, the scribe grimly observes, "the bridge was found cracked (*crainatus*) and the water-course of the Thames was seen below."   So much alarm was created that an Act was "made by the Maire and Aldermen concernyng the passage of carts and carrys over London Brigge" (1425).   After deploring the "grete perell and febleness" of the causeway, the Act ordains that "noo persone from hens forthward chace nor dryve no carte ne carre shodde with iron over the sayd brydge upon payne of imprisonment of hys body and to pay 6s. 8d."   A similar tale is unfolded in the City legislation of 1482, when danger to the bridge in general, and the "grete toure at Drawbrigge" in particular, was so much apprehended that, as before, the heavier kind of vehicles were forbidden to cross except "for grete necessite and defence of this sayd Citie"; regulations were laid down as to the fishermen who frequented the stream near the bridge (a subject we shall recur to); and whereas much damage had resulted from vessels being moored to the sterlings, it was

ordered that "no ship lyeng at Fresshe Wharf, nor in other places on the
est syde of the brygge, lay nor caste no anker in the sayd soleies, nor upon
the stadelynges, nor nye unto the same by the space of 20 fathom."
Meanwhile, a disaster to one of the arches occurred in January, 1436-7, for
we find 4*d.* was bestowed on John Byndere "for timber found by the
breaking of the bridge"; a "chowte" (shoute, or barge) was hired to carry
stones from the broken tower to the Bridge House; and carpenters were
toiling night and day to avert an extension of the injury. A new wooden
arch was built in 1473. The instability of the arches may supply an
explanation of an entry under 1492: "To John Johnson in reward byrause
the Kynge's great gonne [gun] shulde not pass over the bridge, but rather
by another wey, 5*s.*"; the other "wey" probably necessitating a circuit by
way of Kingston. Masons were employed in 1497 to mend "the second
pere [pier] on th' est side next unto the drawbridge." A report of the
wardens "on viewing the foundation of the new pier" was in 1504 written
and presented "to the Lord Mayor and Sheriffs and others of the Council."
A new source of peril was pointed out in 1523 in a report made by the
master carpenter, the warden, and the master mason of the works. They
considered that great hurt was done to the woodwork in consequence of the
obstacle to the river-current created by "the mill now lying in one of the
gullies which breaketh the right course of the stream." This mill probably
formed part of the waterworks. Stone for two new arches was purchased in
1530, and in 1548 fresh piles were driven "at the starling called Chapel
Point." A committee was appointed early in Elizabeth's reign "to view the
defaults of London Bridge." The Common Council was, in 1619, informed
by the master that much damage was done by "the negligent guidance of
hoys, barges and boats passing through the arches," and the consideration
of the matter was referred to the "Committee for Letting the Lands and
Tenements belonging to the Bridge House." Again the perpetual subject
arises in 1657, when the repair of the arches was referred to the "Committee
for the Bridge House," and in 1665, when the "Committee for Letting the
Bridge House Lands" were directed "to view the defective arch of the bridge
complained of by the master, and to take some other workmen besides the
workmen of the Bridge House to assist in the view." The year after the
Great Fire not only the defective arch, but the drawbridge, gave anxiety to

the Common Council, the arch being "dangerous for passengers," and the decay threatening to spread still further. It was estimated that the repair of the arch would entail an outlay of £220. The stonework of the six cellars on the bridge and one rib or arch were also damaged by the Fire. The same melancholy note was sounded in February, 1673-4. A committee of the Court of Common Council was appointed, consisting of Sir William Peake, Sir George Waterman, Mr. Alderman Ward, Mr. Pilkington, and five Commoners, to consult with the bridge-masters, City surveyors, and other persons as to the ways and means of restoration.

Apart from the jeopardy in which the bridge residents were placed by the defects just described, the nature of the architectural plan of the bridge made accidents inevitable to passengers by water.

Under the year 1428-9, William Gregory's "Chronicle of London" gives the following account of an accident which happened to the Duke of Norfolk and his retinue when shooting the bridge: "The vij day of Novembyr the Duke of Northefolke wolde have rowyde thoroughe the brygge of London, and hys barge was rentte agayne the arche of the sayde brygge, and there were drownyde many men, the nombyr of xxx persomys and moo of gentylmen and goode yemen [yeomen]." Howell, in his "Londinopolis," published in 1657, records an old satire upon the bridge: "If London Bridge had fewer eyes it would see far better." This refers, of course, to the number of its arches and the dangers of passing through them. In Ray's "English Proverbs" is another quaint saying to the same purpose: "London Bridge was made for wise men to go over and fools to go under." The dangers of shooting London Bridge about the year 1663, are thus alluded to in the amusing "Travels of M. de Monteonys." Speaking of the boats which plied on the Thames to carry passengers to the City or Westminster, by way of avoiding the rude English coaches and the ruder paved streets of London. "They never," he says, "go below the bridge, although there is not any place to which they cannot be had. But it is considered dangerous for these small boats to go under the bridge when the tide is running up, for the water has then an extreme rapidity, even greater than when it is returning, and the two currents are united." In describing his visit to the Tower he states that neither in going nor returning did his boat pass under the bridge, for the tide being running up there was a fall of more than two feet. The passengers left the boat, crossed to the other side of the bridge, and then re-entered it, whilst the waterman, he adds, had no difficulty in descending the fall, but a great deal in mounting up it again.

After the city was restored from the desolation caused by the Great Fire, a greatly increased commerce and consequent increase of the traffic over London Bridge caused considerable inquiry to be made as to the possibility of increasing its breadth. A tradition exists that the cross over the dome of St. Paul's having been cast in Southwark, the street of London Bridge was too narrow, and its numerous arches too low to allow of its being brought that way into the City.* Some remarks by Pennant are worth citing as evidence of the condition and aspect of the bridge about the middle of the 18th century: "The houses on each side of the bridge-way," he says, "overhung and leaned in a most terrific manner. In most places they hid the arches and nothing appeared but the rude piers. I well remember the street of London Bridge, narrow, darksome, and dangerous to passengers from the multitude of carriages: frequent arches of strong timber crossing the street from the tops of the houses, to keep them together and from falling into the river. Nothing but use could preserve the repose of the inmates, who soon grew deaf to the noise of falling waters, the clamour of watermen, or the frequent shrieks of drowning wretches. Most of the houses were tenanted by pin or needle makers, and economical ladies were wont to drive from the St. James's end of the town to make cheap purchases." Three vacancies were left on each side between the houses and opposite to each other, to enable passengers to obtain a view of the river east and west, and also to step out of the way of carts and coaches. As there was no regular footway over the bridge, it was the most usual and safest custom to follow a carriage which might be passing across it.

The history of London Bridge during the 18th century chiefly consists of doubts whether the bridge would stand, surveys of its buildings, repairs, reports of architects, schemes for its alteration, and controversies concerning the erection of a new bridge.

* Mr. R. Garraway Rice, F.S.A., informs me that the dome and cross of St. Paul's were made by Andrew Niblett, and probably at the Merton Copper Mills, Mitcham, of which he was the proprietor.

§ 6.   The Drawbridge.

Between the sixth and seventh piers of Peter of Colechurch's Bridge, counting from the southern end, an aperture allowed the passage of vessels which, in consequence of high tide or the height of their masts, could not sail under any of the arches. The opening was crossed by a wooden bascule, which was raised to admit ships, or to prevent the inroad of a hostile force. This movable appliance, like the main bridge, passed through many vicissitudes. The books for the year 1388 speak of the construction of a new drawbridge. Some years elapsed before it was completed, for in 1406 we find a reference to the removal of "le Fauxbrigg," which we may presume to have been a temporary causeway for use during the preparation of the new bascule.

In 1413 mention occurs of an officer who superintended the working of the bascule, and watched the vehicular traffic over the main bridge. For "keeping the passage of carts and ships at the bridge," Nicholas Holford received 21s. 3d. In another entry for the same year the keeper of the passage is also described as clerk of the chapel, and he seems to have received a separate salary for each of these oddly contrasted employments. Only eight years went by before repairs were called for, as in 1421 the wardens are charged for "mending the trap upon the drawbridge." Shortly afterwards the approach to the City was strengthened by the erection of a strong tower. Stow says that "the tower on London Bridge at the north end of the drawbridge (for that bridge was then readily to be drawn up, as well to give passage for ships to Queenhithe, as for the resistance of any foreign force) was begun to be built in the year 1426." It must be to some other tower that allusion is made in the bridge accounts under date of February, 1426-27, when, in expectation of the state entry of the Duke of Bedford, workmen were employed to "mend the battlements and the lower battlements at the drawbridge." Expenses were incurred in March, 1441-42, for "making le drawebrigge upon the brigge," an entry which apparently indicates the construction of a fresh bascule. Some twenty years subsequently the fabric was in good working order, as an entry under 1461 shows that a sum of 10s. 2d. was received from the passage of ships under the drawbridge, each ship paying the high toll of 2s. Possibly the odd 2d. points to some irregularity in the management. Certain it is that the Common Council deemed it necessary, in 1463, to pass an Act "concernyng the drawynge of the draughte brydge of London," by which it was provided that the bridge-masters should take for each drawing 6*d.* and not more, and if they should refuse to admit any vessel when required they should forfeit the sum of 3*s.* 4*d.*, "to be levied on the goods of the said masters." But ere long the wardens were denied the luxury of overcharging by the decay of the bascule itself. No tolls were received from ships in 1480 because the bridge could not be drawn. It was not absolutely immovable, but its feeble condition may be judged from the fact that the Common Council expressly ordered that it should not be raised except for the protection of the City from a foe. The bascule and its machinery were in so sorry a plight in 1497 that Sir William Martyn and Thomas Ward, and divers commoners may well be pardoned for spending as much as 18*s.* 11*d.* on a repast after "avewing the remedye of the drawbridge toure." The "remedye" requires to be interpreted as *suggested* remedy, for in the next year's accounts the further sum of 12*s.* is set down for a repast to divers Aldermen and commoners "avewing the daunger and jeopardye of the drawebridge." The work of restoration proceeded but leisurely, and when an emergency arose in 1500, a heroic effort had to be made to meet the sudden call, as the following entry will reveal:—To the carpenters working out of due time as well by night as by day in mending and repairing "of the full ruynous draw-bridge, and thereof making sure for to be drawen alle redye for the Kinge's berkis [barks] to have hadde passage through, and in other works, 16*s.* 6*d.*" The structure was not in use in 1506, and though carpenters and labourers were employed upon it, the 12*d.* they received from the wardens was only payment for removal of broken rails and other wreckage caused by a gale. At this period the wardens consoled themselves for the loss of the ships' tolls by renting two chambers in the drawbridge tower, each tenant paying 3*s.* 4*d.* In 1526 the bascule was still closed to shipping, and the account books intimate that this state of things is likely to continue "till the time the stonework of the drawbridge tower be amended." When London apprehended an invasion of rioters in 1549 a false or makeshift drawbridge was ordered to be provided "with all spede," "to be usyd for a season in case nede shuld requyer," the intention being, as we may conjecture, to destroy the useless drawbridge on the approach of the rebels. Fortunately, however, "nede" did not "requyer," and the bridge of timber which the masters constructed in 1557 "at the drawbridge" was evidently not a movable one. It was newly planked in 1575, an operation which Stow himself may have witnessed. And, to take a considerable leap onwards, we find that matters remained in much the same condition till July, 1666, when the question of making a drawbridge upon London Bridge was referred to the Committee for the City Works and to report. An order was made in the following month for the drawbridge to be made "with all convenient speed." The speed was not remarkable, judging from the fact that in 1667 the master carpenter reported that the timber was in a state of decay and the repairs would, he estimated, cost £200. A new bascule was completed in May, 1672, only, however, to be replaced, fifty years later, by another. This picturesque feature of London Bridge finally disappeared in 1748.

§ 7.   Gates and Towers on the Bridge.

It will be convenient, at this point of our narrative, to glance at the gates and towers on the bridge, and some of its minor adjuncts, reserving till presently our remarks on the Chapel and houses. That the bridge was safeguarded by gates in the 13th century is evident from the story of an incident in the Civil Wars of Henry III's reign. When Simon de Montfort was seen to be approaching the City from the south, John Gisors, one of the King's adherents, fastened up the bridge and flung the keys into the river. The gates, nevertheless, were battered down; a crowd of sympathisers rushed out to join De Montfort, who then without difficulty made his way into the City. One of the gates alluded to no doubt belonged to the tower which stood over the first arches at the Southwark terminus. "This gate," Stow informs us, "with the tower thereupon, and two arches of the bridge, fell down, and no man perished by the fall thereof, in the year 1436; towards the new building whereof divers charitable citizens gave large sums of money." The bridge accounts thus refer to the disaster under date January, 1436-7 :— "Paid for the hire of one chowte (shoute) to carry stones from the broken tower to the Bridge House, 14*s*. 8*d*."

LONDON BRIDGE FROM AN ENGRAVI

On the second pier from the Southwark side is the Bridge Gate with traitors' heads upon it ; further north, between
Stone Tower on which the heads of traitors were until then displayed.   The remains of St. Thomas's C
gap is Nonesuch House.   The dangers of navigating the bridge are graphicall

BY JOHN NORDEN, ABOUT A.D. 1600.

sixth and seventh piers, is the Drawbridge ; adjoining this is the " new frame," built in 1577 on the site of the Great
l, with a modern dwelling house above, are seen on the large centre pier.   On the north side of the third
icted in an overturned boat, whose occupants are seen struggling in the water.

In 1471 the Bastard Falconbridge and his "Kentish mariners," as Stow terms them, assaulted this restored entrance, and burned both it and thirteen houses on the bridge. Over this gate the traitors' heads were fixed in 1577, having been removed from the tower north of the drawbridge. They are represented in this position in Norden's View of London Bridge (opposite). Sensitive citizens, who turned with disgust from the contemplation of these savage relics, could find a more cheerful object of study in the newly gilded and coloured "portitures and armes," for decorating which, in 1581, a painter received £3 15s. The gates were watched by a porter. An entry in the records for 1382-3 shows that "John Dunston, servant of the Mayor, was appointed keeper of the gate upon London Bridge." In 1557 mention is made of payment to a porter for keeping the gates. The bridge gatehouse was let, in 1665, to one Thomas Heath. No remarkable event appears to have occurred at the southern gate for a long period. A great fire in September, 1725, destroyed many houses at the southern end of the bridge, and severely damaged the gate. A report of the Committee for letting the Bridge House lands dealt, in May, 1728, with a project for enlarging and re-building the gateway. "We find," runs this document, "that the said gate is now but 13 feet wide, and to enlarge the same so that two carts or coaches may pass through together, the middle part thereof must be entirely taken down." The estimated expense was £1,000. Without further delay operations were commenced, and the new structure was completed before the close of 1728. Two posterns were provided for foot passengers. Over the portal were placed the royal arms, at the base of which appeared the inscription, "This gate was widened from eleven to eighteen feet in the mayoralty of Sir Edward Becher, Knight. S.P.Q.L." It did not enjoy a remarkable longevity, for in 1754 it had become dilapidated, and in 1766 it was, with the rest of the City gates, finally removed. A bronze token is extant which bears on its obverse a view of the bridge gate, with the legend "Bridge Gate as re-built, 1728"; on the exergue, "Taken down, 1766." The reverse is adorned with a figure of Justice.

The Great or Stone Gate, to which we may now turn our attention, was a more imposing structure. It stood on the north side of the drawbridge. Upon its battlements the traitors' heads were formerly placed, and it was

THE BRIDGE GATE IN 1616, FROM VISSCHER'S VIEW OF LONDON.

therefore sometimes known as Traitors' Gate. Stow, as we have before noted, gives 1426 as the year of its erection, but in another passage he observes that the tower at the drawbridge was "newly begun to be built in the year 1426." It is obvious that some kind of tower must have accompanied the drawbridge from its first establishment. To the previous tower reference appears to be made in an item of the bridge accounts for 1392, where three shields of the arms of the King and Queen are mentioned as being hung over the Stone Gate, in anticipation of a royal pageant.

Next year the wardens went to some little expense in ornamenting the face of the tower with effigies of King Richard II and his consort. The "images" were cut in freestone by Thomas Wrenk, and set within "tabernacles." Wrenk also executed three shields of the arms of the King and Queen and St. Edward, which were placed beside the statues. The sculptor received £10 for his work. Double that sum was awarded to the artist who coloured the statues, shields and protecting tabernacles. In order to throw the new embellishments into strong relief, a layer of white plaster was spread over the wall of the tower around the figures and coats of arms. A more gruesome addition to the tower sent a shudder through the citizens who thronged the bridge in the autumn of 1416. Benedict Wolman, a London "hostiller," as we learn from an "inquisition" preserved in the City records, had been concerned with others in a plot to compass King Henry V's death, and to replace him by Thomas Warde, called Trumpyngtone, who was alleged to be none other than the long-concealed Richard II. Wolman was sentenced to death, and hanged at Tyburn, his head being set upon London Bridge, at the place called "Le Drawebrugge." A few days afterwards the head of William Parchemyner [Parchment-maker], or Fyssher, was impaled on the battlement. Parchemyner was an accomplice of Sir John Oldcastle. In those troubled times the masters did well to look after the defences of the bridge. To their laudable attention to details we may perhaps attribute the mending of the "port-coleys" in the Stone Gate, in 1425-6, an operation which entailed the moderate outlay of 3*d.*

In 1426 the tower adjoining the drawbridge was re-built. "John Reynwell, mayor of London," Stow informs us, "laid one of the first corner stones in the foundation of this work, the other three were laid by the sheriffs and bridge-masters: upon every of these four stones was engraven in fair Roman letters the name of Ihesus.   And these stones I have seen laid in the bridge storehouse since they were taken up."   Gregory's Chronicle also states that in this year (1426) the "tower on the draught brygge of London was begoune.   And the Mayre layde the fyrste stone, and mo othyr aldyrmen with him."   When we turn to the bridge records, indications are manifest that a new undertaking was being energetically planned and executed.   Expenses are set down for a breakfast at the Bridge House for the auditors, divers aldermen and commoners, together with the Recorder, Chamberlain, John Carpenter (the Common Clerk), and Richard Osebarn.   Round the table an important discussion took place "as to obtaining a benevolence from the executors of Richard Whityngton for a relief for building the tower anew at the drawbridge."   As Carpenter was one of these executors his presence was especially welcome.   A week afterwards axe and hammer were at work, and 3s. 4d. was paid to Walter Lokmaker, smith, for taking away the old "ßeill" of the great Stone Gate, and fixing the new iron one.   Geoffrey Crotenden received £4 12s. for twelve great "corbelstonys of kardston of Kent" for the new tower to be built at the drawbridge.   Other loads of stone and supplies of lime and sand for the "castle" also appear in the accounts.   The executors of the will of John Burton, late citizen and mercer of London, handed to the bridge-masters, in 1493, the worthy mercer's bequest of 112s., to be applied for the construction of a battlement on the Stone Tower next the drawbridge.   A yet larger legacy was handed to the bridge-masters, in 1523, by the wardens of the "mystery of grocers" in the name of the late "Syr John Crosby, Knyght and alderman," towards the cost of widening the roadway at the Great Gate, with the stipulation that the memory of the donor should be perpetuated in "armys wrought in freestone at the seide place."

In the 13th year of Henry VIII the "Grete Gate" was adorned with four new statues of SS. Peter, Paul, Michael and George, in freestone, which were "set in howsinges of frestone."   The figures were the work of "Mathewe Peter, Spanyarde," foreign talent being apparently preferred to native.   A year or two later the effigies of two lions, which ornamented the gate, were gilded with fine gold by Andrew Wrighte, painter, for the sum of 5s.   Further testimony to the care which was then being bestowed upon this portion of the bridge is seen in the gift of £20 from Sir William Butlar, Knight and alderman, towards the cost of enlarging the way and void ground at the Great Gate, a condition being attached that Sir William's arms should be wrought in freestone, and the tablet erected "at the said place." In the accounts for 1531 we find reference to glass for the new tenements at the Great Gate. The history of the Stone Gate was now nearing its end. In April, 1577, the decayed tower and arch were taken to pieces, the accounts indicating that £38 16s. 7d. was paid to the labourers engaged in the operation. "Then," says Stow, "were the heads of the traitors removed thence, and set on the tower over the gate at the bridge foot towards Southwark." Upon the site of the vanished tower arose the handsome " Frame," to which we shall refer later on under the subject of the bridge houses.

A pretty custom was in vogue in the reigns of Henry VII and Henry VIII, of decorating the gates of the bridge and Bridge House with leafy boughs and garlands of flowers on Midsummer-day. On one occasion the records speak of 3s. 11d. expended in thus beautifying the Bridge House Gate. In more parsimonious times only 8d. was disbursed; but another year found the wardens in a liberal enough mood to add 2d. for "pokkes to undersett the jessemen" [pots for holding jessamine].

Besides the statues which embellished the Stone Tower, there stood on the bridge two figures of saints, which the citizens would probably salute with pious reverence as they passed along the bridgeway. On the west wall rose an image of St. Thomas of Canterbury. This is alluded to in an entry in the books for 1492: "To Laurence Emler, for the workmanship of the image of St. Thomas, wrought in stone, standing upon the wall on the west side of the said bridge, 40s.," and a marginal note intimates that this statue was "newly-made" by Emler. A new pier was constructed in 1529, and its position is marked in the records as on the west side of the "void rome [room] upon London Brigge under the ymage of Saynt Thomas there." The other effigy was that of St. Catherine, which was erected in the reign of Henry VIII. Under date 1521, Mathewe Peter, the Spanish sculptor already mentioned, is stated to have received 8s. for carving " an image of Seint Katerine, in freestone, whiche ys set over an arche in th' est side of the brode loke [broad lock] in the honour of the Quene's Grace of Englande."

A few words may be added here with respect to some minor adjuncts of the bridge. The rental of 1358 fixes the locality of the compter or accountant's house on the west side of the bridge at its northern end, between the Chapel and the staples of the bridge towards London. In the accounts for 1526 an entry relates to the Storehouse upon London Bridge, and three loads of lime are noted as being delivered there; but the exact site of this building it is not easy to determine. Another building over the precise character and purpose of which a veil of obscurity rests was the Pin House. Both in 1547 and 1553 candles were purchased for some unexplained use at the "Pynhouse." Stocks and a cage for the discipline of the unruly formed part of the furniture of the bridge, and are represented in an engraving in some editions of Foxe's "Martyrs" as standing in close proximity. That the Common Council were heedful of sanitary matters in the reign of Richard II is shown by an order of the court, directing that the latrines at the bridge should be kept and repaired by the wardens. On the cognate subject of sewers the accounts do not greatly enlighten us. There is an item in the statements for the year 1498 concerning oak planks, which were used for the "common sewar" within the borough of Southwark. The "cloaca" is alluded to in a deed of the year 1294, and seems to have been also known as "le cluse" (sluice), and was apparently a kind of gutter.

The payment of 20*d.* to "four carpenters for hanging up the gates by night on London Bridge" (Bridge House records, 1554) serves as a quaint reminder of the custom of closing the bridge portals after dark.

§ 8.   The Chapel.

Next in interest to the bridge itself is the famous Chapel dedicated to St. Thomas of Canterbury, and familiarly called St. Thomas of the Bridge. This was erected on the tenth or centre pier, which measured 35 feet in breadth and 115 feet from point to point. The building was 60 feet in length by 20 feet broad, and stood over the parapet on the eastern side of the bridge. The western front facing the Bridge Street was 40 feet in height, having a plain gable surmounted by a cross; and was divided by four buttresses into three parts. The centre of these divisions contained a rich pointed arched window of one mullion, with a quatrefoil in the top, and the two sides were occupied by the entrances to the Chapel from the Bridge Street, each being ascended by three steps.

The interior consisted of two chapels, one above the other; the upper chapel was lofty, being supported by fourteen groups of elegant clustered columns, and lighted by eight pointed windows. Below each of the windows were three arched recesses, separated by small pillars; the

WEST FRONT OF THE CHAPEL OF ST. THOMAS ON LONDON BRIDGE.

roof was originally formed of lofty pointed arches. The eastern end of this beautiful building formed a semi-hexagon, having a smaller window in each of its divisions. The lower chapel, or crypt, was constructed in the bridge itself, and was entered from the upper chapel and the street, as well as (at low water) from the sterling surrounding the pier. It was about 20 feet in height, with a roof supported by clustered columns, from each of which sprang seven ribs, whose intersections were bound by fillets of roses and clusters of regal and ecclesiastical masks. This chapel also contained a rich series of windows similar to, though much smaller than, those above; and the floor was paved with black and white marble. Under the Chapel staircase, in the middle of the building, were buried the remains of Peter of Colechurch, but neither brass plate nor any inscription marked the site of his tomb.

London seems to have rivalled Canterbury in its devotion to St. Thomas. This is not surprising, as Becket was the son of a prominent London citizen, and his rise in fortune must have been watched with particular interest by his fellow citizens, whilst the horror with which the country generally received the news of his murder was, for the same reason, intensified in the City of London. The "martyrdom" of Becket took place on the 29th December, 1170, and he was canonized in 1173, only three years before the foundation of the bridge. In dedicating the Bridge Chapel

INTERIOR OF THE UPPER CHAPEL.

to St. Thomas, Peter of Colechurch's decision may have been affected by some shrewd elements of worldly wisdom. The good priest's task was heavy enough: copious funds were required; and the Archbishop's was a name to conjure with. Public bodies in London vied with each other in doing honour to the Saint. The City in its corporate capacity placed itself under the patronage of St. Thomas, whose effigy, with that of St. Paul, appeared on both the Mayoralty and the Corporate seal. The latter seal contained the legend *Me que te peperi ne cesses Thoma tueri* (Cease not, O Thomas, to protect me who gave thee birth). The Hospital of St. Thomas of Acon in Cheapside was also founded by Becket's sister in his honour, close to the site of his birthplace, about twenty years after his death. In 1466 the authority of Rome was invoked to replenish the bridge coffers, and "Master Godard, of the Order of the Friars Minor," was rewarded for two Papal bulls which seem to have been procured through his instrumentality. The first granted "an indulgence for forty days to those who should yearly visit the chapel on the feast of St. Thomas the Martyr, and on the day of translation of the same from the first vespers to the second vespers, and give to the repairs of the

INTERIOR OF THE LOWER CHAPEL.

chapel." The second extended the indulgence to one hundred days to those who should in addition pay visits on Good Friday and the Assumption of the Blessed Mary the Virgin.

The Chapel, as already stated, was built by Peter of Colechurch, and formed part of his design for the erection of the bridge, as is shown by the extension eastwards of the Chapel pier. It was the first and also the most beautiful of the buildings on the bridge. No particulars of its construction are preserved, but it would appear that only one of the two apartments (probably the lower) was at first used for religious purposes, as the accounts for the years 1384 to 1397 contain many items of the cost of building the "new chapel." In 1384-5 300 feet of Portland stone was supplied at 6*d.* a foot for a stall, in 1388-9 "twenty great pieces of hard stone from Kent called noweles" for the steps of the new chapel cost 15*d.* each, and in the latter year "140 feet of hard stone called skeutable" was bought at 6*d.* per foot. With the increase in the number of endowed chantries further additions became necessary; in 1392 the wardens paid £4 14*s.* 4*d.* for twenty-one cartloads of stone from Reigate for the new chapel, including carriage to the "Breghous." What may perhaps have been a third chapel,

L

situated probably in a corner of the two larger chapels, is mentioned in 1387-8, when a small (sanctus?) bell was bought for the little Chapel. In September, 1396, the large sum of £14 3*s.* 6*d.* was spent on forty-three cartloads of Reigate stone for the "upper vault," the battlements, and "le vys" (*i.e.*, the vise or spiral staircase) of the new Chapel. The great number of windows in both chapels made the provision of glass a heavy expense. The accounts for 1397 show that 69 feet of white glass was provided for two windows, costing 54*s.* 7½*d.*: besides 37½ feet of white, and 150 feet of stained glass containing images and shields, costing together £6 17*s.* 6*d.* A payment for mending broken windows was made in 1418 to Hugh Wyse "Docheman glasyere." Other payments for decorative repairs occur. In 1420 "J. Londones, peyntour," received 13*s.* 4*d.* for painting a pane in the chapel vault. In 1427 certain shields hanging on the "perclos" (or screen) in the chapel were repaired. These probably contained the arms of benefactors. A payment of 10*s.* occurs in 1426 for painting the image of the Virgin. In 1489 a substantial gift was received from Anneys Breteyn, widow, of £40, as an instalment of £60 "towards the new making of the two stone walls with two images in tabernacles thereupon standing in the void room on the north side of the said chapel." The west side of the Chapel was in need of extensive repair in 1533, when new "brestes of stone work" were made.

It is time to turn from the Chapel to its occupants. These were, in the early days of its history, the members of the Fraternity of St. Thomas, who are variously described in the bridge records as the "Master and Brethren of the Bridge of London," the "Chaplains, Brethren and Sisters of the Bridge of London," "Brethren and Proctors of London Bridge," etc. Peter of Colechurch was the first head of the Fraternity, and Godard, the chaplain, a friar minor, appears to have succeeded him as ecclesiastical superior. The number of chaplains varied from time to time, as new chantries were founded. In 1350 four chaplains were officiating in praying for the souls of benefactors. The earliest accounts, for 1381–2, give the weekly wages of four chaplains as 11*s.* 5½*d.*, and that of the clerk of the Chapel, who was, as we have seen, a very useful official, as 15*d.* In 1494 there were two chaplains and four clerks, each of whom received 20*d.* weekly. One John Coventre, a chaplain, who was too old and feeble to perform divine service, received in 1418 a pension "for term of his life." In 1303 Sir Robert Fitz Walter obtained from the Corporation the grant of a tenement in Colechurch Street, charged with the maintenance of one chaplain in the bridge Chapel. Other chantries were established for John de Lyndeseye in 1334, by Ralph de Lenne in 1349, and by John de Hatfield in 1363.

In 1419–20 the priests of the Chapel were "unjustly and maliciously suspended," whereupon the wardens purchased an absolution for them from the Bishop of London, at a cost of 6s. 8d. The liberties and privileges of the chaplains were again attacked, and a Papal bull was procured for their confirmation in 1465–6. The number of Flemings and other "Teutons" residing in London at this period is shown by entries in the accounts for 1468–9 and the following year, of the receipt of 4s. from a certain friar minor, for license to celebrate in the chapel and hear the confessions of persons of the Teutonic tongue and preach to them in Lent. In 1480–1 a sum of 5s. was received, for a like privilege, from a Dutch friar.

The salient features of the method of divine service in the Chapel may be now reviewed, and it will be convenient to connect the scattered notes at our disposal in chronological order. Naturally the great celebration of the year took place on the day of the Translation of St. Thomas of Canterbury, July 7th. It was then, no doubt, that the little edifice was crowded with devout citizens, from the dignified Alderman to the rough-clad petreman. So far as the limited resources of the chaplains permitted, everything was done to make the occasion attractive, even to the hiring of some specially gifted chorister. Thus, under 1408, we light upon the entry in the accounts: "Paid to a chanter, and his expenses and food on the feast of the Translation of St. Thomas, beyond the oblations received at the same feast, 2s. 6d." Three years later expenses are allowed for the chanters in the Chapel on the day of the festival. A full choral service is indicated in a memorandum of 1414, where, in addition to the ordinary chanter and clerks, mention is made of aid rendered by William "Chauntor" and other chanters for vespers and other musical offices. A breakfast for the choir formed part of the disbursements. In the month of April, 1417, a sum of £4 was paid "in aid of a new pair of organs for the chapel." The epithet "new" points to the previous existence of an organ.

One can pleasantly exercise the fancy in imagining how the passing boatmen would linger near the arches to listen to—

> "the pealing organ blow
> To the full-voiced quire below."

On Christmas Day, too, the Chapel must have been full of animation, "divers men and boys" being called in to assist the choir. At these and other seasons the oblations of the worshippers were collected, and the amounts duly entered in the wardens' books. At times the musical abilities of the clerks of St. Nicholas, or the Company of Parish Clerks, were requisitioned, as in December, 1416, when they attended upon the wardens "in the counter on the bridge at the time of the account," and gave some kind of musical entertainment, in the form, perhaps, of glees and madrigals. Their modest fee came to 14*d.* At the coronation pageant of Edward IV's queen, also, and at other celebrations, twenty-five members of this society were present on the bridge, the choir of St. Thomas's being, of course, insufficient to cope with such great occasions. In 1491 the organs "standing in the lower chapell" were repaired. Though the edifice, as we shall presently see, was broken up in 1554, the services were continued till within a few years of the Chapel's disappearance. In 1541 the purchase of a "holy water sprinkle" for a penny is recorded. One priest and one clerk were conducting the usual ministrations in 1548, and the accounts allow for such items as singing bread, wax for candles, and the like. But, in 1550, the strains of chant and anthem echoed for the last time from the walls of St. Thomas's Chapel. The organs were removed. "To Howe, organ-maker," wrote the clerk who kept the bridge-masters' books, "for brokerage of the organs that were in the chapell by hym solde to a Portingale [Portuguese], 2*s.*"

When, towards the close of the 14th century the new Chapel was in course of construction, appropriate changes took place in the belfry. John Beauchamp, plumber, stripped the belfry and Chapel of its old lead, and some thirty years afterwards a sanctus bell was purchased for 2*s.* 4*d.*, and a little later a carpenter was engaged to hang bells in the Chapel. The reverse process was carried out in 1548, and the terms of the entry in the records are suspiciously suggestive of agitating incident, possibly of a threatened seizure by the Crown : "To fyve carpenters and one labourer working by one morninge in taking downe of the belles in the steple upon the bridg, the bellframe, and conveighing of the same home unto the Bridge House, iij*s*."

We may now take a cursory view of the furniture of the Chapel, first, however, pausing to make one or two notes on a subject that closely and personally interested the attendant clergy, viz., their vestments. The blessing of a vestment in 1421 cost the wardens the modest sum of 8*d*. Ten years later the worn vestments were repaired at an expense of 8*d*., and for 26*s*. 8*d*. a cope was brilliantly adorned with an orphrey. Elsewhere in the records we remark the purchase of two new vestments for feast-days for 30*s*. An altar-covering of "steyned" cloth brightened the Chapel in the summer of 1417. For painting an altar-cloth Heathe, "the King's painter," was employed in 1546. Coloured cloth also draped the font. At Lent, 1416, the crucifix was hidden from view by two specially procured yards of "bokeram" [buckram], 22½*d*. Of the Communion-plate only scanty particulars can be gleaned. A newly-made chalice was blessed in 1429 for a fee of 8*d*. This chalice, with a paten, weighing 16½ ounces, was fashioned for 43*s*. by Robert Bosam, goldsmith, the careful clerk recording the price per ounce as 2*s*. 8*d*. A memorandum in the Small Register mentions two chalices gilt within and without, and one gilt within only. The respective values were 53*s*. 8*d*., 38*s*. 8*d*., and 31*s*. To turn now to the use of lights: it appears that two torches were bought in 1392, although, of course (excepting that of Peter of Colechurch), no burials took place in the Chapel. Tapers and candles occur in the accounts of 1461; the tapers were intended for the feast of the Purification, the candles "for burning about the sepulchre of Our Lord Jesus Christ in the chapel at Easter." The weight was 20¼ lbs., and the cost 20*d*. A canopy of canvas was procured in 1521 to protect the "braunche of lampis" or candelabrum when not in use. From undated records we draw the following items: A hanging lamp burning before the Body of Our Lord Jesus Christ, and a yard of "felewet" serving from the canopy upon the Body of the Lord, 13*s*.; and to a certain man for making a canopy hanging in the Chapel upon the Body of Christ, 10*s*.

Some information of interest is found respecting the service books. Three books of the Chapel were bound in 1392 for 8*s*. A more elaborate reference occurs in 1397. The interesting items may be reproduced : For writing two new antiphonars (chant-books, with music) for the Chapel, and two calendars for the same, 6s. 4d.; for four clasps of latten gilt, and four "tyssues" of silk bought for the same, 12s.; skins for covering the same, together with making and sewing, and eight great buttons with "tasseles" of silk, 18s.; and one mass-book. John Walcote, a "lymnour," or writer, received in 1415 a fee of 9s. 4d. for "lymnynyg" a secular legend or lection, and we must vainly regret that this and similar specimens of the Chapel books are not now extant. Next year Richard More, "bookbynder," was paid 15s. for binding two new legends, "one secular and the other of the saints, together with covering of them." Another glimpse of the mediæval bookbinders' craft is afforded in the item (1423): To Roger Douns, for binding a missal and gradual, and for cleaning and glosing the back of the same, 5s. 6d. The correction of a missal cost the wardens 10s. 8d., the "correction" apparently being on a scale of some magnitude. The particulars of the Chapel furniture must close with a glance at a miscellany of articles and materials not readily classified. A faldstool was painted and covered for 7s. 8d., and a new "holywater scopp" was bought in the same year, 1385. The purchases in 1396 included a new key and a "havegooday" of iron, with two plates of iron for the same, for the outer door of the new Chapel. The following entries occur in 1531: To Henry Colvyle, goldsmith, for a new chalice weighing 12¼ ounces, 61s.; for a censer of latten, 3s. 4d.; Isebrande Johnson, joiner, for a new border and "creste" for the roodloft, 20s.; to Richard Rownanger, painter, for gilding the crucifix, Mary and John, two "angells," and the border and crest of the said loft with "fyne golde" and "for payntyng of the parclose wythin and withowte with vermelon," £6 3s. 4d.; and lastly, for colouring the Chapel roof with stone colour. The goods of the Chapel tempted some burglars, in 1528, to acts of sacrilege, and the money laid out by the wardens in consequence amounted to 34s.

A house was provided for the chaplains, and a curious provision was made for their personal comfort in the will of Isabella la Juvene, who left "to the pittance of the chaplains, brethren and sisters of the house of the Bridge of London, for their table on the day of my death, half a mark." In 1384, 32lbs. of "pewter-vessel" was bought for the chaplains, the price being 8*s.* A breakfast (*jantaculum*) in the Chapel took place in 1404 at at the time of an inquisition of divers writings and muniments relating to an unpaid quitrent.

In 1539 40 we hear the first knell of the Chapel's approaching doom in the change of its dedication, 2*s.* being paid "to a paynter dwellynge in Southwarke for defasynge and mendynge of dyvers pyctures of Thomas Beckett in Our Lady Chapell upon the bridge. The clerical staff had become reduced to one priest and one clerk in 1541 42. In 1543 "a brotherer [broderer]" received 13*s.* 4*d.* for the "altering of the marterdom of Thomas Beckett unto the image of Our Lady." A law-suit sounded a mournful anticipation of the end, and a committee of Common Council met to debate " concerning the staying of Ashley's suit touching the chapel on the bridge." The final sentence came in 1549. " It is agreid," runs a City minute of 22nd January, 1548 9, "that Mr. Wylford and Mr. Judde, surveyours of the workes of the brydge, shall to-morowe begyn to cause the chapell upon the same brydge to be defaced, and to be translated into a dwellyng-house, with as moche spede as they convenyentlye maye." For a year or two, nevertheless, the wretched remnant of the once beautiful edifice lingered on, being in the charge of a watchman, " Hew" Boswell, who kept guard over the condemned walls at 2*s.* a week. In 1553 the agents of destruction appeared on the scene. Masons and carpenters take stone from stone and beam from beam. Labourers carry chalk and rubbish and boards, and make the place "clean"— a cleanness that might have drawn tears from the shade of honest Peter of Colechurch. The history winds up with this prosaic record : " 1566 67. Received the 25th January, of Drewe Momperson, in part payment of 40 marks for a licence to set over the lease of his house, the late chapel upon the bridge, for the term of years to come that was granted to William Bridger, grocer, his predecessor deceased, £6 13*s.* 4*d.*"

§ 9.   The Bridge Houses and Shops.

Singular picturesqueness and animation were lent to the old bridge by the houses which lined each side of the thoroughfare. It is impossible to assign a date to the first appearance of these buildings, but the records certainly point to the erection of dwellings on the bridge before a quarter of a century had elapsed after the death of Peter of Colechurch. So early as the 5th of Henry III (1221) a grant was made to the bridge of London of land in the parish of St. Olave, Southwark, "which [the land] lies between the land of the bridge towards the east and the land of Thomas de St. Christopher towards the west from the highway leading to the houses of the bridge." The document is witnessed by Serle Mercer, Mayor. Two years later the frontage of one of the bridge houses is noted as measuring $8\frac{1}{4}$ yards. From entries in the Register of Deeds which may be assigned to the early part of the 13th century, we ascertain that enterprising tradesmen had already availed themselves of the excellent business situation of the bridge thoroughfare. A grant was made by Andrew, son of Bastian, butcher, to the Fraternity and the proctors of the bridge of "one shop upon the bridge between the shop of Andrew le Ferun and the shop of the bridge." About 1250, a grant was made by "Eufemia, daughter of Andrew le Ferun, to Michael Tovy, warden of the bridge of London, and the brethren of the same place," of "all right in her tenement adjoining the stone gate of the bridge of London on the south, which Andrew her father held of the master and brethren of the bridge aforesaid." The witnesses were Ralph Trey, Rich. Joye, Walter de Cheswyk, and others. Another London lady figures in a deed which, as shown by the signatures of Sir Michael Tovy and Robert de Basing, "proctors of the said bridge," appertains to the same period. Alice, sister of Robert le Barbour, made over "to God and the bridge of London, and the brothers and proctors of the same bridge, a place with a house built thereupon, upon the bridge of London in the parish of St. Magnus, at the head of the same bridge towards the east, next the way which leads to the quay of Colrad on the south." The dimensions are recorded as 8 yards by $4\frac{3}{4}$ yards. Another deed alludes to "the houses built at the head of the bridge of London towards Suwerk in the east, between the house of Anger, the husband of Beatrice la Fraunceise, towards the south, and the cross standing over the next pier *(pilarum)* towards the north."

The citizens were properly mindful of the stability of their bridge, and a transaction dating at the close of the 13th century evinces their watchfulness over the tenants of the bridge. This deed takes the form of a covenant between Henry Poteman and his wife Dionisia, on the one side, and Sir John Bretoun, knight, then warden of the City, Robert de Basyng, William de Betoigne, John de Cant [Canterbury], Richard Aiswi, William le Mazelin, Adam de Rok, Thomas Romain, John de Dunstapl, aldermen of the City, and Adam de Fulham, then alderman of the said bridge, on the other. The fishmonger and his wife agree to embed, in a strong foundation of stone and lime, four wooden posts which support one of the bridge houses. This building apparently overhung the stream and adjoined Poteman's house, "which is next the street leading to the sluice (*cloaca*) of the said bridge on the west part."

The traffic over the bridge doubtless made the keeping of a hostelry in the vicinity of the bridge a profitable speculation. The "Bear," at the bridge foot, in the parish of St. Olave, built by Thomas Drynkewatre, taverner of London, and leased by him to James Beaufleur, citizen of London, on 7th July, 1319, sustained for three ensuing centuries a great reputation as a house of entertainment. But the City fathers, if they bore no ill-will to good liquor, were minded that it should be honestly sold ; and, in 1320, certain "regrators" (*i.e.*, forestallers in the public markets or elsewhere) were forbidden by the Mayor and Aldermen to sell ale on London Bridge. In King Edward III's time (1358) a shop, with a garden attached, in the possession of the wardens, and situated "between the garden of the Bridge House on the north side and the highway on the south, and the ditch called "le goter" on the east, brought in a rent of 10s. It should be noted that, in addition to the yearly rent, an incoming tenant was called upon to pay a "gersum" or fine. An example of a "gersum" for a shop on the bridge occurs in the accounts of 1389.

It is curious to learn that the wardens occasionally received fines for injuries done to the bridge houses by passing vessels, probably at unusually high tides. Thus, in 1386, John Seut was mulcted in the sum of 10s. for damage effected by a ship belonging to him. Again, in 1465, a foreign sailor was required to pay a forfeit of 12*d.* "for mending the windows of a tenement upon the bridge broken by him with his ship." Double that sum was paid in to the wardens' account in 1527, by a Frenchman, for "brosing [bruising] of a lytell house upon the Brigge House wharthe by rysing and fallyng of his shippe lying at the said wharfe."

With regard to the amount laid out upon the erection of the bridge tenements, it may be of interest to note that in 1390 Henry Willom, carpenter, was paid £49 "for making nine new shops next the Bridge House, and finding timber by contract." The masonry for the foundations seems to have entered into a separate account. Our description of the bridge finances made allusion to a carefully drawn up list of the houses and their rental in 1460. We may here add a few particulars extracted from the same inventory. The number of the tenements in the different sections is set down as follows :

The beginning at the east of the bridge ...		...		32
,,	west	...	...	31
The middle	east	...	...	18
,,	,, west	...	...	18
The end	east	...	...	15
,,	,, west ,,	...	...	15

Eight women are named as tenants, several being widows. A fair proportion of the householders were responsible for the rent of two tenements. In some cases the trade carried on at the house is indicated, the industries embracing those of "haberdassher," "jueller," "cultellar" [cutler], bowyer, "armurar," "pynner," "fleccher," "taillour," "peyntour," and goldsmith. The tenants were, of course, subject to certain restrictions and conditions. "No person," ran an ordinance of Common Council in 1236, should "hereafter make any alienation of nothing longing to the brigge withouten the consent and speciall licence of the wardeins of the said brigge for the tyme being, on peyne of forfeiture of his title and right in the same thing so aliened." The practice of sub-letting, as might be expected, came into vogue, but it was forbidden by an order of April, 1557, which enjoined upon the bridge-masters to see that tenants did not "set over the terms of their leases." The leases were for a considerable period made out by the wardens at their own discretion, but the Common Council apparently saw good reasons, in 1528, for directing that all leases should henceforward be submitted to the Court for approval. Another regulation, which doubtless tended to the comfort and safety both of the tenants and the public, required the inhabitants of the bridge dwellings to hang out lights after dusk. This by-law belongs to the reign of Charles I.

Not the least attractive page in the history of the bridge tenements is that which relates to the traders' shops, which by various quaint signs appealed for the patronage of the wayfarer and the citizen. The bridge records of the 14th century refer to the industries of cutler, pouch-maker, glover, goldsmith and bowyer. Bright and picturesque must have been the scene on London's great river-street, with its bustling crowds, the gay dresses of the citizens' wives, as they hurried from shop to shop, and the stream of horsemen and vehicles passing to and from the City and Southwark. In the 15th century, as we gather from hints in the records, there flourished on the bridge, in addition to the trades already named, the arts and crafts and profession of the draper, spurrier, grocer, and "sergeaunt licentiate." At that time, and later, we meet with the signs of "The Three Shepherds," "The Botell," "Floure-de-Lice," "Hors-hede," "Ravyns-hede," "Bell," "Toppe and George," "Bore," "Cheker," "Princes Hous," "Castell," "Bulle," "Whyte Horne," "Whyte Horse," "Blak Bulle," "Panyer" "Tonne," "The Nonnes," "Holy Lambe," "The Chalcs" [chalice], "Catte," "Bores-hede," "Seint Savyoures," "Redde Rose," "Three Cornysshe Chowys" [choughs], "Saynt Johne's Hed," "Green Dragon," "Bell," "Pie," "Our Lady," and the "Cardinal's Hat." The Cardinal's Hat would appear, judging from two references, to have

THE SIGN OF THE ROEBUCK ON LONDON BRIDGE.

possessed elegantly decorated casements, for, in 1480, "glass with two images in it" was put up at this establishment, and, about forty years later, the wardens went to the expense of "glazing the tenement at the sign of the Cardynalle's Hatte without the gate upon the bridge." In the 17th and 18th centuries London Bridge was, like St. Paul's Churchyard and Paternoster Row, a favourite locality for booksellers. Amongst the signs of these shops met with on the title-pages of old books, are : "The Three Bibles," "The Angel," "The Looking-glass," "The Black-boy," and "The Golden Globe," which was the sign adopted by William Herbert, the well-known editor of Ames's "Typographical Antiquities." Other tradesmen kept shop at "The Pedlar and his Pack," "The White Horse," "The Dolphin and Comb," "The Roebuck," "The Breeches and Glove," "The Lamb and Breeches," "The Anchor and Crown," "The Bible and Star," and "The Locks of Hair." Besides the above, the names of other houses are preserved in tokens of the 17th century, issued by tradesmen carrying on business on London Bridge. "Such are "The Lion," "The Sugar Loaf," "The Bear," "The Dog," and "The White Lion."

THE SIGN OF THE ANCHOR AND CROWN ON LONDON BRIDGE.

The latter name reminds us that considerable danger was sometimes occasioned to passers-by through insecure signs coupled with a high wind. The sufficient reward of 4*d.* was paid, in 1562, "to one that brought home a lyone blowen downe upon London Bridge."

It is not surprising to hear that trouble now and then arose in connection with the stalls, which the traders of the 16th and 17th centuries persisted in setting up in the bridge thoroughfare. A committee was appointed, in January, 1580-1, "for reformation of the annoyances of the stalls of the shops on London Bridge," and they decided that no stall should be above four inches "without the principall," that is, four inches beyond the shop-front. And in 1667 a cobbler's stall, which had been set up without permission of the committee, was ruthlessly pulled down. The bridge folk, as well as the committee, had their grievances. The traffic sometimes showed a tendency to disorder, and blocks were caused by knots of obnoxious loungers. A complaint was made to the Common Council, in October, 1658, that "by reason of the irregular passing and repassing of coaches, carts and cars, and the standing of costers and [sic] mongers, and other loose people there, continued stops are made upon the said bridge, whereby several abuses are daily committed there, and the inhabitants very much prejudiced and hindered in the despatch of their business in their several trades."

The architecture of the bridge houses calls for no detailed description. The buildings as represented in old engravings appear lofty though somewhat narrow in width, the roofs gabled, chimneys tall, windows latticed, the aspect of the exterior being generally plain and unadorned. A minute account of a dwelling house "in the middle west part of London Bridge" is given in a document found in the Bridge House muniment-room, and dated 18th May, 1613. The house contained a hanging-cellar, shop and counting house attached, hall and chamber over the shop, a "little dark chamber," kitchen, a little void room, a chamber behind, three little rooms over the kitchen, and three other chambers. The lease ran for twenty-one years.

No little activity seems to have been evinced in the erection of new houses during and for some time subsequent to the reign of Henry VII. The carriage of loads of "framed timber" figures in the accounts of 1496, and "tile and brick" were delivered at the store-house. Next year carpenters were "garnishing and furnishing" the new tenements. The year 1505 saw further additions "at the north end." At the south end "two great tenements" were constructed in 1508. In Southwark, close by, the building of a house of two stories cost the wardens 43*s.* 6*d.* Two aldermen, in 1532, made an official inspection of the decayed structures adjoining the Chapel, and recommended in their report the erection of "four newe tenementes of lyke proporcion and buyldynges unto the newe buyldynges of late made upon the north syde of the same brydge." The painting of "two new houses at the Drawbridge" cost the wardens £88 15*s.* in 1579.

The 16th century was signalised by the construction of two notable buildings, (1) a new gate, and (2) Nonesuch House.

The tower which stood on the northern end of the drawbridge had become so decayed that in April, 1577, it was replaced by a new building; and the heads of the traitors, which had formerly stood upon it, were re-erected on the tower over the gate at the bridge foot, Southwark. The new building consisted of a gate and tower; the first stone was laid by Sir John Langley, Lord Mayor, on the 28th August, 1577, and it was finished in 1579. It was a beautiful building, having all its fabric above the bridge formed of timber, and formed a second Southwark Gate. There are not any extensive references to the work in the bridge accounts. But evidence of the changes in progress is furnished by such entries as, in 1577, "Labourers for pulling down the stone house upon London Bridge, £38 16*s.* 7*d.*"; "carriage of fifty-four loads from the stone house," etc., and in 1579, various expenses for "watching at the newe frame." The term "frame" was applied to any mansion largely consisting of timber.

But the glory of the gate of 1579 was quite outshone by the magnificence of a wooden palace which spanned the bridge on the City side of the Chapel, and was proudly called Nonesuch House. It is said to have been constructed in Holland entirely of wood, and brought over in pieces, being erected on the bridge with wooden pegs only, not a single nail being used in the whole fabric. Built on the seventh and eighth arches of London Bridge from the Southwark end, it overhung the parapet on each side, leaving a clear passage 20 feet wide underneath its structure in the centre. This magnificent building was crowned with carved gables, cupolas, and gilded vanes, and two sun-dials were placed on the top of its southern side.

The date of its erection cannot be fixed with certainty, and Thompson, in his "Chronicles of London Bridge," inclines to place it in 1585; but the evidence of the bridge records throws the completion of the new buildings nearly fifty years back. This statement, however, is made on the assumption that the "Frame" referred to in the accounts can be identified with Nonesuch House. "To Richard Rownang, painter"—runs an entry in 1509—"for painting and mending of a Trinite and ij aungellis, set in the new Frame upon the bridge, 5s.," and "to him also, for painting of two vines with fyne golde set upon the types in the said Frame, the piece 2s.—43s. 6d." In 1529, we come across the item, "To Isebrande Johnson, joiner, for cutting and carving of the transfiguration of Jeshu set in the newe Frame upon London Brigge," 30s., and again "carving two angels for the same Frame, 12s.; carving three lintels for the same Frame, 2s.; carving four spandrells in four great brackets for the same Frame, 2s. 8d.; cuttyng, carvyng, and embowyng of sundry haunces and braketts for dores and wyndows for the said newe Frame, 17s. 4d." If our hypothesis be correct, we may assign to the same structure the "armes and scotishons [escutcheons] for the fore fronte of the new buildings upon the bridge," for which the wardens disbursed 6s. 2d. in 1542, nor is it at all singular that so elaborate a building should be in progress for many years. Another entry for the same year is full of items which lend unusual brilliance to the prosaic pages of the records. They are grouped together as appertaining to the "new buildings," and include the fixing of the King's arms and the City arms, painting and gilding of eighteen vanes with fine gold in oil with sundry arms, and garnished with fleur-de-lis, "sett upon the fyngalls" (i.e., the spires of the roof); painting and gilding "a great lyon holdynge a great fayne in his clowes, with the Kynge's armes crowned with a crowne imperiall and garnyshed with flowers-de-lyces"; coating with "lead colour in oyle" the pedestals of the vanes; painting and gilding the royal arms "in a garter, crowned with a lyon uppon the one side, and a dragon uppon the other side, and the Kynge's poseye [posy] under it, with fyne golde and lyce sett in a frame with a flower-de-lyce uppon the hed, giltte"; priming and colouring in oil "two scotchons, one of the armes of the Citie and one other of Saynt George"; and painting thirty-one "cases with lockes, and seventy-two barres, all read." It must be mentioned that some of the decorations here enumerated undoubtedly belonged to Nonesuch House, and this affords good ground for identifying the "newe Frame" with Nonesuch House. The celebrated mansion was repaired in 1648, the entry of that year specifying it by the name of "None Such"; the expenses amounted to £10. In the same year, and in 1649, the workmen were busy rebuilding the houses which had lain in ruins since the fire of 1632. Even then the gaps were not completely filled, and to that circumstance was probably owing the fact that the great fire of 1666 did not inflict much damage on the bridge thoroughfare.

Among the celebrated persons who resided on London Bridge is said to have been John Bunyan, but the statement is not supported by authority. It is, however, a well-established fact that Hans Holbein, Henry VIII's great court painter, lived on the bridge, as did also Peter Monamy and Dominic Serres, marine painters, and Laguerre, the engraver.

§ 10.   Waterworks and Fishing.

Scattered through the Bridge House records of the 15th and 16th centuries are a few allusions to a subject, the importance of which increased with the steady growth of the metropolis, viz., that of the water supply. The item "expenses of labourers at the waterworks" occurs in the accounts for 1479-80. An engineering novelty attracted the curiosity of the City fathers in 1497. It was a hydraulic machine of Flemish invention. There is a touch of enthusiasm in the description given of the apparatus by the bridge accountants: "To Symon Harries, for a vyce of bras bought in the countrey of Flaunders conteyning theryn right connyng and crafty conseites of ghematrye [geometry] in conveiaunce of water oute of ryvers, wellis, or pondis, up unto the highest partees of castellis, toures, or eny other places; the whiche necessarie and full convenient instrument remayneth here in store to the use of the said bridge: price thereof vij li" (£7). Repairs to the waterworks are mentioned in the accounts for 1510, and in 1559 various tools employed at the works cost the wardens £3 17*s.* 11½*d.* The water-works are possibly alluded to in a quaint entry in the accounts of 1558 which record payment of 4*d.* "for twoo powles [pails] for the water drawenge at the legg [ledge] on the bridge."

We have already seen in the case of the notable brass engine that the civic authorities readily accepted useful suggestions even when they happened to have a Continental origin. London, in the time of Elizabeth, was indebted to Holland for an ingenious method of water supply. In 1582 water-works were erected under the arches of London Bridge, one Peter Morris, a Dutchman, having conceived the plan of utilizing for this purpose the force of the torrent as it rushed through the narrow arches. By means of an engine he conveyed the Thames water in leaden pipes over the steeple of St. Magnus' Church into Thames Street, New Fish Street and Gracechurch Street, for the supply of the inhabitants in those districts. At the north-west corner of Leadenhall Street the main was conveyed into a standard which ran four ways, towards Bishopsgate, Aldgate, the Bridge, and Stocks Market. To improve the supply of water, which was not always plentiful, Bernard Randolph, Common Serjeant of London, left money to the Fishmongers' Company "towards conducting the Thames water for the good service of the commonwealth in convenient order."

Four wheels were, in course of time, fixed in the stream for the purpose of raising water. This antiquated device survived for more than two centuries, and it is curious to learn that, shortly after the accession of George III, the navigation of the great arch was rendered dangerous by eddies caused through stopping the two adjoining arches on the north side by the grant of a new arch to the water-works. At this time the question of the removal both of the bridge and water-works was again being discussed in the public press, and a Committee of the Court of Common Council was sitting to examine and report upon a petition from the proprietors of the water-works for permission to erect and rent a wheel in the fifth arch at the north end of the bridge. In the petition it is stated that the leases of the four arches used for the purposes of the water-works were to terminate in the year 2082, the earliest having been let in the year 1582, for 500 years, and the remainder taking only the unexpired term. The opinions of several eminent engineers whom the

Corporation consulted were divided as to the effect which the grant of a fifth arch would have upon the security of the bridge and the navigation of the river ; but ultimately, in June, 1767, the arch was granted on certain specified conditions. The water-works existed until the year 1822, when an Act was passed for their entire removal, the Corporation being authorised to pay £10,000 to the proprietors, in compensation, out of a loan raised upon the security of the Bridge House estates. Under the provisions of the Act, the licenses of the old company were rendered void, and all their machinery, buildings, etc., transferred to the New River Company.

The records afford a sufficient excuse for glancing at the subject of fish and fishing as a feature in the history of the bridge. Allusion is made in a deed dated 1294, to a "quay called Fishwarf," in the parish of St. Magnus, and one Stephen Pykeman is named as its owner. The retail trade in fish was placed under restrictions as to place of sale, an order having been made by the Court of Aldermen in 1283 (as appears by an entry in the City records of later date) that meat and fish should not be sold elsewhere than in the house called "les Stokkes" and "other places deputed in the same City." Against this by-law Bennet Thorne and Agnes Greiland offended in 1322, and, as the archives gravely report, "John Sterre and Roger-atte-Vigne, wardens, come before the Mayor, Aldermen and Commonalty, and present" the evil-doers for selling fish contrary to the order of the Mayor and Aldermen just cited. The "other places" where alone fish might be vended to the good housewives of the City appear to have been Bridge Street, the stalls near Woolchurch-haw and old Fish Street. The trade thus regulated embraced, of course, all species of fish, from river or sea. From the Thames itself a copious supply of the finny spoil was drawn. Both as a testimony to the alertness of the bridge-masters as business men and to the purity of the mediæval Thames, it is interesting to note that in 1382 the wardens received a rent of " 20s. from the farm of the fishery under London Bridge."

The peace of the City fathers was for a long period troubled by disputes and offences arising out of the Thames fishery, the chief transgressors being a class of fishermen known as Petremen or Petermen. An Act of Common Council about the year 1400, is entitled "An Acte concernyng

Petermen and other fysshing in the Thames." It decrees that "none fish in the Thames with anglys nor other engines, but only with nets of assize [of a mesh fixed by law] and only at times seasonable, nor near any wharf of the bridge, from the Temple to the Tower, nor on the other side of the Thames by the space of twenty fathoms, under penalty of imprisonment and forfeiture of their nets and the fish so taken, and further, of the nets, angles and other engines being burnt in the Cheap." Much annoyance was experienced by the guardians of the bridge through the habit of fishing close up to the "stadelynges" [starlings].

An offset to the worry thus engendered was found in the fines which sometimes fell to the wardens' exchequer. Thus, in 1461, a fine was paid in by an unlucky citizen "for fishing next the stadelynges against the order of the Mayor and Aldermen." We observe that the irrepressible Petermen are again aimed at in the legislation of 1482, "grete and many inconvenientes" having been occasioned to the "stadelinges and ground workys of the same brigge by petermen, layers of wylchons and other fysshers lieing almost dayly and tydely in tyme of yere at the said stadelynges." But raids upon the perverse Petermen were still found necessary, as is indicated in this entry in the accounts for the year 1509: "Fines of Petermen for fishing and rugging at the bridge, and with their nets and engines daily hurting the same contrary to divers acts thereof made, 2s. 4d." In 1517 the indifference of the Petermen to the welfare of the bridge drew a further Act from the Common Council, wherein it was laid down that "no manner of persons, fishermen or others, cast any manner of nets within the ryver of Thamis on the este part of the said brigge betweene the said brigge and Botulphes Wharf on the north side of the said ryver, and the Briggehouse Wharff on the south side; nor on the west parte of the said brigge bytweene the same brigge and Old Swan on the north side, and the water-gate of seynt Mary Overye and the sayd brigge on the south side," under penalty of 6s. 8d. for each misdemeanour. Similar prohibitions were issued against the use of wylchyns or other engines.

§ 11.   The Bridge House.

The mainspring and centre of administration of the affairs of the bridge lay in the Bridge House. "This house," in Stow's opinion, "seemeth to have taken beginning with the first founding of the bridge either of stone or timber." A very early mention of it occurs in the will of Isabella la Juvene, A.D. 1272, according to the terms of which the benevolent lady leaves property to the house of the bridge (*Domui Pontis London*). In the 15th century the accounts show that a quitrent was payable by the wardens. Under November, 1414, an entry runs as follows :—"Paid to William Milton, renter, for the rent of the Earl of Arundel for quitrent issuing from the tenement of the bridge called 'le Brighous' in Southwark, 10*d.*" And again, in 1480, we note a "quitrent paid to the Earl of Nottingham and George Neville, Lord of 'Bergevenny,' going out of that place in Southwark called the Briggehous, 16*d.*" The building is alluded to in the books of 1414 as the House of the Wardens; and in a map of Southwark, *circa* 1542 (No. 74 of the Duchy of Lancaster Records), it is marked as the "Brusthouse." The area occupied by the house and the subsidiary buildings and garden, was bounded on the north by the river; on the south by the thoroughfare once known as Barms Street, and now as Tooley Street; on the east by Battle Bridge; and on the west by "a great house of stone and timber," so Stow describes it, "belonging to the Abbot of St. Augustine without the walls of Canterbury, which was an ancient piece of work, and seemeth to be one of the first built houses on that side the river over against the City." St. Olave's Church stood on the west of this "Abbot's Inn of St. Augustine."

The inmates of the House were occasionally and unpleasantly reminded of their proximity to the Thames by an invasion of flood-water. In 1376, for example, a gang of labourers was hurriedly summoned when a raging tide "did drowne all the neither [nether] romes within the Bridge House." Some injury was done to the river-side wall of the House in 1382 by a vessel, the skipper of which, a Flemish mariner, was mulcted of 6*s.* 8*d.* by way of compensation to the wardens. It is interesting to learn from the Small Register, that at the close of the 12th century, the wardens had a distinguished neighbour in Henry Fitz Ailwyn, the first Mayor of London. Fitz Ailwyn gave a licence to one Adam Barbour to make a certain upper room over the quay of the said Henry next the head of London Bridge. Belonging to, or named after the Bridge House, was a dock, which is referred to in an item of the accounts of 1501 : "To Richard Cokkes, fishmonger, towards his costs in making of a new wall of hard stone and brick between his garden and the Bridge House Dock, in Southwark," £6 13s. 4d. A wharf abutted on the river at this point, and is mentioned in 1439, when labourers were hired to carry piles from the wharf of the Cardinal to "the wharf of the Bridge." Later on we come across an entry which relates to the payment of watermen for towing "a great boat" to the Bridge House, the vessel having broken from its moorings and been driven eastward from the Bridge House Wharf. From the minutes of the Bridge House Estates Committee for 1667, we find that there were at the Bridge House five wharves, viz.: Hannott's, Wilson's, Ramsey's, the timber wharf and the Pumpbearers' wharf, the latter belonging to the New River Company. The wharves and warehouses at the Bridge House, as we learn from the same source, were let out ; one warehouse bore the name of the Old Lodge ; another is referred to as Half the Old Gatehouse. Adjoining the river, also, was the Bridge House Yard. Here, at one time, a shelter was put up at the end of the crane-house, for the use of the shutemen who might return wet and fatigued from night duty on the river. The little refuge was erected at this spot so that the shutemen might land directly there, instead of awakening the porter at the gate. The wardens thoughtfully provided the shelter with a fire-place at which the watermen might make "a fire of the chips in the yard"; but, it was cautiously ordered, "there must be no dwelling nor hospitality." Another open space in the vicinity was known as Golders Yard, the rent of a chamber in that yard being accounted for in the books for 1538. The water was reached by the Bridge House Stairs, where persons arrested on the river or on the high seas were often landed, as in 1559, when about eighty pirates were brought to shore, and immured in the Marshalsea prison. They were afterwards tried and condemned at the Admiralty Court, which was then held in the Borough.

Of inns in the vicinity of the House casual mention is made in the following entries : 1496, "For a millstone put in the horse-mill at the Crowne ayenste the Bridge House gate," 7s. 7d.; and 1515, "Cleansing a ditch between the corner tenement at the Bridge House and the Ram's Hedde there."

Having glanced at the environs of the House we may now approach the building itself.   An inspection of the section of Agas's map, which faces page 1, will impart a general idea of the aspect of the place in the early years of Elizabeth.   The exterior, with its unornamented doors, windows and roof, is severely plain ; nor can any picturesque details be discovered in the gate which looks out upon a short alley turning off Barms Street.   A shop which flanked the entrance is described in the accounts of 1387 as vacant.   New tenements were built next to the gate in 1389. This portal, as we have previously noticed, was decorated every Midsummer-night with garlands and greenery ; and, on these occasions of enlivenment, the frugal wardens unloosed their purse-strings to the extent of at least $1\frac{1}{2}d$. for appropriate illuminations.   That was the sum laid out in 1482 "for three pounds of Midsomer candell spended within the Briggehous Gate and in the Porter's Logge."   The item "Candles for the lanterns at the gates" now and then occurs.   At the beginning of the 15th century we meet with an official, "John atte mere," whose versatile talents enabled him to combine the duties of "cook and keeper" of the Bridge House.   A periodical sixpence was allowed this functionary for feeding the dogs who assisted him in guarding the premises.   In 1495 the books indicate that $20d$. a week was paid to the porter of the Bridge House, with an additional $10d$. for "keeping and feeding the hounds."   His lodge, as a later allusion informs us, was provided with a lattice, though which the porter's watchful eye surveyed the outside world.   It is pleasing to remark that the Bridge House porters were not altogether neglected in their declining years.   In 1601, for instance, the wardens agreed to pay Thomas Garrett, a retired porter of the Bridge House, "$12d$. a week towardes his reliefe in regard of age and poverty for the space of one year next following."   For more than two hundred years the expenses of "meat for the hounds" are regularly set down.   Sometimes a slight variety is lent to the subject by descriptive details, such as, in 1416, the purchase of a new dog "of white colour," or the arrival of sundry "mastyf houndes" in 1529.   These eminently useful servants of the wardens, however, did not always cherish due regard for the reputation of the House.   The candid historian must record that, in 1634, the wardens were under the painful necessity of paying William Leet "towardes his cure, beinge hurte by the Bridghouse dogges," $20s$.   A similar entry casts a shadow over the pages of the accounts for 1635, whereby it appears that 50*s.* was given to Thomas Hollowaye " towardes the charge of his dyet and cure, haveinge received very manye wounds by the Bridghouse dogges."

The accompanying illustration represents the Bridge House as it appeared in 1827, viewed from Bridge Yard, Tooley Street.

It is time now to take a brief glance at the interior. The details we are able to lay before the reader are mainly drawn from the records for the

THE BRIDGE HOUSE, AS SEEN FROM BRIDGE YARD, IN 1827.

16th century. In 1521 the building was freshly glazed with "49 feet of new glass with postellis and prolictes in the hall window within the Bridge House, and 159 feet of new glass with arms and flowers within the same hall, parlour, and counting-house." Cloth for covering the counter in "the counting-house in the Bridge House" is an item of the useful order; of a more decorative character were the 35 yards of cloth with which a new chamber was hung in 1462, Ralph Reynold, "peyntour," receiving 20*s.* for painting the drapery. As, we may presume, punctuality was a virtue on which the wardens and their subordinates prided themselves, it was meet that 36s. 10d. should be paid "to a Frenchman dwellyng in the brugh of Suthwerk for a clocke and dyall, with all thynges ther unto belongyng, sett and occupied within the Briggehouse." Later on, Bright Awsten drew a quarterly fee of 20d. "for kepinge the clocke" in order. In the 15th century the Bridge House folk had been advertised of the passing times and seasons by means of two bells, which were purchased in 1409. Conspicuous among the furniture of the House was an image of St. Thomas, for which a "tabernacle" was made for 5s., by Wyche de Feyse, carver, in 1520. Four years after the extensive new glazing above referred to, the hall was brightened with hangings of "redde saie," and the "border" was painted and decently draped with "vj ellis and a half of fyne canvas." Other embellishments took the form of a green carpet "for the Towne-housse." This Town-house was doubtless so called from being the chamber in which the Sessions were held by the Lord Mayor, Aldermen, and Recorder, and other City business connected with Southwark was transacted. An illustration of the stand used for the Lord Mayor's sword is given on page 49. For twelve "grene ensshyns [ensigns] marked with the Bridge House marke in velvytt and fringe," the wardens expended 28s. 8d. The arms of the City Companies were made for the hall by Richard Scarlett in 1583; they were perhaps employed for mural decoration. At the same date, curtains were bought "to kepe the Prince's armes in the hall." In some apartment, the position of which our information does not enable us to point out, legal business was transacted at the time of the commencement of the Civil War. Under February, 1642, we read that there was "Payed unto Joshua Carpenter, towards the charge of layeing in oyle colour the tymber worke of the justice his house within the Bridghous," the sum of £6 13s. 4d. Before taking leave of the interior, we may observe that leather buckets were kept at hand in case of fire.

The agreeable subject of the garden may next be considered. To this pleasant spot the records contain numerous allusions, commencing from the close of the 14th century, at which period the ground was enclosed for protection against trespass. Adjoining gardens were held by John White, vintner, and the Abbot of Battle, towards the 15th century. The products of the garden were varied. At one time we are told of half a bushel of beans being sown ; at another, of vines repaired, pruned, and "bound." For "making the beddis," sowing seeds, and planting herbs and plants 27s. 3d. was spent in 1504. Ever and anon a small disbursement was incurred for "wedars" [weeders], who were employed by the porter. Among the blossoms which beautified this enclosure may be mentioned such old-fashioned favourites as the gilly-flower and rosemary. Those interested in floriculture may like to know that in January, 1408-9, six great "appulympes" were bought for the garden of "le Brigge-hous," and money was laid out on six "hupes," and for the wages of a labourer "stubbyng and settyng" thereof. There were then two ponds in the garden, which required occasional cleansing. In the time of Henry VIII some development in the bridge-masters' taste was exhibited in the erection of "a fountain of brickwork." While dwelling on these lighter aspects of life at the Bridge House, we may remark that the masters kept a "game" of swans. The accounts for June, 1434, jot down the expenses for the marking of the "swans of the bridge" by the King's swan-master ; for a breakfast which formed the usual accompaniment to the "swan-upping"; for the hire of two men navigating two boats at Stratford "for the swans"; for a swan-mark entered in the King's book, and for the services of the swan-master's men in following many swans for the bridge. Unfortunately the "mark" in use for the bridge swans cannot be found. It seems likely that the herd or keeper of the swans had his office at the east of the bridge, and that to this circumstance may be attributed the names of the localities now known as Old Swan Pier and Swan Lane. The right of keeping swans on the Thames was esteemed a high privilege, and is at present exercised by the Crown and the Companies of Vintners and Dyers. When and for what reason the Corporation ceased to exercise this privilege does not appear.

Building material and various machines were kept in the Bridge House stores. The plant seems to have been occasionally let out for hire by the wardens. On apparatus and materials used in the operations connected with the bridge some observations have been already made. Further items embrace Flemish tiles, large purchases of which are entered under 1414, the tiles being manufactured at Lewisham Tile-house, and tin, of which metal the wardens bought 8 lbs. in 1530, from John Jan, pewterer. Lead was probably manipulated in the Plomery House, a building which occupied a place within the Bridge House area. In 1517 a new store-house was constructed of timber. A fully detailed list of articles in the custody of the wardens in 1350 will be found in the Appendix. The Corporation succeeded in inducing King Henry VI to issue, in 1431, a writ to collectors of the fifteenth in the county of Surrey not to compel the citizens of London to pay the fifteenth for timber and other stores for the bridge. The City records for 1547 (Letter book Q) contain orders concerning the sale of bridge stores at current prices. An engineering operation of an unusual kind seems suggested in a statement under date 1519, which relates to the raising and conveying "a great house" called the Newe Lodge within the Bridge House from the garden there to the water-side next the Thames.

A novel and interesting chapter in the history of the Bridge House relates to its use as a place of storage for corn. The most remarkable incidents in this connection belong to the 16th century. It should be premised that the Corporation, out of consideration for the necessities of the poorer citizens, established granaries where, in time of dearth, wheat was furnished to the London bakers at a fixed and moderate price. At the same period houses were let in the vicinity to merchants of the Steelyard and others for the storage of wheat. Thus, in the accounts of 1514, appear a rental of 16s. 8d. from a Spaniard for the hire of a void house within the Bridge House "to lay in whete by 9 wekes, 16s. 8d.," and of 12s. "from William Farmer for the like." Some five years later much activity was displayed in providing twelve "bays" for "garnardes," or granaries, within the Bridge House; and the work of this department had become so onerous as to necessitate the creation of a "clerk of the garnardes." An item of 1520 suggests a busy scene: "Labourers delivering wheat and meal." Meanwhile the London bakers were jealously watching the action of the authorities, and evidently dreaded the effect upon their trade. Their discontent found expression of such a character that the City was moved to stern reprisal. "Forasmuch" runs an ordinance of the Common Council in 1520, "as it is righte well knowen that the bakers of the City, of pure malyce and envye daily, in divers parts of the City, sow scismes and grugges against the purveyors and buyers of whete conveyed to the garnardes at the Briggehouse for the good provision of the said City, and allege that such whete there now beyng is not swete, but partly ynfecte and corrupt, as by their bill of complaint to the Mayor, etc., more fully appears. Upon which the Mayor, etc., have seen and tried the same whete and pronounced it good, swete, and holsom for manys [man's] body." The sting of the document lies in its tail, it being finally decided that all the said bakers be " exempte " from the Common Council until it shall be otherwise ordered—which appears to be a sentence of disfranchisement. It must be confessed that the bakers had not erred on the side of courtesy. They had appealed to Cardinal Wolsey, and informed him that several of their trade had been committed to Newgate because they objected to the musty condition of the official wheat at the Bridge House ; and they even impeached the fair fame of the bridge-masters and an alderman, for seeking to make private gain out of the sale of corn to the bakers. In addition to the " exemption " decreed by the Common Council, we learn that the tradesmen who refused to purchase their wheat from the Bridge House were condemned to a fine of £10. In 1522, a new oven for the use of the City was erected, and freestone was squared for ovens and chimneys. Considerable impetus was imparted to the enterprise by the generosity of a City goldsmith, Sir John Thurston, or Throstone. Sir John, who, Stow tells us, had formerly been an embroiderer, and was Sheriff in 1516, left a legacy of £200 for providing ovens. The testator's wish was duly carried out by his executors. " There be certain ovens built," writes Stow, " in number ten, of which six be very large, the other four being but half so big." The goldsmith's bequest, however, did not completely defray the cost, which was made up from the City funds, as the following note in the accounts of 1523 will show : " Received of Master John Barnarde, Chamberlain of London, for half a fifteenth granted by the Commonalty of London within the City of London, towards the costs and charges of the said ten new ovens and howsinges for the same, as making of new mills to be set at the bridge for the said City." The benevolence of Sir John Thurston was recognised in memorial scutcheons. To Robert Magesdon was paid 12*d.* " for the workmanship of vj shildys [shields] of freestone conteigning in every shilde the Goldsmythes' armys of the City, for to be set upon the ovens within the Briggehous," and " To Mathewe Peter, Spanyarde, for the workmanship of v shildes of freestone conteigneng in every shilde the armys of Sir Thurston [*sic*], Knight, late cytezen and goldsmythe of London, for to be set also upon the ovyns within the same Briggehous, 10s." The example of Sir John Thurston incited another philanthropic citizen to a like liberality. Sir Stephen Genyns, Knight, late Aldermen of the City of London gave £66 13s. 4d. for the purchase and storage of a stock of wheat "to be laide within the garnardes of late new buylded withyn the Briggehous of London for the profite and advantage of the commonalty of the saide Citye for evyr." Such pride did the citizens take in their corn-store that in 1525, they indulged in an expense of 13s. 4d. "to Roger Silvester, marbular, for ij platis of copper and gilte, graven with sculpture for mencion to be made of the begynnyng of the newe garners within the Briggehous and the fynysshing of the same, and set in the same works." A disbursement of a less pleasant character was incurred in answering a citation against Mr. Rise by the parson of St. Olave in Southwark for tithe of "the mill late lying in London Bridge." Nor did the corn business prove a profitable one. In six years ending 1525, the wardens lost in the sale of wheat, rye, and beans, the amount of £203 17s. 4½d.

Richard Gresham, mercer, is recorded, under the same date, as giving 20s. towards the repair and maintaining of the "garnars." The voice of the bakers was again uplifted in 1526. Always, they urged, their trade had been at liberty to make and sell bread unhindered, and since the days of Edward II they had been allowed to buy wheat in the open market; but now their industry was harassed by the restriction of purchasing only the Bridge House wheat. Their opposition even took the embarrassing shape of delay in paying for the corn they so unwillingly applied for, and the accounts of 1530 intimate that divers sums were owing for wheat delivered out of the Bridge House.

The lapse of half a century did not reconcile the London bakers to the quality of the Bridge House wheat, for in 1578-9, we find the wardens of the White Bakers' Company making solemn notification to Lord Burleigh that 800 quarters of wheat in the garners were unwholesome and unfit for food. In 1578, in consequence of the increased hardships suffered by the poor, each of the City Companies was called upon to furnish a quota of corn, to be kept in the granaries and sold at cheap rates in times of scarcity, and the Companies, not too willingly, subsequently assessed themselves to supply a stock of corn according to their means. The precepts were, in all cases, sent to the Companies by the Lord Mayor. When Sussex and Kent yielded a bad harvest, and the supply was rendered yet scantier by exportation, the Lord Mayor besought the aid of Burleigh in restraining the outward movement of corn supplies. But the year of famine was followed by a year of plenty (1583), and the Mayor, Sir Edward Osborne, asked the Lord Treasurer's permission, "on account of the prospect of a plentiful harvest," for the City store of cereals to be transported and sold secretly, to the advantage of the Companies. There was then in the Bridge House a total of 1,000 quarters, as appears from a statement made after an inspection by the Master, Wardens and Ancients of the Bakers' Company. Though the permission was accorded, the Mayor was made aware that the Queen was not inclined to favour the exportation. Granaries constructed of chestnut wood were set up in Tooley Street in 1587, and stood till 1802. The year 1588 was a season of scarcity, and four mills were erected on the starlings on the east side of London Bridge close to the Gate at the Southwark end. The machinery was worked by water-wheels. Hither the poorer citizens were allowed to bring their meal to be ground at a moderate charge. In 1594 the shadow of famine again fell over London; and "it being now winter time," writes Stow, "the Lord Mayor, Sir John Spencer, called upon the Companies, viz., those of them that had not laid in their proportion, to do it within so many days, corn being then brought in from foreign parts." Some disquietude was occasioned in this year by the extraordinary action of Admiral Sir John Hawkins, Treasurer of the Navy. Hawkins demanded of the Lord Mayor the Bridge House, with its granaries, ovens, etc., for the use of the queen's navy, and baking biscuits for the fleet. The Lord Mayor addressed a remonstrance to Lord Treasurer Burleigh, stating that the City would be deprived of its provision for the poor if he lent the granaries, that the companies would neglect to lay up the corn they were enjoined to, and that grain must either be bought from the meal-sellers, or the merchants would be discouraged from importing any more. He added that the ovens of the Bridge House were required for baking bread for the City poor at reduced rates. It was not, however, until further remonstrance of the

Lord Mayor to the Lord Treasurer, that the admiral desisted from his demand.

In the 17th century there do not seem to have occurred any noteworthy episodes in connection with the corn-stores. A report of the Bridge House Estates Committee, which was considered by the Common Council in 1656, touched upon the granaries, and states that there were " many buildings in the Bridge House, some whereof are converted into warehouses, and in possession of the eminent Companies of this City, being intended for granaries in time of dearth, but now either lent or farmed out by them to bakers, corn-brokers, and others." A further report in September, 1656, reveals the existence of "much abuse done by the granary keepers and under officers of several companies letting out the granaries to bottle-merchants and others at considerable rents, which they put in their private purses; and some of the Companies have not, for years, laid up corn for the good of the poor, and such purposes as they ought." A view of the granaries was taken in 1667, and a list drawn up of the forty-three companies who stored corn there.

The accompanying illustration shows the granaries as they appeared in 1830.

A brewery was attached to the Bridge House. To this Stow has the following reference: "Sir John Munday, goldsmith, then being Mayor (1522), there was of late, for the enlarging of the said Bridge House, taken in an old brewhouse, called Goldings, which was given to the City by George Monex, sometime Mayor (1514), and in place thereof is now a fair brewhouse new built, for service of the City with beer." The accounts speak of this place as the byre-house or bere-house, and locate it at the eastern end of the Bridge House. The bere-house was utilised, in 1534, for the storage of salt and wheat, and it may or may not have been the "salt-house" which, in 1537, was let for a term of about four years to William Dolphin, draper. At any rate, Monoux's building had terminated its career of usefulness by 1593, if we may judge from an entry of that year, relating to a Committee of six aldermen and fourteen commoners, together with the bridge-masters, appointed to view a spot for the erection of a brewhouse at the Bridge House.

By a not unnatural transition we may pass from the topic of the brew-house to that of the feasts which have left copious and sometimes amusing traces in the Bridge House records. These convivial gatherings usually formed a pleasant conclusion to such tedious functions as viewing stores and auditing the balance-sheet. To take an early instance, we read that on 18th April, 1409, the expenses amounted to 48s. 4d., "upon the coming of the Mayor, Recorder, and other aldermen, with their officers and servants,

ANCIENT TIMBER WAREHOUSES OR GRANARIES, AS SEEN FROM
THE BRIDGE HOUSE GARDEN IN 1830.
From a water-colour drawing by Harvell, preserved in the Guildhall Library.

to the Bridge House to view the store of the bridge there." A good table was spread for the City dignitaries when, in 1421, they looked over the stores; and the Corporation thoughtfully provided "victuals" for the carpenters and other servants going with the Mayor and Aldermen up river towards the west to destroy "les weres" [weirs]. The audit breakfast was a movable feast, being held at various times in the year. Their *déjeûner* in the year of Agincourt cost 47s. 1d. ; three years afterwards the bill, which included a charge for fish, ran up to £3 0s. 7½d. Possibly in 1423 the examination of the items was peculiarly fatiguing, for two repasts were held, one at "le Briggehous," the other at "le Guyhalde" [Guildhall] ; when the expenses, including the adjourned breakfast, amounted to 117s. 3d. About two years later the scene of an official repast, is laid in "le Grehound" in "Eschepe." There were present the wardens and masters, Robert Thornton, William Bray, Peter Chirche and John Bongay, with others ; but this does not appear to have been an auditors' feast, as the company had assembled at the Greyhound "to talk in council upon matters of the Chapel, and for giving an answer to the Bishop of London." About this time a substantial repast was partaken of, at a cost to the Bridge House funds of £4 19s. 6d., by the auditors and their friends, among the company being John Coventre and Robert Whityngham, Alderman William Melreth, John Higham, Thomas Buteller and John Bakun, the Chamberlain, the Recorder, Richard Osgood, and John Carpenter, the famous Common Clerk. The *menu* embraced meat, fish, bread, ale, wine, pullets, rabbits, "heronsewes," partridges, small fowls, salmon, fruits, etc. Another bill of fare is adorned with such items as "lupis soolys, lampreyys, welkys, whyttyng, sturgeon, halybutte, lomprons," eels (salt and fresh), spices and sauces. A certain chamber in the Bridge House, attractively styled "le Herber" [arbour] was, one evening in 1426, festively prepared for the Mayor and "many aldermen," who sat down to a hearty supper after "surveying the land encroached by Robert Cok and his ancestors, between the common latrene and Oistre Gate, and also surveying the arches of the bridge, and the store of stone and timber at the Bridge House." At the audit-breakfast held in May of the same year, Alderman Sir William Sevenoak lent for the decoration of the banqueting hall a picture, an accident to which is thus referred to in the accounts :—"Paid John Peyntour for mending in his art one picture lent by William Sevenok for the breakfast of the auditors, because it was damaged, 4d." In 1429, the Bridge House arbour was gaily draped with tapestry for the auditors' repast. At another breakfast of that year the dishes included beef, mutton, geese, capons, "shovelers," egrets, maribons, "hegherons," "blaunderell," etc. A hired "pasteler," or pastry-cook, lent his aid, and when the June sun ripened the "weberys" [wimberries] women would collect them from the hedges for the auditors' table. The audit repast of 1438 must be enrolled among the notable events in the history of the Bridge House feasts. It was the last of a series, no more being hinted at in the accounts till the year 1461. The dishes included "beef merybones, chinis de pork, signets, little pigs, geese, teelis, snyts and ploveris." The first year of Edward IV saw the revival of the breakfast "for the chaplains, clerks, carpenters, masons, and other ministers and servants of the bridge, as of old time accustomed." Forty shillings was the customary allowance for the audit feast in the time of Henry VII, a sum which indicated more frugal habits on the part of the officials, or greater economy on the part of the wardens. In the earlier years of Elizabeth the sum allowed annually for the audit dinner was £15. which, from the guests' point of view, compares favourably with the meagre dole of Henry VII's days!

From some unexplained cause the accounts were "not as yet ready to be audited" in June, 1653, and the stern decree went forth from the Common Council that no dinner should be provided at the City's charge until the accounts were duly prepared. The second audit feast of 1666 was held in May at the "Sunn" in Fish Street. Little did the gay company imagine that in less than four months the "Sunn" and all Fish Street and a large part of the City would be reduced to ashes. The guests at the feasts held under the auspices of the wardens appear to have been summoned with proper state and ceremony. We find that 6s. 8d. was paid, in 1554, to Mr. Grene "the Lord Maire's officer for warenyng of gestes and the saide awditours." More than a century later (1666) the augmented fee of 40s. was given to the "Common Cryer" for performing a like function. When, in 1581, the Lords of the Council were invited to dine with the Lord Mayor, a number of "showtmen, now called scavelmen" were despatched, to duly advertise their Lordships. An order was made by the Common Council, in 1556, that £100 yearly should be contributed from the Bridge House exchequer towards the expense of the Lord Mayor's banquet in Guildhall. The wardens of 1581 entertained the Lord Mayor, the sheriffs, the Surveyor, Thomas Hennedge, and others at the rural spot of Stratforde-Bowe.

P

§ 12.   Relations with the Ward, Parishes, and Southwark.

Of the municipal divisions in which the localities mentioned in the present chapter were situated, the chief were the Bridge Ward Within and Southwark. All the houses on the bridge lay within the Bridge Ward Within; but it should be observed that the bridge was divided between two parishes, the southern portion, as far as the drawbridge, falling within the parish of St. Olave's, Southwark, and the remainder being attached to the parish of St. Magnus.

Turning our attention first to the connection of the Bridge House with Southwark, we find one of the earliest items in the extant records suggesting a want of amity between the wardens and some of their ecclesiastical neighbours. It runs thus: August 1st, 1404. To William, for boat hire for carrying the Mayor and Recorder to the Chancery to prosecute a commission to inquire as to scouring the ditches between the land of the bridge and the land of the Abbot of Bermondsey. Another important neighbour, in the parish of St. Mary Overy (which touched the bridge foot on the west), was more obliging. The accounts for June, 1416, record that 20*d.* was paid to the porter of the house of the "Blessed Mary of Overey" for the easement for permitting the boats and "shoutes of the bridge to go by the gate there in the night time." The passage through the arches of the bridge was beset with risk, especially after dark, and in the case just cited the shoutemen were no doubt glad to avoid the danger by harbouring for the night in the creek of St. Mary Overy. Under 1489 we find the entry of a quitrent for a garden in "Horse a Downe," *i.e.*, Horselydown. A large transaction took place in 1550, when the lordship of Southwark was purchased for the sum of £980 8*s.* 9*d.* out of the Bridge House exchequer. The City by this means attained the end at which it had aimed for some two centuries, viz., jurisdiction over Southwark. King Edward VI's charter made over to the Corporation the control of legal cases arising in the borough, and of markets and fairs; and assigned to the City various messuages, lands and rentals. Shortly after obtaining these new powers the City dignified Southwark with the title of Bridge Ward Without. The inhabitants of this ward, however, were not endowed with the privilege of electing any representatives upon the Common Council. The office of Alderman of the Ward is usually accepted by the senior Alderman, and confers upon its holder the title of Father of the City. The then recent extension of the City's authority over Southwark seems to receive a little illustration in the entry under 1584, "Setting the year of our Lord and a mark on the Court House, 16*d*."

The Bridge House itself stood in St. Olave's parish. An interesting link between the bridge-masters and the ancient church of St. Olave's is supplied by the will of William Est, dated 1421. By this deed certain property is given to the wardens in order to provide "one fit chaplain to say divine service in the church of St. Olave," the money, beyond what is necessary for the chaplain, to be available for the repair of the bridge. In case of remissness on the part of the wardens in carrying out the directions of the will, the administration is to pass to the City Chamberlain, and the funds to be utilised for the endowment of a chaplaincy for the chapel of the Guildhall.

Southwark Fair was held in mediæval times, and was not suppressed till the year 1743. Its lively scenes are depicted in a painting by Hogarth. By Edward VI's charter, above alluded to, the City's authority over the fair was recognised, and the date fixed for the 7th, 8th and 9th days of September. On this topic the bridge records furnish a variety of side-lights. It is clear that the celebration of the fair extended to the bridge, for, in 1461, 3*s*. 3*d*. was received from divers artificers for their stallage on the bridge at the time of the fair in Southwark. Further statements to the same effect are the following: 1486, 4*s*. received for toll at "Our Lady Feire" for standing upon the bridge; and, 1499, 7*s*. 8*d*. "leveid and gaderid of divers artificers stonding and selling their wares and chafres on the said bridge in the tyme of Oure Ladye Faire in Southwerke." During the fair, the Lord Mayor and Sheriffs used to ride to St. Magnus's Church, after dinner, at two o'clock in the afternoon. They were attended by the Sword-bearer, wearing his embroidered cap, and carrying the pearl sword, and, at the church, were met by the Aldermen clothed in their scarlet gowns, lined, without their cloaks, the Lord Mayor being vested with his collar of SS. without his hood. After evening prayer, the whole of the company rode over the bridge in procession, passed through the fair, and continued either to St. George's Church, Newington Bridge, or to the stones pointing out the City liberties at St. Thomas's of Waterings. They then returned to the Bridge House, where a banquet was provided, after which the Aldermen took leave of the Lord Mayor, and all parties returned home. The bridge-masters gave a supper on these occasions to the Lord Mayor's officers.

Before quitting Southwark, it may be remarked that, by the charter of Edward VI. land to the extent of some acres "of meadow in divers parcels in St. George's Fields" was acquired by the Bridge House. The Fields lay to the south and south-west of the bridge. They formed the remnants of a marshy tract which originally covered a wide area from Deptford to Lambeth. This land was neglected for a long period, being chiefly employed as a meagre pasturage, but after Westminster and Blackfriars Bridges were constructed, its value was readily recognised and turned to account. That the Fields were under the supervision of the Bridge House Estates Committee in the 17th century can be concluded from a report presented in March, 1698-9, "touching certain boundary marks in St. George's Fields"; and in the following year the Committee prepared a report "touching St. George's Fields and other lands belonging to the Bridge House."

The bridge occupied three of the fourteen precincts into which the Bridge Ward Within was divided. The ward took in the blocks of houses at each side of the northern bridge foot, and then extended in a narrow strip to the junction of Lombard Street and Gracechurch Street. Of this ward John Horn was Alderman in 1276, and, in 1368, the famous William Walworth. Overlooking the bridge from the east rises the venerable church of St. Magnus. Not altogether happy were the relations between the Bridge House and St. Magnus. The following entry, dated 26th August, 1413, needs no explanation :—" For the hire of four horses for three days, with other gifts and expenses by the wardens, to Tonbrigge, to speak with the Archbishop of Canterbury and inform him of the unjust claim made by the rector of St. Magnus for the oblations in the Chapel of the bridge." The Archbishop does not seem to have succeeded in appeasing the parties. Next year the wardens bore the expense of £7 19s. 7d. in the suit of Robert Malton, rector of the church of St. Magnus, touching the Chapel on the bridge. A few months afterwards a lawyer's account appears among the items, and a fee is duly handed "To Master John Combe for his counsel at the Roman Court in the suit of the rector of St. Magnus against the wardens of the Chapel." Various payments for inhibitions against the rector of St. Magnus for the unjust summoning of the chaplains of the Chapel on the bridge impart a militant aspect to the records of 1425-6. All the details of legal conflict are not to hand, but the following extract from the books of 1508 suggests a decisive *coup* on the part of the wardens:—"To Walter Smith, for purchasing a bull of confirmation from the Court of Rome concerning the exemption of the Chapel and the ministers of the same." At any rate, peace ensued, and some twenty years later a remarkable change comes over the scene, for we discover the choir of St. Magnus "singing evensong in the Chapel at our Lady's Fair before the Mayor and his brethern," their "reward" amounting to 3s. 6d. A similar function was performed by the clerks of St. Magnus "on the Nativity of Our Lady, as hath been accustomed," in 1542.

"A greate house" within Churchyard Alley, in this parish, was tenanted, in 1555, by Agnes Doughty, who paid the wardens a rent of 50s. In 1597 the bridge-masters held premises over the cloister of the church of St. Magnus, adjoining two tenements belonging to the Bridge House, the rent, payable to the Churchwardens, amounting to 18s.

Bridge Street traversed the bridge, and was continued northwards through and beyond St. Magnus parish. It was, in Stow's days, "commonly called (of the Fish Market) New Fish Street." A very early document (*circa* 1223) relates to the "release," by Katherine, relict of Adam Eliwaker, of her interest in her "husband's shop, lying between the land of Robert de Fulsham on the east, the King's highway on the west, the land of Walter de Fulsham on the north, and the way which leads to the Tower of London on the south, in the parish of St. Magnus the martyr in Brugestrete." The fishmongers of Bridge Street were a fierce and turbulent set, and did not scruple to use swords, knives and staves in their frequent quarrels. In March, 1365, the Mayor and Sheriffs held an inquiry into "a certain enormous affray in the parish of St. Magnus, in the ward of Brugestrete," in which Giles Pykeman, citizen and fishmonger, was so badly beaten and wounded that his life was despaired of. Giles had probably transgressed against the customs of the trade. But if the fishmongers broke laws, they could also make them; for when the quality of fish was in doubt or the customs of the trade called in question, the fishmongers of Bridge Street and Old Fish Street were summoned to act as assessors or jury. And that their occupation did not discourage the pursuit of law and literature is evidenced by the fact that Andrew Horn, afterwards City Chamberlain, the most learned lawyer of his day, and writer of the "Liber Horn" and the "Mirror of Justices," kept a fishmonger's shop in Bridge Street in 1315. A singular prosecution took place in 1311, when Hugh Mattrey, a citizen, privately purchased lampreys of a Portsmouth merchant, and stowed the fish away in his house, with the intention of re-selling at an illegitimate profit. The offending Hugh was admonished that the lampreys ought to have been exposed for sale immediately after arrival, under the wall of St. Margaret's Church in Bridge Street. Upon his promising amendment, and confirming his oath by touching holy relics, his trespass was forgiven.

Going a little further afield we may trace certain connections between the Bridge House and the Ward of Farringdon Within. Some trouble arose in 1462 with respect to a house "standyng at the end of Seint Nicholas Fleshambles next towards Chepe, belonging to the brigge of London. Though only just built, its equilibrium was threatened by "large gettes hangeing over the strete there," and the walls began to crack and gape so alarmingly that the wardens applied for a grant of two additional feet of the "common grounde towards the est for to bring up a story fro the tremer or gette there redy made." These measures of precaution were allowed. Again, the will, dated Feb., 1503-4, of John Randolf, citizen and mercer, makes reference to lands, etc., rented at 20s., held from him by the bridge-masters in the parish of St. Nicholas Fleshshambles. Towards the reparation of Christchurch the wardens contributed in 1609.

In olden times the City claimed a right in the management of the River Lee, as affecting the commerce of London. The tie between the City and the Lee was strengthened by the grant to the bridge-masters in 1238 of a mill on that river. "John, son of Richard, son of Renger of London, by intuition of divine love and for the health of his soul, and for the health of the soul of Richard his father, and the souls of his ancestors" confirmed his father's gift of a mill at Stratford, called Seynmille, to "the church of the Blessed Thomas the Martyr upon the Bridge of London, and the brothers there serving God, and for the maintenance of the same bridge." Subsequently, according to Stow, the wardens enjoyed part possession of certain mills near Stratford, and the Master of St. Thomas of Acon also had an interest in other mills. This property brought with it no little anxiety, for the owners of the mills were held responsible for the repair of a chalk causeway, trenches, and wooden bridges in that locality. In 1312 the bridge-keeper and the master of St. Thomas of Acon were called upon by a royal writ to give substantial reasons for not fulfilling their duties in keeping the causeway and bridges in decent condition. The bridge-master denied his liability, but the decision went against him. All this, however, was very ancient history, and no question arising out of the bridge-masters' ownership of a Stratford mill occurs in the records in later times.

We may close this section by quoting an entry which, with our present knowledge, must remain obscure. It alludes to the old custom of beating the bounds: "1666. Paid by order of Sir Thomas Bludworth, Lord Mayor, to ten of the Aldermen's coachmen for goeing with their masters the bounds that day, being Ascension-day, at vj*s.* viij*d.* a peece," in all £3 6*s.* 8*d.* The occasion was undoubtedly a special one. It was not, as at first sight might appear, connected with the Great Fire, as the ceremony took place at least four months before that event.

§ 13.   Historical Incidents.

In the story of old London Bridge we hear repeated, from time to time, the noise and alarm of wars and civil commotions, and meet many evidences of the rude and turbulent spirit of bygone days. An untoward incident occurred in July, 1263. "Queen Eleanor," writes Blaauw, in his "Barons' War," "anxious to enjoy the greater security of Windsor under the protection of her son, ... had embarked from the Tower to effect her passage by the Thames. The Londoners, however, assailed her when the barge approached the bridge with every mark of foul indignity and hatred ; the rudest curses, the most opprobrious accusations were shouted at her, while mud, broken eggs, and stones were thrown down with so much violence as to compel a retreat to the Tower.   The personal affront . . . . implanted so intense a spirit of revenge in Prince Edward, that his resentment fatally influenced the battle of Lewes.   The first shock of the battle was . . . . fiercely given by Prince Edward, whose impetuosity spurred him forward to revenge upon the Citizens of London their late insults to the Queen, his mother :

    ' And vor to awreke is moder,
      to hom vaste he drou.'—Rob. Glove."

In August, 1305, after King Edward I's return from his fourth expedition into Scotland, London Bridge received the ghastly ornament of the head of William Wallace.   This appears to have been the earliest instance of a barbarous practice, which was continued through many subsequent reigns.   In these early times the traitors' heads were fixed on poles on the tower at the north end of the drawbridge.   The rising of the peasantry in the reign of Richard II was an ominous event for the City, and for the bridge by which the advancing and victorious rebels were preparing to enter London.   On the 13th June, 1381, Wat Tyler, with his followers, after having burnt the Stews in Southwark, at the foot of London Bridge, were checked in their attempt to cross the bridge by William Walworth, Mayor, who fortified the place, caused the bridge to be drawn up, "and fastened a great chaine of yron acrosse, to restrain their entry."   The Kentish men were, however, re-inforced by the Commons of Surrey, and the citizens, fearing their threats to fire the bridge, granted them admission.   A less dangerous disturbance in 1426 left a curious vestige in the accounts of the Bridge House.   A tumult had occurred at the bridge gate, and a carter, who probably had goods to deliver for the wardens' use, had prudently put up at a neighbouring inn till "le fray" had subsided ; and he afterwards applied for and duly received the sum of one penny for the expense of his horses' provender at the friendly hostelry.

In 1450 occurred the rebellion of Jack Cade, who encamped on Blackheath, with his Kentish followers, in the month of May.   The citizens were induced to open the bridge gates to Cade, who entered with his rabble on

the 2nd July. As he crossed the drawbridge, he cut with his sword the
ropes which supported it. In Shakespeare's stirring picture of this
rebellion, a messenger tells King Henry:

> " Jack Cade hath gotten London Bridge ; the citizens
> Fly and forsake their houses."
>
> (Second part of HENRY VI, *Act* iv, *Scene* iv).

Cade soon lost the goodwill of the citizens by outrages upon their
property; and on the 5th July the Mayor and Aldermen summoned the
City forces to defend the bridge. They also sent for assistance to Lord
Scales at the Tower, who dispatched the valiant Matthew Gough to their
aid. The rebels, however, forced their way to the drawbridge, and set
fire to the houses at the Southwark end of the bridge. In the conflict,
John Sutton, alderman, and many of the citizens, besides Matthew Gough,
were slain, and numbers of women and children lost their lives by fire or
drowning. The struggle continued all through the night, the Londoners
being sometimes beaten back to St. Magnus's Church, at the north end of
the bridge, and at other times driving the Kentish men back into Southwark. A truce was agreed to towards the morning, and soon afterwards,
a general pardon having been procured for Cade and his followers, they
began to disperse. Their leader was, however, slain by an esquire of
Kent, and his head placed on the bridge gate. Some years later a
significant item in the wardens' accounts refers to "six malles of lead,
with pikes of iron," which the bridge-masters had provided for the defence
of the bridge.

Amid the strife and distraction of the reign of Edward IV, the
wardens were kept continually and uneasily on the alert. In 1470, when
Edward had fled to Flanders, and George, duke of Clarence, Richard,
earl of Warwick (the " King-maker "), George, Archbishop of York, and
divers lords, knights, esquires and other persons hastened to London to
release the aged Henry VI from the Tower, the bridge-masters discreetly
refrained from offering any resistance. They took care, however, that the
interests of the bridge were represented in the persons of a body of
stalwart sentinels and artillerymen. For their services in " watching and
attending upon [Aldermen] George Ireland and Thomas Stalbrooke, keeping
the gate upon the bridge" during four days and four nights, John Mills and

William Pye received 6*s.* 8*d.* each; "for watching and attending there for three days and three nights." Roger Payne and William Pykerell were paid 5*s.* each. The wages of four gunners amounted to 18*s.* 8*d.* Eighteen pence was disbursed in dragging the guns and "other habiliments of war" to the bridge. Six pounds of "gunne poudre," at twelve pence a pound, figures grimly in the accounts.

But it was not long before the "gunne poudre" was needed again. In the following spring, Thomas Neville, usually known as the Bastard Falconbridge, having collected some ships and a number of desperadoes, landed in Kent, hoping to surprise London and enrich himself with the plunder of the City. He arrived in Southwark in May, and gave out that he came to set at liberty King Henry VI, who was again imprisoned in the Tower. On the 14th he attacked the bridge, and burned the gate and all the houses up to the drawbridge. Here he met with a stubborn resistance, the citizens being commanded by Ralph Jocelin, alderman and draper, who was afterwards made a Knight of the Bath by King Edward IV. Falconbridge and his adherents were compelled to retire, and were followed by Jocelin and the citizens along the waterside beyond Ratcliff, many of the insurgents being slain or captured.

The Bridge House accounts for this eventful year yield lively proof of the excitement caused by the onslaught of "the most wicked rebels and traitors of the King." When "Thomas Facomberge, lately called Bastard Facomberge, and Nicholas Gascoyne," and their adherents reached the bridge they were saluted by "guns and other ordnance from Guyhalda [Guildhall] of London," the carriage of which was calculated at two shillings, "and for 38 lbs. of gunpowder 38*s.*" Four gunners, when the riot had subsided, were paid 20*s.* for each twenty-four hours of their anxious watching. Twelve new bows at 20*d.* each, and fifty-one sheaves of arrows at 18*d.* the sheaf, doubtless did fatal execution among Falconbridge's following. Horsemen were sent out to reconnoitre the enemy on their approach, and follow them on their retreat, each "spy" being rewarded with a fee of 13*s.* 4*d.* Twelve sacks of stone and wool were brought from "Ledenhalle to the bridge" (at a cost of 2*s.* 2*d.*) and used as a rampart in which the rebel shots buried themselves harmlessly. Across the drawbridge were suspended huge sheets of canvas (the forty-one yards were priced at 17*s.* 1*d.*), which were soaked with vinegar to quench the "wildefire" flung by the rebels. The vinegar thus usefully employed cost 27*s.* A strong cable for "binding and fixing" the drawbridge is set down at 22*s.* 6*d.*; and for the cord from which the Leadenhall woolsacks were hung 2*s.* 6*d.* was paid. Twelve pence was well spent on the boring of three port-holes, through which the defenders projected their "gunshotte." With the same conscientious exactness we find the wardens accounting for sums paid to a special troop of City Liverymen for acting as garrison in the tower, "next the said drawbridge," for candles which shed a light on their vigils, for the supply of "payles" and "bolles" [bowls] and "loads" of water thrown upon the burning houses, for the removal of the "robissh" left by the conflagration, for the commissariat of the labourers, and to "George Ireland and Thomas Stalbroke, aldermen, being there for the safe keeping and defence of the City, and other good men of the City attending upon them from Saturday, 11th May, to Wednesday following.' These precautions seem to have been remarkably effective. Certain faithful lieges of the King were killed and wounded, but only "Richard Gamell, citizen and bowyer," is named among the slain. For the destruction of the "fourteen tenements situate upon the bridge in the parish of St. Olave, between the drawbridge and the Stone gate newly constructed," the Mayor and Aldermen may have looked for compensation from the King, to whom a letter, composed and written by John Parker, scrivener, (for 6*s.* 8*d.*), was despatched by a mounted messenger; the hire of the latter from London to Coventry amounting to 4*s.* Some twenty years later the accounts mention a formidable store of four tons of "ragge" for gunstones, the material being furnished by the royal gunners for 4*s.* 8*d.* In 1497, apparently in anticipation of the rebels under Audley, a number of carpenters were hurriedly set to work to render the bridge "diffensible." Insurrections in various parts of the country in 1549 again threw the City into a state of alarm, and a "false drawbridge" was erected "in case nede should requyer, by reason of the sterrynge of the people (which God defende) to caste down th'other."

London Bridge again suffered siege early in 1554, during the rebellion of Sir Thomas Wyatt. He arrived in Southwark at the head of the City trained bands, whom, by pretences, he had induced to desert to him, on the 3rd February. Meeting with no opposition in Southwark, some of his soldiers completely wrecked the Bishop of Winchester's Palace and destroyed his extensive library, whilst their leader laid two pieces of ordnance at the bridge foot, and dug an extensive trench between the bridge and his forces. In order to reconnoitre the bridge, Wyatt broke down the wall of a house adjoining the gate, and obtained access to the porter's lodge, whom he compelled by intimidation to allow himself and his followers to enter the street for observation. He found everything well prepared for his reception. Sir Thomas White, the Lord Mayor, had been assisted by Lord William Howard, as Lieutenant of the City; Queen Mary remaining meantime at Guildhall. The drawbridge at London Bridge was cut down and thrown into the river, the bridge gates shut, ramparts and fortifications raised round them, and ordnance planted to defend them. The Lord Mayor and Sheriffs, well armed for the conflict, had ordered all persons to shut their shops and windows, and to stand ready harnessed at their doors for any event which might occur. After reporting to his followers the active measures of the citizens, Wyatt decided, upon consultation, to withdraw his forces to Kingston, and, crossing the Thames there, to enter the City from the west. He entered London on the 7th February, but after a sharp engagement, was compelled to surrender at Temple Bar, and was executed on the 11th April, on Tower Hill.

The religious troubles of Queen Mary's reign are curiously reflected in an incident which occurred in 1555. A woman was put into the cage on London Bridge for refusing to offer prayers in St. Magnus' Church for Pope Julius III, who was lately dead. Foxe gives an illustration of this circumstance, from which it appears that the stocks and cage stood by one of the archways on the bridge, in a vacant space which looked on to the water. The fate of a more distinguished and unhappy woman was connected with the history of our bridge in 1586. On the 4th December, the sentence of execution passed on Mary Queen of Scots was read at London Bridge, in the presence of several of the nobility, the Lord Mayor and Aldermen, the City officers, the principal part of the gentry of London, and the most eminent citizens, habited in velvet, with gold chains, all mounted on horseback. The subject of the defence of the bridge again appears in the accounts (1570), in the form of "a table conteyning the instruments and gynnes [engines] apperteyning to the Bridghousse." The

Armada year leaves but one trace, and that of a convivial character, on the records. On the 2nd March, 1588, "a dinner for the aldermen and others at the muster in St. George's Fields," was given, for which the wardens paid thirty-one shillings. After the defeat of the Armada, eleven of the captured standards were hung on London Bridge towards Southwark, on Monday, September 9th, 1588, being the day of the fair, to the great rejoicing of all who saw them. The Civil War only seems to have disturbed the bridge on one occasion. In 1647 the Parliamentary army gained possession of the City by way of the bridge. Colonel Rainsborough was sent, with a brigade of horse and foot and cannon, to possess Southwark and the works at that end of London Bridge. On his arrival he found the bridge gates shut, the portcullis lowered, and a guard within; but upon placing a counter guard with two pieces against the gate, in a short time the great fort was surrendered.

The perils of flood and fire, no less than those of war, frequently affected the fortunes of the famous bridge. In 1281 a severe and lasting frost, such as no man living could remember the like, carried away five arches of the bridge. The year was marked by an accumulation of ice in the Thames, which placed the bridge in jeopardy, and impelled the wardens to write a note on the subject to the Mayor, Aldermen and Common Council. Each of the three following centuries was memorable for a similar crisis. The year 1564 was remarkable for a severe frost, which lasted from the 21st December to the 3rd January. On New Year's Eve people "went ouer and alongst the Thames on the ise from London Bridge to Westminster. Some plaied at the foot-ball as boldlie there as if it had beene on the drie land, and both men and women went on the Thames in greater numbers than in anie street of the citie of London." An extreme frost on the river Thames occurred in the year 1608, when a fair was again held on the ice. Another severe frost occurred in the winter of 1683-4, when the river was converted into a solid mass of ice, "to that degree," says Maitland, "that another city as it were was erected thereon; where, by a great number of streets and shops with their rich furniture, it represented a great fair with variety of carriages and diversions of all sorts; and, near Whitehall, a great ox was roasted whole on the ice." Printing-presses were set up upon the ice, and coaches plied from Westminster to the Temple, sledge races, horse and coach races, puppet plays and interludes, and even bull-baiting took place upon the ice during this remarkable frost. In the month of November, 1715, a severe frost happened, which continued until February in the following year. During this frost a fair was again held on the Thames, with booths, shows and printing-presses, and views of the river are preserved, showing a long line of tents upon the ice. In the autumn of the following year, a violent gale of wind from the W.S.W. prevailed, which reduced the stream of the Thames so low that many thousands of people crossed it on foot, both above and below the bridge, and passed through most of the arches. The winter of 1739–40 was the scene of another frost-fair upon the Thames, during which multitudes disported themselves on the ice, though some lost their lives by their rashness.

Another menace to the stability of the bridge was sometimes found in an abnormal tide. A curious little tract, reprinted by Gough in his "British Topography," relates "a wonderfull and unusual accident that happened in the river of Thames, Friday, Feb. 4, 1641, there flowing two tydes at London Bridge within the space of an houre and a halfe, the last comming with such violence and hideous noyse that it not only affrighted but even astonished above five hundred watermen that stood beholding it on both sides of the Thames. Which latter tyde rose sixe foote higher then the former tyde had done, to the great admiration of all men."

Almost from its birth the structure raised by Peter of Colechurch had been imperilled by the devouring flames. The new bridge was scarcely finished when it was almost destroyed by a serious fire, which occurred in Southwark, on the 10th July, 1212. Stow relates that the fire arose at the south end of the bridge, but was carried by a strong wind to the north end. Many passengers, and other persons attracted to the bridge by curiosity, were caught between the two fires. "Then there came to aid them many ships and vessels, into which the multitude so unadvisedly rushed that the ships being thereby drowned, they all perished. It was said that through the fire and shipwreck there were destroyed above three thousand persons, whose bodies were found in part or half burned, besides those that were wholly burned to ashes and could not be found." There is little doubt that this sad calamity arose in consequence of the wooden buildings with which the bridge was then covered; but it is improbable that the number of the victims was so great as the honest old chronicler states.

On the 21st November, 1504, a fire broke out at the northern end of the bridge, by which six houses were destroyed. It was probably on the occasion of the repairs necessitated by this fire that there were placed on the bridge the stones described on page 43. An entry in the accounts may refer to this conflagration: —" To William Ayleworth, 'bogeman,' for carriage of ten pipes of water for the fire on the bridge, 12*d*." Several other persons were also remunerated for assistance rendered. If the inference may be drawn from two items of different date, it would seem to have been the wardens' custom to remit for a period the rents of houses seriously damaged by fire.

On the 11th February, 1632–3, a dreadful fire broke out in the house of John Briggs, a needle-maker, at the north end of the bridge, which consumed all the buildings, on both sides, to the first gap on the bridge. Forty-two houses were destroyed, owing to the difficulty of obtaining water, the Thames being almost frozen over. In the vaults and cellars below, the fire remained glowing for nearly a week. Very little wind prevailed, otherwise the greater part of the City must have been consumed. A list of the inhabitants of the houses burned in this fire shows that the shop-keepers, at this period, were chiefly haberdashers, hosiers, silkmen, glovers, girdlers, mercers, hatters and drapers. One house on the east side was re-erected in 1639, but the rest of the tenements were not re-built till 1647. The disaster was reported on by a special committee of Common Council on 18th February, 1632–3. They described the area wasted by the flames as 354 feet in length and 15 feet in breadth, and recommended that this space should be widened to 18 feet, and that, until the re-construction of the houses, a substantial wooden fence 10½ feet high should be put up on each side, with recesses five feet deep provided at intervals for the sheltering of foot-passengers from the traffic of carts and the rush of "beastes made wild and furious through the indiscreete and violent usage of their drivers." This fire deeply impressed the mind of one Susannah Chambers, who left by her will, dated 28th December, 1640, to the parson of the parish church of St. Magnus on or near London Bridge, the yearly sum of twenty shillings, for a sermon to be preached on the 12th day of February, yearly, in that Church in commemoration of God's merciful preservation of the said Church of St. Magnus from ruin in the late and terrible fire of London Bridge.

Comparatively little harm was done by the Great Fire of 1666. Pepys relates that, on the morning of the 2nd September, he went on the Tower battlements, whence he saw "the houses at the end of the bridge on fire, and an infinite great fire on this and the other side the end of the bridge, which, with other people, did trouble me for poor little Michell and our Sara on the bridge." The damage to the bridge itself was chiefly confined to the destruction of the large square building which terminated its northern end, and the demolition of the wooden piles and passage which had been erected after the fire in 1633. Of St. Magnus's Church nothing remained but some of the walls, and the buildings in front of it were destroyed even to the water's edge, whilst on the western side of the bridge, the waterworks and tower, numerous houses lining the river, and the ancient building of Fishmongers' Hall, were reduced to smouldering fragments. Temporary sheds were erected for the convenience of the burnt-out tenants of the bridge houses. These structures had a frontage of from 32 to 49 feet, and possessed cellars. Rent was paid by the occupiers. The repairs to the piers and arches cost the Bridge House £1,500, before the leaseholders could attempt to rebuild the premises destroyed by the Great Fire. When this was effected, tenants soon offered themselves to take building leases of sixty-one years, and in five years the north end was completely rebuilt with houses four storeys high, and a street of 20 feet in breadth between them. Arrangements were also made with the tenants of the property at the south end of the bridge, by which those buildings were re-constructed uniformly with the houses on the north end. The drawbridge appears to have remained, although it had long since ceased to be opened for the admission of vessels through the bridge.

One of the last fires on London Bridge took place on the 8th September, 1725, beginning at the house of a brushmaker, near St. Olave's Church, Tooley Street. It burnt down all the houses on that side of the way as far as the bridge gate, with several of the buildings on the other side.

The more romantic and picturesque side of the history of the old bridge may now be briefly reviewed. As a sample of the romantic incidents linked with the bridge may be mentioned the story of Osborne's leap. Stow, speaking of Sir William Hewet, a clothworker, Lord Mayor in 1559, says: "This Mayor was a merchant possessed of a great estate of £6,000 per annum, and was said to have had three sons and one daughter, to which daughter this mischance happened, the father then living upon London Bridge. The maid playing with her out of a window over the river Thames by chance dropped her in, almost beyond expectation of her being saved. A young gentleman named Osborne, then apprentice to Sir William, the father, which Osborne was one of the ancestors of the Duke of Leeds in a direct line, at this calamitous accident leaped in and saved the child. In memory of which deliverance, and in gratitude, her father afterwards bestowed her on the said Mr. Osborne with a very great dowry." Osborne's leap has formed the subject of pictorial representations preserved at the seat of the Duke of Leeds, at Mercers' Hall, and elsewhere; but no further corroboration of Stow's account is to be found, nor does it appear that Sir William Hewet ever had a house on London Bridge. His son-in-law, Edward Osborne, was descended from a respectable family settled at Ashford, in Kent.

From time to time the routine of life on the bridge was relieved by the gaiety and colour of royal ceremonial and pageants. The famous jousting between an English and a Scottish knight, as a display of the valour of their respective countries, took place on London Bridge, on St. George's day, the 23rd April, 1390. The English champion was Lord Wells, who was then King Richard's ambassador in Scotland, his antagonist being Sir David Lindsay, Earl of Crawford. The King himself was present, and had to witness the defeat of his subject by the prowess of the Scottish lord.

On the 29th August, 1392, London Bridge witnessed a still more magnificent ceremony. Some months before this, Richard, who had impoverished himself by luxury and extravagance, had seized the charter and liberties of the City, on the refusal of the citizens to furnish him with a compulsory loan. The citizens found it necessary to submit to the King's demands, and obtained restitution of their rights and privileges on

R

payment of the large sum of £10,000. The reconciliation between the King and the citizens was completed by the King's state visit to London, and his magnificent reception by the citizens. Four hundred of the principal Londoners, well mounted, and habited in one livery, met the King at Wandsworth, and at Southwark the procession was met by the Bishop of London and the City clergy, followed by 500 boys in surplices. "When the train arrived at the gate of London Bridge, the greater part of the inhabitants, orderly arranged, according to their age, rank and sex, advanced to receive it, and presented the King with a fair milk-white steed harnessed and caparisoned in cloth of gold, and hung with silver bells; whilst to the Queen was presented another white palfrey, likewise caparisoned in white and red."

The bridge accounts show that 23s. 4d. was paid for "three shields of the arms of the King and Queen painted upon tables (*super tabulas*), and hung over the stone gate upon the coming of the said King and Queen to London," and "5d. for 'oker' and 'cole' bought for washing the said gate at the same time." A novel spectacle attracted crowds to the bridge on the 15th April, 1413, the coronation day of Henry V, as will be gathered from the subjoined entry in the accounts: "Divers expenses, 'steyning' painting linen cloth and plates and other things for the giant, together with other workmen and chanters, with their apparel, on the coming of the King at his coronation to London Bridge, £9 13s. 10d." Two years afterwards a curt statement of expenses indicates that the bridge was decorated on the triumphal return of Henry from Agincourt, with the captive French monarch in his train. In 1421 the bridge resounded with preparations for again welcoming King Henry after his victorious campaigns across the Channel. The giant's head was replaced by a newly carved one; images were repainted and gilded; stores of tinsel were purchased; gaily coloured costumes of linen were prepared for bevies of maidens who should greet the hero; so great was the press of the work that artificers toiled day and night. In the spring of 1427 a similar excitement prevailed before the return of the great Duke of Bedford from the French wars. "Crokis" and "pastural" sticks were purchased for idyllic scenes. Ornamental turrets were erected, and groups of juvenile choristers were trained to sing to the accompaniment of organs. The effigy of a princess surrounded by attendant ladies stood in a prominent position, and attached to the figure was an inscription consisting of David's words, "*Dux itineris fuisti in conspectu ejus et plantasti radices.*" Twelve other effigies of celebrated personages were fixed on the bridge-way, and corresponding shields bore appropriate arms and names. The curious list of heroes deserves repetition :- -"Abraham the Patriarch; Isaac the Patriarch; Jacob the Patriarch; Joseph, Prince of Egypt; Moses, leader of the Hebrews; Joshua, leader of the sons of Israel; John, Duke of Bedford; Judas Maccabæus; the centurion of the Roman Senate; St. Alban the Prince; Henry, first Duke of Lancaster; Hector, Prince of Troy; Hercules the Prince. Henry VI's coronation procession passed the bridge in November, 1429, the young monarch being saluted by a choir of lay-clerks and boys, and a mimic queen, who, sceptre in hand, was attended by maidens and pages. Interesting features in the ceremonial "at the coming of the King" (Henry VI) in May, 1430, were a giant clad in glittering robes of "Kendale glance"; antelopes surmounting towns and bearing the English and French badges, and a symbolic group representing "Nature, Fortune and Grace, with their maids." King Edward IV crossed the bridge in state on his coronation day, when sand was strewn upon the roadway. Elaborate details in the accounts relate to the festivities at the coronation of Edward's Queen. They included gold paper, "red bokeram," "tynfoille," "vermelon" [vermilion], "verdgrece" [verdigris], red wax, black chalk, "six kerchyfs de plesaunce for the apparel of six images of women," and "vj balades" presented to the Queen, for writing copies of which one John Genycote was rewarded with the fee of 3*s.* As before, the proceedings were enlivened by a choir of men and boys. An expensive pageant [the Bridge House records again tell us] celebrated the entry into London of "the Lady Princes of Spayne" (Katharine of Aragon). A somewhat obscure entry recording the payment of 3*s.* 7*d.* for "standing on the bridge, and in a vacant tenement at the Standard in Chepe at the coming of the King through the City towards Westminster, the Vigil of the Nativity of St. John the Baptist" may point to the grand ceremonial muster of the Midsummer watch.

The bridge funds contributed, in 1522-23, one-fifteenth and a half to the cost of the City's welcome to Charles V, Emperor of "Allmeyn" (Germany). In the last year of Henry VIII's reign the bridge was decorated "against the coming of the Lord Admiral of France," and at the coronation of Edward VI the wardens again gave "a fifteenth and a half" towards the City's special disbursements.   Towards a pageant in Queen Mary's time (1554), the bridge authorities modestly contributed the cost of "poles, etc.," in Cheapside.   Queen Elizabeth's coronation pageant drew £4 from the bridge exchequer.   For "plate, lynnen, glasses, etc., used att the tent in St. George's Fields att the King's most excellent Majesties comeing to London" on the historical 29th May, 1660, the bridge-masters paid, "by order of the Court of Aldermen," £7 0s. 4d.

OLD LONDON BRIDGE AFTER THE REMOVAL OF THE HOUSES AND THE CONSTRUCTION OF THE GREAT ARCH.   A.D. 1758.

CHAPTER II.

Last Days of Old London Bridge, its Successor and Sister Bridges.   A.D. 1750 to A.D. 1894.

§ 1.   Old and New London Bridges.

IN November, 1749, the new Westminster Bridge was completed, having been commenced in September, 1738.   London Bridge was not now the only bridge crossing the Thames in the metropolitan district. The contrast presented by the broad road and convenient approaches of Westminster Bridge caused the attention of the Corporation to be directed to the great inconvenience of their own bridge.   A large party in the Common Council were in favour of pulling down the old London Bridge and erecting a new one in its place ; but the majority decided to retain the original structure, and enlarge it by pulling down the houses and removing some of the arches.   A committee appointed to consider the best means of rendering the structure safe and convenient, reported that the foundation was still good, and that the edifice might, with suitable repairs, be rendered as serviceable as Westminster Bridge, being capable of receiving four carriages abreast, with a good footway on each side.   Mr. George Dance, the City Clerk of the Works, who had been ordered by the committee to survey the bridge, produced a plan involving the removal of the houses and other alterations at an estimated cost of £30,000.

A Bill was accordingly promoted in Parliament by the Corporation for effecting these improvements, and for raising money to enable the trustees to carry them out   The Act received the royal assent on the 27th May, 1756, and provided for a clear roadway over the bridge 31 feet wide, with two footpaths each 7 feet wide, and a stone balustrade on either side through the entire length of the bridge. It also authorised the imposition of an additional toll for the payment of the expenses incurred by the alterations. The tolls were afterwards found to be difficult of collection and a great hindrance to commerce and navigation, and in the following year another Act was passed, granting a sum of £15,000 towards the re-building of London Bridge, and abolishing the additional tolls created by the previous Act. Under the same legislative authority great facilities were afforded to the navigation of the river by throwing the two arches in the centre of the bridge into one. The appearance of the bridge after its re-construction in 1758 is shown in the illustration at the beginning of this chapter. A further sum of £30,000 was appropriated by a later Act in 1767 for the redemption of the original tolls on London Bridge, which were then leased by Mr. Edward Neale; but the lessee having raised his demand on account of an increase in the tolls, an Act of 11 George III, 1771, provided for their continuance until 1782, when the tolls were finally to cease. The plans for these improvements were much aided by an Act passed in 1755 for removing the ancient market held in High Street, Southwark, to a new site in Rochester Yard.

While the repairs of the bridge were in progress, a temporary wooden bridge was erected on the western side of the bridge, into which it opened at each end. This structure was unfortunately destroyed by fire on the night of Tuesday, 7th April, 1758, and considerable damage was caused to the drawbridge and other portions of the original edifice. Some suspicion seems to have arisen that the mischief was intentionally caused. The Corporation lost no time in taking steps to repair the destruction caused by this conflagration. Orders were given for the immediate construction of a new temporary bridge, and upwards of 500 workmen were constantly employed upon it, through whose exertions the bridge was re-opened on Wednesday, the 19th of the same month, and the whole of the new wooden bridge was ready for carriages in less than a month after the fire.

During the progress of the alterations it was found that the removal of the centre pier, and the excavations around and beneath its sterlings, had dangerously weakened the adjoining piers and the new great arch. In this emergency the Corporation applied for advice to Smeaton, the celebrated engineer, who immediately travelled from Yorkshire to survey the bridge. His advice was that the Corporation should buy back again the stones of the City gates, and throw them into the water to guard the sterlings. These gates had been sold in the year 1760, and were then partly taken down. So promptly was Smeaton's advice followed, that the stones were bought the same day; horses, carts and barges were instantly procured, and the work commenced immediately, although it was Sunday morning.

The cost of re-constructing the bridge amounted to nearly £100,000, and the improvements effected were not without corresponding drawbacks. In the beginning of 1763, when the smaller arches were stopped up with ice, the whole force of the tide rushed so violently through the great arch, as to tear up the bed of the river, and expose the foundation piles, the damage thus occasioned costing £6,800 to repair.

One of the latest poetical productions connected with old London Bridge was written by the famous Anne Killegrew, celebrated by Dryden. It is printed in Southey's "Specimens of the later English Poets," and is entitled "On my aunt, Mrs. A. K., drown'd under London Bridge in the Queen's barge: anno 1641."

Notwithstanding the expenditure of £100,000 on the re-construction of London Bridge just mentioned, the present century opened with a renewed agitation for better bridge accommodation, and in 1800 "The Third Report from the Select Committee upon the Improvement of the Port of London" was printed. It stated that the great, continual and ineffectual expenses of the old bridge, its irremediable insecurity, and the dangers of its navigation, had induced the committee to collect information and provide designs for the building of a new one. Designs for a new bridge were accordingly obtained. The attention of the Corporation was called to the matter in 1812, when the owners of coal craft and others interested in the navigation of the river presented a petition setting forth the great loss of lives and property which annually occurred, as well as the delays and inconvenience occasioned to the navigation of craft through the state of the bridge, and the want of an adequate waterway under it. London at this time only had a population of 959,000; nevertheless, the traffic across the old bridge in one day of July, 1811, amounted to 89,640 persons on foot, 769 wagons, 2,924 carts and drays, 1,240 coaches, 485 gigs and taxed carts, and 764 horses. The dangers of the bridge owing to the narrowness of the arches were considerable, the fall of water at times being no less than five feet.

The above-mentioned petition was referred to the City Lands and Bridge House Estates Committee, who reported on it in December, 1814, with suggestions from Messrs. George Dance, William Chapman, Daniel Alexander, and James Montague for the improvement of the bridge and enlargement of the waterway. The subject was again referred to the Committee in the following July, but nothing further was done until the year 1816, when the owners of coal craft again petitioned the Corporation. It was then decided that the Corporation should await the completion of Southwark Bridge, which was in course of erection. Petitions, however, continued to be presented at the Guildhall and in the House of Commons, and in 1820 a Select Committee was appointed to consider the question. In the following year the whole matter was discussed in Parliament; various plans were considered, and the Corporation resolved to apply for a Bill in the next session to sanction a plan for enlarging the waterway of the bridge, but not for building a new one. In August, 1822, an Act was passed for removing the London Bridge Waterworks, and this, coupled with the recommendation of a Parliamentary committee for the erection of a new bridge, determined the Bridge House Committee to adopt a bolder course. They proposed to apply to Parliament for power to erect a new bridge, if such a measure should be decided upon. In July, 1823, an Act was passed "for re-building London Bridge, and for improving and making suitable approaches thereto," and it was left to the Corporation to carry this into effect. Previously, in 1821, premiums of £250, £150, and £100 were offered by the Corporation for the best three designs, the decision being placed in the hands of a committee consisting of John Nash, John Soane (afterwards Sir John Soane), Robert Smirke, and William Montague. The premiums were awarded to Messrs. W. Fowler, T. Borer, and C. A. Busby, but one of the designs, of John Rennie, F.R.S., was ultimately adopted on the recommendation of a committee of the House of Commons. Mr. Rennie died in 1821, but the works were carried on by his sons, Mr. (afterwards Sir John) Rennie and Mr. George Rennie. The contract was given to Messrs. Jolliffe and Banks, who undertook to construct the bridge within six years, about 100 feet to the westward of the old bridge, for the sum of £426,000. The old bridge was to remain until the new one was completed. The first pile was driven on the 15th of March, 1824, and in digging for the foundations some interesting antiquities were discovered, including a beautiful silver statuette of Harpocrates, now in the British Museum. The first stone was laid, upon the completion of the cofferdam, by Lord Mayor Garratt, on the 15th of June, 1825. In the cavity of the foundation stone was placed, amongst other things, a Latin inscription, of which the following is a translation : —

"The free course of the river being obstructed by the numerous piers of the ancient bridge, and the passage of boats and vessels through its narrow channels being often attended with danger and loss of life by reason of the force and rapidity of the current, the City of London, desirous of providing a remedy for this evil, and at the same time consulting the convenience of commerce in this vast emporium of all nations, under the sanction and with the liberal aid of Parliament, resolved to erect a bridge upon a foundation altogether new, with arches of a wider span, and of a character corresponding to the dignity and importance of this royal City ; nor does any other time seem to be more suitable for such an undertaking than when in a period of universal peace, the British Empire flourishing in glory, wealth, population, and domestic union, is governed by a Prince the patron and encourager of the arts, under whose auspices the Metropolis has been daily advancing in elegance and splendour. The first stone of this work was laid by John Garratt, esquire, Lord Mayor, on the 15th day of June, in the sixth year of King George the Fourth, and in the year of our Lord 1825. John Rennie, F.R.S., architect."

Three medals were struck in official commemoration of the event.

The bridge is thus described by Sir John Rennie : "It consists of five semi-elliptical arches ; two are of 130 feet, two of 140 feet, and the centre, of 152 feet 6 inches span and 37 feet 6 inches rise, is perhaps the largest elliptical arch ever attempted. The roadway is 52 feet wide. This bridge deserves remark on account of the difficult situation in which it was built, being immediately above the old bridge, in a depth of from 25 to 30 feet at low water, on a soft alluvial bottom, covered with large loose stones carried away by the force of the current from the foundation of the old bridge, the whole of which had to be removed by dredging before the cofferdams for the piers and abutments could be commenced, otherwise it would have been extremely difficult, if not impracticable, to have made them water-tight. The difficulty was further increased by the old bridge being left standing to accommodate the traffic whilst the new bridge was building ; and the restricted waterway of the old bridge occasioned such an increased velocity of the current as materially to retard the operations of the new bridge, and at times the tide threatened to carry away all before it. The great magnitude and extreme flatness of the arches demanded unusual care in the selection of the materials, which were of the finest blue and white granite from Scotland and Devonshire. The piers and abutments stand upon platforms of timber resting upon piles about 20 feet long. The masonry is from 8 feet to 10 feet below the bed of the river."

The time occupied in the erection of the bridge from the driving of the first pile was seven years five months and thirteen days, and, owing to the difficulties and dangers referred to by Sir John Rennie, forty lives were lost during the progress of the works, upon which upwards of 800 men were employed. The bridge has been described as unrivalled "in the perfection of proportion and the true greatness of simplicity." In 1826 the Corporation obtained an Act of Parliament authorising the Commissioners of the Treasury to grant £42,000 out of the Consolidated Fund for the purpose of widening the bridge 6 feet.

The bridge itself was but a comparatively small part of the work undertaken by the Corporation. The approaches were a much more costly affair, and in order that these might be carried out in a thoroughly satisfactory manner application was made to Parliament for the continuation of the coal dues. This, after an "unprecedented" opposition in the House of Lords, was in substance agreed to, the period for the extension of the duty of sixpence per chaldron being limited to twenty-one years. The Bill also contained powers for raising a sum not exceeding one million pounds upon the credit of the coal duty.

The new London Bridge was opened with great ceremony by King William IV and Queen Adelaide, on August 1st, 1831. The King commanded that the procession should be by water, with the double view of benefiting the men employed on the river and of enabling the greatest number of his subjects to witness the spectacle. The arrangements on the river were entrusted to Admiral Sir Thos. B. Martin, and on the bridge and its approaches to the London Bridge Committee. A triple awning was erected at the London end of the bridge, extending from a magnificent pavilion the whole width of the bridge as far as the second pier, and covered with the colours of all nations. A throne was placed

NEW LONDON BRIDGE.

in the royal tent and tables were laid for the royal family, while under the canopy were two rows of tables capable of accommodating 1,500 persons. The river was lined with craft, including eight City barges, newly gilt and decorated with the gayest flags, and each provided with a band of music. Tiers of seats were erected on the terrace of Somerset House, and every building which could command a view was thronged with spectators. The King and Queen and other members of the royal family assembled at St. James's Palace about two o'clock, and proceeded in carriages to Somerset House, business being entirely suspended along the line of route. A guard of honour of the Foot Guards, with their band and the bands of the Household Troops, were stationed in the square of Somerset House, and when their Majesties appeared on the steps descending to the platform from which they were to embark, the cheers were almost deafening. The scene as the royal barges passed up the river, amidst the firing of cannon and the enthusiasm of multitudes of people, is said to be "indescribable." While the company on the bridge awaited the arrival of the King and Queen they were entertained by a military band, by the German minstrels, by "the celebrated siffleur," and by "that still more celebrated performer, Michael Boai." The royal barge was moored at the stairs on the London side of the bridge, and upon stepping ashore, the King, addressing the chairman of the Bridge Committee and Mr. Routh, said: "Mr. Jones and Mr. Routh, I am very glad to see you on London Bridge. It is certainly a most beautiful edifice, and the spectacle is the grandest and the most delightful in every respect that I have ever had the pleasure to witness." Upon reaching the top of the steps the City sword was tendered to His Majesty by Lord Mayor Key. The chairman of the committee at the same time presented the King with a gold medal, by William Wyon, of the Royal Mint, commemorative of the event. The members of the committee who took part in the reception of the King and Queen, were attired in blue coats with buttons impressed with His Majesty's portrait, and white waistcoats and trousers.

The ceremony of opening was performed by their Majesties walking over the bridge. Just as the royal procession had reached the Surrey side of the bridge, Mr. Green "ascended in his celebrated balloon," which descended in the evening at Charlwood, in Surrey. On the return of their Majesties to the pavilion a banquet was provided, at which the Lord Mayor proposed the health of the King and Alderman Sir C. S. Hunter that of the Queen. The Lord Mayor then presented a gold cup of great beauty to the King, who said, taking the cup: "I cannot but refer on this occasion to the great work which has been accomplished by the citizens of London. The City of London has been renowned for its magnificent improvements, and we are commemorating a most extraordinary instance of their skill and talent. I shall propose the source from whence this vast improvement sprang: "The trade and commerce of the City of London."

The royal procession on its return was joined by several of the City barges, and there was a renewal of the scene already witnessed, including the cheers of the people, the firing of artillery, the ringing of church bells, and other tokens of loyalty and respect. The Duke of Wellington, who had befriended the Corporation in Parliament, and assisted in obtaining the necessary approaches, was invited to the ceremony. He, however, declined the invitation, as he had on a recent occasion been informed by " the highest authority in the City," that his attendance upon the King was likely to create a disturbance, for which the City authorities could not be responsible. The country at this time was in the throes of the Reform agitation, when the Duke's windows were broken by the mob. The City, however, showed its appreciaton of the victor of Waterloo, by erecting a bronze equestrian statue of the Duke of Wellington in front of the Royal Exchange. At the same time a granite statue of William IV was put up at the corner of the new street named after the King.

The old bridge was not entirely removed until 1832, when the bones of the builder, Peter of Colechurch, were found beneath the masonry in the foundation of the Chapel. A portion of the stone was purchased by Alderman Harmer and used in building his seat, Ingress Abbey, near Greenhithe, and many snuff boxes and other memorials were turned from the pile wood.

The actual cost of the bridge and of the approaches and improvements on both sides of it was as follows: Removal of old London Bridge, with necessary alterations during the progress of the works at the new bridge, £35,500; cost of building new London Bridge, including land arches, abutments, and paving, £680,232 12*s.* 10*d.* ; cost of the approaches and improvements on both sides of the bridge, £1,840,438 7s. 1¾d.; total, £2,556,170 19s. 11¾d. Of this sum the Corporation contributed out of the estates charged with maintaining London Bridge, and raised upon the credit of those estates, £820,318 2s. 5½d.; the Government contributed, with the sanction of Parliament, £192,000; the amount raised upon the coal and wine dues was £1,000,000; the amount granted by the Corporation out of their own estates towards completing the approaches was £16,421; and the amount realised by the sale of surplus land, etc., was £626,930 18s. 10¼d. A total expenditure of £1,840,438 upon street improvements produced a return of £626,930 in the shape of old materials, surplus ground, etc., equal to 34 per cent., reducing the gross cost of the approaches to the net cost, £1,213,508. These street improvements included, on the south side, Borough High Street to the Town Hall, and a portion of Tooley Street, and on the north side Upper Thames Street, Fish Street Hill, Eastcheap, King William Street, Princes Street, Lothbury, Gresham Street, Moorgate Street, and a portion of Threadneedle Street, with several other minor alterations.

As early as 1853, a proposal to widen London Bridge was seriously considered, and in 1858, the Bridge House Estates Committee having examined the stability of the bridge, and the designs and plans sent in by various architects for widening it, brought up a report on the subject. It appears from this report that Sir John Rennie, who superintended the construction of the bridge, thought it inadvisable to widen the bridge, because, firstly, the bridge was never calculated to have the additional weight upon it, which would be occasioned by constructing footways to overhang on both sides; secondly, the bridge had attained its final bearings, and it would be injudicious to disturb it; thirdly, the overhanging sidewalks would disfigure and entirely alter the architecture of the bridge; fourthly, the proposed widening would be of little advantage, unless the approaches to the bridge were also enlarged.

Mr. Thomas Page and the City Architect were, however, of opinion that the bridge could be satisfactorily widened, and the City Architect did not think it would be necessary to alter the approaches to the bridge. He estimated the cost at £25,000.

Wishing to avoid so great an expense, the committee determined to try a re-arrangement of the traffic, and the present method was inaugurated by which drays and heavy wagons pass near the kerb, while lighter vehicles use the middle of the road. The enforcement of this rule by the City police rendered a widening of the bridge unnecessary, and the reference was ultimately discharged.*

§ 2.   Blackfriars Bridges (Old and New), Holborn Valley Viaduct, and Southwark Bridge.

London Bridge was the only bridge across the Thames till 1749, when the ferry-boat which used to ply between Lambeth and Westminster was replaced by a bridge designed by Charles Labelye, the See of Canterbury, to whom the ferry belonged, receiving compensation to the amount of £2,205. Westminster Bridge was soon afterwards followed by Blackfriars Bridge, which was begun by the Corporation in 1760. As in the case of Westminster Bridge, considerable opposition was made by the Watermen's Company, whose interests were inimical to those of the general public, and by a number of bargemen and market gardeners. In 1756, however, an Act of Parliament was passed, and the design of Robert Mylne, a young Scotchman who had studied architecture at Rome, and who had just returned from a tour of Europe, was accepted. Mylne's bridge was of Portland stone, and consisted of nine semi-elliptical arches, the centre one a hundred feet wide with a rise of 41 feet 6 inches. The total length of the bridge was 995 feet, and its width 45 feet. Between the arches, double Ionic columns, supporting small projecting recesses, were placed against the face of each pier. A literary controversy arose over the plans, in which the conflicting claims of semi-circular and semi-oval arches and of iron railings as against stone balustrades were warmly discussed, Dr. Johnson and the poet Churchill in these matters taking the side of Mylne's opponents. The foundation stone was laid by Sir Thomas Chitty, Lord Mayor, October 31st, 1760, amongst

---

* This was a reversion to an old practice, as appears from an entry in the City Records (Repertory "Drake," fol. 279), requiring the Constables and Beadles of Christ's Hospital to attend at each end of the bridge and to take care that carts coming into the City keep the east side, and, going out, the west side; and to see also that carts were not detained by the collection of tolls.

T

OLD BLACKFRIARS BRIDGE.

the articles deposited in the cavity of the stone being a tin plate with a Latin inscription, stating that the bridge was undertaken by the Corporation of London, amidst the rage of an extensive war, and ending with a glowing eulogy of the Prime Minister, in whose honour the citizens unanimously named the new structure the William Pitt bridge. The bridge appears to have soon lost its original name, possibly because Lord Chatham before its completion had fallen into disgrace, and, while still the greatest Englishman, was no longer the all-powerful Prime Minister of England. The name by which it has been since known marked the association of its site with the Order of Black Friars or Dominicans, whose magnificent monastery formerly adjoined the City end of the bridge. Blackfriars at this time presented a picture of squalid poverty and degradation, due largely, no doubt, to the contiguity of the four prisons, Ludgate, the Fleet, Newgate and Bridewell. In making the approaches, the Fleet Ditch, which was a sort of City gehenna, and continued open from Fleet Street to the Thames, was arched over, and the filth was hidden out of sight. This ancient and swift-flowing stream now runs under new Bridge Street as a common sewer, and enters the Thames on the west side of Blackfriars Bridge.

The total cost of constructing the bridge and its approaches was £230,000, including £12,250 paid to the Watermen's Company, as compensation for the abolition of the Sunday ferry. The bridge itself cost £152,840. The great arch was opened on the 1st October, 1764, when the Lord Mayor, Sheriffs, Aldermen and others, rowed under it in the City barge. Foot passengers were allowed across in 1766, and the bridge was finally completed and opened on November 19th, 1769. The funds for the work were raised by loan, on the security of the tolls and the Bridge House Estates, the loan to be repaid by tolls levied on the bridge. Until June 22nd, 1875, there was a toll of one halfpenny for every foot passenger and one penny on Sundays. The toll-house was burnt down in the riots of 1780, when all the account books were destroyed. Mylne, the architect of the bridge, who was appointed Surveyor of St. Paul's Cathedral, built a handsome residence for himself at the northern foot of Blackfriars Bridge, on the site now occupied by the Ludgate Hill Station of the London, Chatham, and Dover Railway.

Owing to the use of Portland stone in the construction of the bridge, extensive repairs were found to be necessary in 1833, and a sum of £105,158 was expended on the work of restoration. The roadway of the crown was lowered several feet and the approaches at either end were raised. At the same time the picturesque open balustrade was replaced by a dull, heavy parapet. The works were not completed until November, 1840.

Even then the bridge was not considered satisfactory, and the Corporation eventually resolved to build a new and much wider bridge upon the site of the old one. The new bridge, designed by Joseph Cubitt, consists of five iron arches, surmounted by an ornamental cornice and parapet. The axis of the new bridge coincides exactly with that of the old one, but the new structure has the following advantages over its predecessor. The roadway over the central arch is only ten feet six inches above that of the banks on either side, or half the rise of the old bridge; the width between the parapets is 70 feet as against 45 originally, and the smaller number of arches give a greater and more convenient waterway. The gradient in the old bridge was at first 1 in 16, but was afterwards reduced to 1 in 24. The steepest gradient in the present bridge is 1 in 40. The central arch is 185 feet clear between the piers, those on either side 175 feet each, and the end arches give a span of 155 feet. The total length of the bridge, clear of the shore abutments, is 923 feet. To form a foundation for the piers metal caissons were sunk into the bed of the river for about 38 feet under low water mark, and filled with concrete for half this height. From these foundations solid brick work was raised to the level of the natural bed of the river, and upon this again was built the pier itself, consisting of solid brick work faced with granite. On each of the stone piers are two columns of polished red granite, one on either side of the bridge. Each column weighs over 30 tons and is 11 feet high. They are the largest ever used in any bridge, and cost £800 each, being nearly 24 feet in circumference. The capitals are of stone ornamented with birds and marine plants, executed by Mr. J. B. Philip. Each arch may be said to be a perfect iron structure by itself. A temporary footbridge, erected at a cost of £42,125, was opened for traffic on June 1st, 1864. The permanent structure, which cost £401,131, occupied in construction five years and five months. The first stone was laid by Lord Mayor Hale on July 25th, 1865, and before its completion the Holborn Viaduct, another great work of the Corporation, was in progress.

NEW BLACKFRIARS BRIDGE.

HOLBORN VALLEY VIADUCT.

The Holborn Valley Viaduct spans the ancient valley of the River Fleet lying between Snow Hill on the east and Holborn Hill on the west. After the Great Fire of 1666 the Fleet was widened and turned into a canal from the Thames up to Holborn Bridge, and here barges were wont to be moored. The steep declivities of Holborn and Snow hills occasioned great inconvenience to the traffic and were the cause of many serious accidents. Various schemes of improvement were propounded from the middle of the last century onwards, and some relief was afforded at the beginning of the present century by what was known as the Skinner Street improvement—a straight thoroughfare which replaced the narrow and tortuous Snow Hill. In January, 1860, the Common Council instructed the Improvement Committee to inquire and report on the desirability of establishing a central railway station in the City of London, in the neighbourhood of Smithfield or elsewhere, and whether the Corporation should take part in the furtherance of such a scheme. The committee, in their report, submitted a design of the then City architect, Mr. J. B. Bunning, for raising part of the valley of the Fleet, and thereby improving the dangerous and inconvenient gradients of Holborn Hill, Skinner Street, and Snow Hill. A scheme for effecting this purpose was brought under the notice of the Government in 1862, and an Act was passed in the following year prolonging the City's 4*d.* coal duty for a period of ten years, the produce to be applied by the Corporation in the first instance to the raising of Holborn Valley and afterwards to such further City improvements as Parliament might sanction. No less than 105 designs were submitted, and Mr. Bunning being dead, the committee invited Mr. William Haywood, Engineer to the Commissioners of Sewers, to assist in the examination of the designs. This gentleman accepted the invitation and withdrew his own design from competition.

It was ultimately decided to construct a viaduct or high level roadway upon the line of Holborn Hill and Skinner Street, the plan involving the entire removal of the then existing surface and the property on both sides. Premiums for the two most approved designs were awarded to Mr. Richard Bell and Mr. Thomas Charles Sorby, and Mr. Haywood prepared a plan for Parliament. The Engineer to the Commissioners of Sewers was engaged early in 1866 to carry out the structural work of the viaduct, the contract for which was obtained by Messrs. Hill & Keddell, for £99,837. The foundation stone was laid on June 3rd, 1867, and as further approaches had to be constructed, an Act was passed for continuing the coal and wine dues for a further period of seven years. The principal work authorised by the second Act was the construction of a new street from the corner of Fleet Street to Holborn Circus. The total cost of the viaduct and approaches, including the purchase of ground, premises, goodwill, etc., was £2,552,406, a considerable portion of which has fallen upon the City revenues, owing to Parliament's refusal to renew the coal dues until the liabilities connected with this great work were discharged.

Mr. William Haywood, in a report to the Improvement Committee, dated 18th November, 1872, says: " In addition to the Viaduct, the following improvements were effected: the Circus at the western end; the six adjacent public ways; Farringdon Street and Road raised and the latter partially widened; construction of Charterhouse Street and Snow Hill as western and eastern approaches between the Viaduct and Farringdon Street; construction of St. Andrews Street between the Viaduct Circus and Shoe Lane; construction of St. Bride Street from Shoe Lane to Fleet Street; and widening of Shoe Lane."

The height of the level of the Viaduct above the former roadways as they existed in 1863 is 32 feet at Farringdon Street Bridge, which spans the deepest portion of the Fleet Valley. From the Circus at its western end to Giltspur Street at its eastern end, the Viaduct is 1,285 feet long and 80 feet wide, the carriage-way being 50 feet and the two footpaths each 15 feet in width. The bridge over Farringdon Street consists of three spans, the arches being supported on granite pillars. Over the two external columns, on each side of the bridge, are granite piers and pedestals surmounted by bronze statues representing the Fine Arts, Science, Agriculture, and Commerce. A public staircase at each corner of the Viaduct affords communication between Farringdon Street and the Viaduct level. Statues representing Henry Fitz-Ailwyn, the first Mayor of London, Sir William Walworth Lord Mayor, Sir Hugh Middleton, and Sir Thomas Gresham are placed on the staircases. In the centre of Holborn Circus is an equestrian statue of the late Prince Consort.

The Queen opened both Blackfriars Bridge and Holborn Viaduct on the 6th November, 1869. Her Majesty was accompanied by their Royal Highnesses, Princesses Louise and Beatrice and Prince Leopold. Galleries had been erected on the bridge, draped with scarlet and white cloth, from which hundreds of spectators witnessed the opening ceremony. The Queen was received by the Right Hon. James Clarke Lawrence, Lord Mayor, the sheriffs, and other representatives of the Corporation. The Recorder read an address, signed by the Town Clerk, in which the hope was expressed that the new bridge would be the means of removing the danger and inconvenience arising from the constantly growing traffic, whilst at the same time the architectural features and sanitary condition of the neighbourhood would be greatly and permanently improved.

The Home Secretary delivered to the Lord Mayor a copy of the Queen's reply, which was as follows :

"I thank you for your loyal and dutiful address. It has afforded me much pleasure again to visit the City of London. Anxious as I have always been to identify myself with the interests of my people, it has given me unqualified satisfaction to assist at the opening of your new Bridge and Viaduct. In these works, at once of great practical utility and of architectural ornament to the City, I recognise the spirit of enterprise and improvement which has ever characterised the citizens of London; and I confidently trust that your anticipations of the benefit which will result to the community may be fully realised."

The Queen having declared the bridge open for traffic, the Royal procession, preceded by the Lord Mayor and Corporation, passed under the Viaduct and through Smithfield and Giltspur Street to the east end of the structure, where two colossal plaster statues, one bearing the palm of victory and the other the olive branch of peace, had been erected. A beautiful volume containing a description of the Viaduct having been handed to the Queen, Her Majesty declared this splendid thoroughfare also open, and thus two of the greatest works ever undertaken by the Corporation for the benefit of the public were brought to a happy conclusion.

SOUTHWARK BRIDGE.

In May, 1811, a Bill was passed for the erection of a new bridge to cross the Thames about a quarter of a mile west of London Bridge, and to be known as Southwark Bridge. The work was undertaken by a private company, and the cost is stated to have been about £800,000, though it would appear from contemporary records to have been considerably less. The architect, John Rennie, F.R.S. (who afterwards built New London Bridge), designed a bridge of three cast-iron arches, the two outer and smaller spans being 210 feet long, while the central and largest arch covered 240 feet. The height of this arch from the water at the highest spring tides is about 42 feet. The roadway is formed of solid plates

SOUTHWARK BRIDGE.

of cast-iron joined by iron cement. This roadway, 42 feet wide, is supported by stone piers, which rest upon timber platforms whose foundations are wooden piles driven below the bed of the river. A new and successful principle in the construction of cast-iron bridges was introduced in this instance by Rennie, namely, the formation by the ribs of the arches of a series of hollow masses, or voussoirs, similar to those of stone. Bolts are rendered unnecessary by the use of dove-tailed sockets and long cast-iron wedges, and the whole mass is so closely tied together

U

by bondstones, vertical and horizontal, that it is well fitted to resist the horizontal thrust. The entire length of the bridge is 700 feet, and the weight of the iron-work 5,700 tons.

Although the Bill for the erection of Southwark Bridge passed in May, 1811, the works were not begun till 1813; they were finished six years later. The first stone was laid by Admiral Lord Keith, April 23rd, 1815, and the final ceremony took place under peculiarly impressive circumstances on March 24th, 1819, the bridge, illuminated with lamps, being declared open as St. Paul's clock tolled midnight.

Although built with the avowed intention of relieving the surplus traffic of London and Blackfriars Bridges, it was estimated by Bennoch that the number of vehicles and passengers over Southwark Bridge averaged less than one-fortieth of the traffic of its sister bridge on the east; London Bridge indeed was only relieved by Southwark Bridge to a very slight extent, and the congestion of traffic was almost as great as before. Several reasons were advanced for the comparative failure of Southwark Bridge. First, the payment of toll, which naturally tends to drive traffic (especially vehicles) over the free bridges. Secondly, a bad approach from the south side. Thirdly, the want of direct communication with the main arteries of the City on the north side of the bridge. Fourthly, the steepness of the approaches to the bridge, and the actual narrowness of the bridge itself.

The first of these objections no longer exists, the second and third have been partially disposed of, and as regards the fourth there has been much discussion in the City Corporation, various plans for reducing the gradient of the approaches having been considered. The bridge, however, still retains its original width of 42 feet, from which $13\frac{1}{4}$ feet must be deducted for the two footpaths, leaving only $28\frac{1}{4}$ feet of roadway.

For thirty years after the completion of Southwark Bridge nothing appears to have been done with a view to facilitating the traffic between north and south London. The difficulties, however, were growing greater year by year. The number of passengers and vehicles crossing London Bridge and Blackfriars Bridge grew by "leaps and bounds," but the bridge at Southwark did not relieve the pressure. In 1849, therefore, the Corporation commissioned the Bridge House Estates Committee to approach the owners of Southwark Bridge (the Southwark Bridge Company) with a view to the purchase of the bridge by the City. The Company stated that the North Kent Railway Company had offered them £300,000 for the bridge, and refused to consider any lower offer. The Corporation was not prepared to pay this price, and the negotiations fell through. Another attempt to negotiate was made by the Bridge House Committee in 1853, but the Southwark Bridge Company now not only declared they would take no less than £300,000, but would not even pledge themselves to accept that amount. The increase in the Company's demand was no doubt caused by rumours that a Committee of the House of Commons was to be appointed to inquire into the "want of additional bridge accommodation." The Committee was actually formed, and its report was laid before the House in July, 1854. It showed an enormous increase of traffic through the streets of London in four years (1850-54), the number of passengers by rail at the London Bridge termini having risen from 5,000,000 to 10,000,000 a year in that time, while the number of pedestrians and vehicles had also greatly increased. The report recommended that tolls should be removed from all roads and bridges as they tended to hinder traffic, and that the expense of maintaining the bridges and roads should be met by a rate levied on the whole Metropolitan district. The Metropolitan Board of Works was constituted in the following year (1855) "for the better local management of the Metropolis," amongst its duties being the carrying out of improvements in connection with roads, bridges, etc.

In 1857 the Bridge House Committee conferred with the new Metropolitan Board of Works in reference to the possible purchase of Southwark Bridge out of the City funds, or to its purchase by the united aid of the Common Council and the Metropolitan Board of Works. The Committee eventually advised the Corporation not to assist in freeing the bridge, and nothing further was done for several years. In the meantime the Southwark Bridge Company showed a desire of getting rid of its burden, and the public agitation against bridge tolls grew apace. The Company, in May, 1864, offered to open Southwark Bridge to the public on terms to be agreed upon, or effect a sale of the property, the price now asked being not £300,000, the previous irreducible minimum, but £200,000. As, however, the Metropolitan Board of Works was about to introduce a Bill in Parliament "to facilitate the traffic of the Metropolis by improving the communication across the River Thames," the offer was not accepted.

In the following month, June, 1864, the Bill above mentioned was introduced, authorising the Metropolitan Board of Works to purchase by agreement Southwark Bridge, and certain other bridges, which were to be open to the public free from toll. It also contained clauses directing the Corporation to contribute £50,000 out of the Bridge House Estates funds towards the purchase money of Southwark Bridge, and to maintain the bridge out of the same funds.

Feeling that this Bill, dealing as it did with the disposal of funds which were under the control and management of the Corporation, was unprecedented and interfered unjustly with the rights of the City, the Bridge House Committee recommended that they should present a petition to the House of Commons against the Bill. This was done and the Bill was successfully opposed. Then followed a series of negotiations between the Corporation and the Southwark Bridge Company. In July, 1864, the Common Council instructed the Bridge House Committee to make inquiries as to the sum of money required to open the bridge to the public free of toll for twelve months. Although the Corporation resisted any arbitrary interference with its rights, it was anxious to arrive at a fair settlement in the interests of the public. Eventually in October, 1864, the Company agreed with the Corporation to open the bridge free to the public for six months for £1,834 and for a further six months at an additional cost of £2,750, the Company in the meantime maintaining the bridge and all the works connected with it. The Corporation agreed to this and the money was paid out of the City's cash, as the Bridge House Estates funds could not be used for such a purpose. The bridge was opened by Lord Mayor William Lawrence, free of toll, on November 8th, 1864, and it has remained toll free ever since.

In March, 1866, the Corporation referred to the Committee of the Bridge House Estates the consideration of the then existing accommodation for passengers and vehicles by means of bridges, more especially with regard to Southwark Bridge and London Bridge. In May the

Committee delivered their report. They had obtained statistics as to the daily number of foot-passengers and vehicles crossing Southwark and London Bridges, taken together and separately, and had also conferred with the chairman and directors of the Southwark Bridge Company with a view to the purchase of Southwark Bridge and the houses and property belonging to it. £200,000 was still demanded as the price of the bridge and other property, and though the bridge was in good condition, it was estimated that repaving, painting and other repairs would cost an additional £5,700. The Bridge House Estates Committee were of opinion that the bridge accommodation for the public was not sufficient, and recommended the purchase of Southwark Bridge for the sum named. This was agreed to by the Common Council, and on June 12th, 1868, the warrant was signed for the completion of the purchase and an order was made for the removal of the toll-houses.

§ 3. Need for bridge accommodation in East London. Various proposals and designs.

In spite of the purchase of Southwark Bridge in 1868—especially completed with the view of relieving the traffic over London Bridge, it was found in a few years that the former bridge, even when freed from toll, did not carry away its due proportion of passengers. Its steep gradients prevented vehicles from taking that route, and the fact that it opened out into no main thoroughfares was a drawback to foot-passengers. The great need of a bridge was east and not west of London Bridge. The late Colonel Haywood pointed out the difficulties in a very lucid report to the Bridge House Estates Committee in 1871. "London Bridge," he said, "is the only roadway across the Thames for the great population which lies to the east of it on both sides of the river. If a straight line be drawn five miles to the north and five miles to the south of this bridge there will be found for the most part to the east of it thirty-seven important Metropolitan districts, which in 1861 had a population of 949,000, and probably now have quite a million, or about one-third of the entire Metropolitan population. In some of these districts, also, the population, as shown by the census, is increasing faster than in any other part of London. It is approached by lines of highway, running for many miles north and south on both sides of the river, and connected with others which form important branches and feeders of traffic towards the east. It is only as they approach the bridge itself that these main lines are impeded by traffic. With one or two exceptions they are ample in width, and have thoroughly good gradients. London Bridge is therefore the most convenient route between the north-east and south-east of London, and has the largest traffic of any bridge in the Metropolis ; nor is it probable, so long as the population increases to the east, that any new bridge on the west or any improvement in the approaches to the existing bridges on the west will materially affect its traffic. A new bridge lower down the river, with suitable approaches, will alone relieve it effectually, and meet the present and future needs of the population. Sooner or later this must be made, and it is even at this time the most pressing Metropolitan improvement. Blackfriars Bridge has direct communication with the north by means of Gray's Inn Lane, Farringdon Road, and St. John's Street, and with the south by Blackfriars Bridge Road and the numerous highways which connect with the thoroughfare at its southern end. The whole are ample in width, and the gradients are for the most part excellent ; the steepest gradient on the bridge itself is on its northern end, which is 1 in 43. Southwark Bridge is under different conditions. Its direct northern approach may be said to terminate at Cheapside, and its southern by the junction of the Southwark Bridge Road with Newington Causeway ; it presents scarcely any appreciable advantage over Blackfriars and London Bridges in respect of distance to the traffic passing between the north, north-east and south, excepting as regards a limited area ; and has disadvantages in respect of gradient which the two other bridges have not." Having gone into a careful calculation as to the relative distances to be traversed by utilising the different bridges, Colonel Haywood came to the conclusion that even if the approaches to Southwark Bridge and its defective gradients were improved, a large increase of traffic to the relief of Blackfriars and London Bridges could not be expected. The late engineer appended a statement showing the vehicular traffic of every description passing both ways over London, Blackfriars and Southwark

Bridges between 8 a.m. and 8 p.m. upon certain days between 1863 and 1870. The following comparisons are selected from this table, the weather being fine on each occasion : —

LONDON BRIDGE.		BLACKFRIARS BRIDGE.		SOUTHWARK BRIDGE.	
Date.	No. of vehicles.	Date.	No. of vehicles.	Date.	No. of vehicles.
June 23, 1863	20,405	June 18, 1863	8,416	June 29, 1863	1,014
Mar. 15, 1866	18,205	Mar. 16, 1866	9,921	Mar. 16, 1866	4,113
Dec. 20, 1869	17,674	Dec. 17, 1869	11,373	Dec. 17, 1869	3,675

It should be remembered that Southwark Bridge was opened toll free in November, 1864, and its daily carriage traffic rose at once from about 1,000 to 3,000 vehicles. Its highest point was 4,113 in 1866, and the subsequent fall was attributed to the opening of new Blackfriars Bridge and the Victoria Embankment. Colonel Haywood concluded his report with three recommendations: First, to lower the arches of Southwark Bridge and the road formation between Sumner Street and Upper Thames Street, and to bring the gradient of Queen Street to 1 in 30 throughout its length. Secondly, to complete the widening of Queen Street. Thirdly, to form a new street from the High Street, Borough, to the Southwark Bridge Road by Union Street.

As early, indeed, as 1843 some relief had been found to the stream of traffic by the construction of the Thames Tunnel—a brick-arched double roadway designed by Brunel—and used for foot passengers, now owned by the East London Railway Company. This work created much interest at the time, being a remarkable achievement of engineering skill. It was originally planned by I. K. Brunel in 1823, the Duke of Wellington being one of the earliest subscribers. The following year the Thames Tunnel Company was formed to execute the work. A shaft was sunk on the Rotherhithe side of the river to the depth of 65 feet, and at the depth of 63 feet the horizontal roadway was commenced. The plan of operation had been suggested to Brunel by the bore of the seaworm *Teredo Navalis* in the keel of a ship, showing how, when the perforation was made by the worm, the sides were secured and rendered impervious to water by the insect lining the passage with a calcareous secretion. With the worm in view Brunel employed a cast-iron shield containing thirty-six frames or cells, in each of which was a miner who cut down the earth; and a bricklayer simultaneously built up from the back of the cell the brick arch, which was pressed forward by strong screws. In this way between January 1, 1826, and April 27, 1827, Brunel completed 540 feet of the tunnel. The engineer, however, now encountered serious difficulties. On May 18, 1827, the river burst into the works, and the water had to be pumped out. When 600 feet of the tunnel had been completed the water rushed in again and drowned six men, carrying Mr. Brunel, jun., up the shaft. At this stage the tunnel was discontinued for seven years for want of funds. Public interest in the scheme, however, continued, and a sum of over £5,000 was raised by public subscription. This, added to a Parliamentary loan, enabled the work to be resumed, and a new shield was constructed. The tunnel was not completed till November, 1841, when the shaft which had been sunk at Wapping was reached. The tunnel was opened as a public thoroughfare for foot-passengers on March 25, 1843. The idea of using it for vehicular traffic had to be abandoned owing to the great expense necessary for that purpose. As it was, the tunnel cost about £454,000. The width of the tunnel is 35 feet and the height 20 feet. Each archway and footpath has a clear width of about 14 feet. The thickness of earth beneath the crown of the tunnel and the bed of the river is about 15 feet. At full tide the foot of the Thames Tunnel is 75 feet below the surface of the water.

In 1871 the Tower Subway was constructed by a joint stock company. It consists of a circular iron tube seven feet in diameter, extending from Great Tower Hill on the north side to near Pickle Herring Stairs on the south side of the Thames. It was intended by the engineer, Mr. Peter Barlow, for a rope-drawn car, but in consequence of several accidents, it is now entirely used by foot-passengers. In spite of the charge of a half-penny for toll nearly 1,000,000 passengers a year are estimated to cross the river by means of the subway.

Public feeling was now growing slowly but steadily in the direction of a new bridge to be built near London Bridge on the east, or at least it was demanded that the latter bridge should be widened sufficiently to accommodate the increased and rapidly increasing traffic. The subject was continually being brought under the notice of the Corporation and the Metropolitan Board of Works, it being for some time doubtful which of these two public bodies would eventually have the responsibility of carrying out this great and much needed improvement. So great became the demand for increased bridge accommodation, that between the years 1874 and 1885 some thirty petitions and other presentations from public bodies were brought before the Common Council urging the Corporation to step into the breach and undertake the construction of a new bridge. One of the earliest of these petitions was presented to the Corporation in 1874, signed by "Merchants, Traders, and others carrying on business in the City of London and the Borough of Southwark, for the widening of London Bridge." The Corporation referred the matter to the Bridge House Estates Committee, with instructions to consider and report upon the best means of affording additional accommodation for the traffic across London Bridge. On January 28th, 1875, the Ward of Candlewick presented a resolution, expressing the opinion that it had become necessary to provide additional facilities for the enormously increasing traffic over London Bridge. Five months later the Corporation received an influential deputation from the Merchants and Traders who had previously petitioned. So urgent became these representations that the Corporation again referred to the Bridge House Committee the consideration of any possible means of relieving the growing traffic of London Bridge without widening the bridge, and without increasing and enlarging the approaches. An alternative suggestion was made for the construction of a subway under the bridge.

In December, 1875, the Bridge House Estates Committee reported on various plans for widening London Bridge and erecting another bridge, and expressed themselves in favour of increasing the width of the existing bridge according to a report which had been examined and approved in the previous September. In January of the next year a *third* petition was presented from "Merchants, Manufacturers and Traders largely interested in the conveyance of goods in and around the eastern part of the City of London." It dealt with the proposed widening of London Bridge, and strongly urged the necessity of another bridge near or east of the Tower. In this view the City merchants were supported by the vestry of St. George-in-the-East and other East-end petitioners, as well as by the vestry of St. George the Martyr, Southwark.

The Corporation, with a strong desire to further the welfare of the city and supply the public need for increased bridge accommodation, at their next meeting referred the merchants' petition to the Bridge House Estates Committee, with instructions to ascertain the relative advantages and probable cost of a bridge over the Thames, or a subway under the river. The same Committee received at this meeting authority to confer with Her Majesty's Government on the subject of these proposals. A week later, in view of the greatly increasing work laid upon the Bridge House Committee by the growth of city traffic and improvements, a Special Committee was appointed, afterwards known as the Special Bridge or Subway Committee. To this Committee was transferred all references made to the Bridge House Committee in relation to additional accommodation for traffic between the north and south sides of the River Thames eastward of London Bridge.

On December 7th, 1876, the new Bridge or Subway Committee presented a report recommending that, provided the requisite funds could be obtained, a bridge over or a subway under the River Thames should be constructed eastward of London Bridge, and that the most eligible site would be that approached from Little Tower Hill and Irongate Stairs on the north and from Horselydown Lane Stairs on the south side of the river. The Committee also recommended that they should be authorized to consider the best means to carry this into effect, and to advertise for designs, premiums to be offered for those most approved. The recommendation in favour of a new bridge, as against the widening of London Bridge, was based on traffic returns over London Bridge furnished by the City Police Commissioner for two weeks in January and February, 1875. These returns show the vehicular traffic over London Bridge to and from the districts which would be likely to be advantageously affected by the construction of a bridge or subway east of London Bridge. From an analysis made by the architect, Mr. Horace Jones, it appears that the average number of vehicles of all kinds passing daily over London Bridge from north to south was at that time about 7,800, of which the proportion of goods traffic was about 4,000. The average proportion going from the north-east to the south-east of London was about 1,570, the estimated proportion likely to use London Bridge being 380, and the proportion likely to be benefited by a new means of crossing the river being 1,190. The returns also showed the number of horses that fell on the bridge during two consecutive weeks, the number of stoppages of the carrying traffic, and the causes of such stoppages. A return was also obtained by the Committee of the number and character of the vessels passing up the river westward of St. Katharine's Docks. From an analysis of this return it appears that the total number of vessels passing up the river during six consecutive working days was 144; the height of the masts of two of these was 40 feet, of eight 45 feet, of thirteen 50 feet, of eleven 55 feet, of thirty-two 60 feet, of thirty-nine 65 feet, of thirteen 70 feet, of seven 75 feet, of eight 80 feet, of nine 85 feet, of one 90 feet, and of one 95 feet.

This report of the Special Bridge or Subway Committee also contained in the appendix an analytical description of the several designs for the relief of the traffic on London Bridge, transferred to the Committee by the Bridge House Estates Committee. Summarized briefly they are as follows :—

1. Low Level Bridge, designed by Mr. Frederic Barnett, having in the middle a kind of loop or dock, without water-gates, allowing small craft to pass always, the swing only to be opened for large vessels. Approaching from each shore about one-third its entire length, the bridge meets the loop, and diverges to the right and left, the traffic passing over one side of the loop by means of one of the swing or swivel bridges, the other swing bridge being left open for a vessel to pass in or out of the loop (and *vice versâ*). The loop is divided by a platform longitudinally with the river, on each end of which turns one of the swings working the two openings by the same movement. By this means Mr. Barnett affirmed that large ships with the highest masts could pass without stopping the vehicular and passenger traffic. The cost was estimated at about £400,000 for works and property.

2. A Movable or Rolling Bridge, to carry vehicles and passengers, proposed by Mr. G. Barclay Bruce, jun. By this arrangement a certain portion of the waterway was always to be left open for vessels. The river was to be divided into seven spans by six piers, on each of which would be fixed rollers and machinery for driving them. The bridge was to be 300 feet by 100 feet. As this kind of bridge might be placed at any level above high water, Mr. Bruce considered that it solved the question of

approaches. He calculated that it could leave the shore every six minutes and carry upwards of 100 vehicles and 1,400 foot passengers. The cost of construction was to be £134,381 and the working expenses capitalized £10,000.

3. Another Bridge similar to London Bridge to be built 100 feet eastward of it, and connected with it at each end, and at intermediate intervals, proposed by Mr. Thomas Chatfeild Clarke. No estimate of cost was given.

4. Low Level Bridge, designed by Mr. John P. Drake. This was to be carried on girders, with a swing middle to turn on a pivot. Bridge to be 50 feet wide. No estimate of cost given.

5. High Level Bridge proposed by Mr. Sidengham Duer, with a pair of hydraulic hoists at each end; bridge to be 40 feet wide and 740 feet long, girders 80 feet above high water mark. The hoists were to be carried out on the principle of the Anderton lifts. No expense would be required for property compensation, as in the case of most high level bridges. The cost was estimated at £130,500 and the working expenses at £1,872 per annum.

6. High Level Bridge of three spans, submitted by Mr. T. Claxton Fidler. The centre span was to be of 508 feet, and the other two spans 180 feet each. The headway was to be 70 feet above Trinity high water. The south approach was to be by means of a spiral ascent.

7. River Railway Line, which Mr. C. T. Guthrie proposed to construct at the bottom of the river, carrying above a framed staging and deck, projecting above the level of high water. The carriage would be driven by machinery and move on the submerged lines between two quays. The estimated cost was £30,000.

8. Subway Double Cast-iron Arch, or "sub-riverian arcade" resting on concrete bed, proposed by Mr. John Keith. Roadway to be 55 feet wide. The cost was to be £509,536.

9. High Level Bridge, proposed by Mr. Edward Perrett, with hydraulic hoists, the bridge to consist of three spans of 267 feet each and 80 feet above high water in centre; staircases to

be provided for foot-passengers. Estimated cost £340,000, with £4,000 per annum additional for working expenses.

10. Two Paddle-wheel Ferry Boats, suggested by Mr. E. Waller (Thames Steam Ferry Company), to ply across, each 82 feet by 27 feet between paddle-boxes. Each boat was to carry twelve two-horse vans and 250 foot-passengers. Estimated outlay £55,000 and £8,000 per annum for working expenses.

None of the above-mentioned designs was approved by the Special Committee, who, as already stated, recommended that they should be allowed to advertise for further designs. The report of the Committee was adjourned for further consideration and finally agreed to in May of the next year.

The year 1877 may be said to be the most important in the discussions as to the advisability of a high level bridge *versus* a low level bridge with some method of passage-way for ships of large size, inasmuch as the Committee in May of that year strongly recommended the adoption of some form of low level bridge. The Special Bridge or Subway Committee had been previously commissioned in February, 1876, to consider the "desirability and the approximate cost of making the approaches to, and of erecting a bridge over, or a subway under, the Thames, east of London Bridge," and on December 7th, 1876, they recommended that a bridge over, or a subway under, the river was necessary and desirable, and asked for power to obtain the necessary funds. In the following January (1877) the Committee was instructed to obtain information as to the gradients and approaches necessary to carry the traffic either over a bridge, or through a subway, across the Thames, with an approximate estimate of the cost, and the report of May contains this information.

Mr. Horace Jones, the City architect, reported fully with regard to the three alternative proposals. He first dealt with the question of a high level bridge with a clear water-way of 82 feet 6 inches in the centre above Trinity high water mark. The architect considered that this height might more or less interfere with about 300 tons burden of shipping per annum, supposing that no alteration was made in the topmasts of the vessels, the total number of tons burden of shipping passing each way being estimated at about two and a quarter millions per annum. Mr. S. W. Leach, engineer to the Conservators of the River Thames, thought a clear headway of 100 feet was necessary, but Mr. Horace Jones pointed out that the additional elevation would greatly increase the difficulties of the approaches. The length of approach to such a high level bridge as the architect suggested, with a gradient of 1 in 40, would, on the north side of the river, be from 2,000 to 3,000 feet, according to the spot selected for its commencement, and on the south side of the river about 3,500 feet. Mr. Horace Jones was of opinion that the high level bridge, if constructed as a suspension bridge, could be kept within a sum of two millions sterling, including the eastern approach or span from East Smithfield, but if a rigid bridge of equally handsome appearance, with approaches, his estimate would be about £2,150,000.

With respect to a low level bridge the architect considered it would be sufficient to take the same height as London Bridge, viz., 29 feet 6 inches above Trinity high water mark. The approach northwards would extend about two-thirds of the way up Little Tower Hill from the river, a distance from the centre of the river of about 1,000 feet; and the approach southward of a length of 1,100 feet from the centre of the bridge, would reach to the continuation of Tooley Street, with a gradient of 1 in 40. Mr. Horace Jones thought it useless to give much attention to a low level bridge to secure economy in the approaches, unless some provision was made for the passage of ships up to London Bridge. This became the chief problem both in the design and estimated cost of a low level bridge, viz., the consideration of the mechanical appliances requisite for the purpose of opening and closing a portion of the bridge. He suggested that the Committee should have a special report on such structures as were in existence which afforded ample, speedy and convenient transit for vessels with little or no inconvenience to land traffic. With the data before him the architect estimated the total cost of a low level bridge, including the approaches and special maintenance, at £750,000.

Mr. Horace Jones estimated the cost of a subway with a direct northern approach from Whitechapel Road, and a special approach from the south side, at £1,500,000. If with a span from East Smithfield, it would be about another quarter of a million.

The architect pointed out that a high level bridge, interrupting slightly the river traffic, would require from the centre of the river, direct north and south, an ascent and a descent together of about 5,700 feet, whilst a subway would at the same gradients and in the same direction require a descent and ascent of about the same distance. The following is the architect's comparative summary of the various routes from the north to the south side of the river, with an ascent and descent of a gradient of 1 in 40 :—

	FEET.
High level bridge, about　　-　　-　　-	5,700.
Tunnel (same depth as Thames Tunnel)	6,280.
Tube or Tunnel (constructed in a way suggested by the architect)　　　-	5,000 to 5,800.
Low level bridge -　　-　　-　　-　　-	2,100.

Having fully considered the question, both with regard to the imperative necessity for the relief of the traffic of the City and the convenience of river navigation, the Committee expressed it as their opinion that the best means to be adopted to meet the wants of and to relieve the continuously increasing traffic of the City, would be to construct a low level bridge, with proper arrangements for affording the requisite facilities for the passage of vessels up and down the Thames. They suggested the erection of the bridge on the site formerly recommended (in December, 1876), viz., that approached from Little Tower Hill and Irongate Stairs on the north side, and from Horselydown Lane and Stairs on the south side. The recommendations of the Bridge or Subway Committee were, after much discussion, agreed to by the Common Council, and the Committee were instructed to consider and report as to the source or sources whence the funds for the construction of a low level bridge and the approaches thereto were obtainable. The Committee at the same time were authorised to confer with Her Majesty's Government, the Metropolitan Board of Works, and any other public body, and with any committee of the Common Council.

Meanwhile, in March, 1878, the Bridge House Committee asked for and obtained authority from the Corporation to seek Parliamentary powers for the raising of funds to widen London Bridge, the approximate cost being estimated at £75,000; but in June they reported that their Bill had been withdrawn at the request of the Government. In October of the same year the Special Bridge or Subway Committee delivered a report containing a summary of their work during the year. The Committee had had under consideration several petitions against the proposed new bridge, amongst the petitioners being the Traffic Committee of the Ward of Billingsgate. A scheme for a high level bridge, to be designated "the Tower Bridge," was put forward by Sir Joseph Bazalgette, the engineer to the Metropolitan Board of Works. This proposal, which excited much public opposition, was presented in the form of a Bill to Parliament by the Metropolitan Board of Works in the latter part of the year 1878, and was successfully opposed by the Corporation and the Thames Conservancy Board. The Committee proceeded to say that in the previous November they conferred with the Works and General Purposes Committee of the Metropolitan Board of Works, and after a full discussion of the question of constructing a new bridge, they, at the suggestion of the Board's committee, authorised the City architect to put himself in communication with the Board's engineer, but the conference did not result in the co-operation of the Metropolitan Board of Works, which the Committee regretted. The Conservators of the Thames were also approached, but they expressed their desire to await more definite proposals before taking action.

A copy of the report presented to the Metropolitan Board of Works by Sir Joseph Bazalgette was handed to the Corporation Committee, who directed the architect to consider it, together with some statistics and information furnished by a deputation from the Wharfingers' Association. Mr. Horace Jones, the City architect, in his report to the Committee dated October 16th, 1878, expressed his personal regret that he had not the pleasure of presenting a joint report with Sir Joseph Bazalgette. In the single interview he had with the engineer of the Metropolitan Board of Works, the only points discussed were the inadvisability of taking a higher gradient than 1 in 40, and the adaptability for a new bridge of the site eastward of the Tower and across to Horselydown Stairs. Mr. Horace Jones gathered reluctantly that Sir Joseph Bazalgette did not propose or desire to pursue the subject jointly with him, and afterwards he (Sir Joseph) presented the report dated March 15th, 1878, to the Metropolitan Board of Works. This report began with a notice of the memorials received from the Whitechapel District Board and the vestries of St. George's-in-the-East and Rotherhithe, and of a report of his own dated December 10th, 1877, approving of the site already suggested by the Special Bridge or Subway Committee of the Corporation, and adopted by the Common Council on May 3rd, 1877, viz., that eastward of the Tower. Sir Joseph, touching lightly upon Mr. Leach's objections to a low level bridge, the interruption to navigation, the height of ships' masts, etc., and quoting from Mr. Horace Jones's report as far as was suitable to his views against a subway, started upon the subject of a high level bridge on the trussed girder principle in an arched form, with the roadway carried across the arch and suspended from it, a design which the City architect pointed out ignored or showed a thorough disregard of all the evidence, views, wishes and interests of the wharfingers and of shipowners trading between the site of the proposed bridge and London Bridge.

The City architect proceeded: "It is quite clear that if the public will submit to have the navigation of the river interrupted in the way Sir Joseph Bazalgette proposes, we may consider whether they will not submit to further interruption or inconvenience by bringing down the bridge to such a level as would successfully compete with London Bridge in obtaining the land traffic. It is true that this must be attended with one result, viz., to approximate the value of the wharf property between the site of the proposed bridge and London Bridge to the value of similar property between Southwark or Blackfriars Bridge and London Bridge, and this would, I fancy, be a question of an expenditure for compensation or a loss of millions to the owners of such property, besides seriously affecting all the trades more or less dependent upon sea-going vessels. It requires only a visit to Bankside to convince any observer of the difference of value between the wharves above and below bridge." Having called attention to an error in the gradients alluded to in Sir Joseph's report, Mr. Horace Jones concluded that a high level bridge would be a costly and extravagant scheme, that if carried sufficiently high to clear all masts, it would be as little used as was the Thames Tunnel, while to adopt a high level bridge of the modified height proposed by Sir Joseph Bazalgette, viz., 65 feet, would on the other hand sacrifice to a large extent the river traffic, and yet be of comparatively small service to the land traffic. Moreover, the distance to

be travelled would be very considerably longer over a high level than over
a low level bridge.

Sir Joseph Bazalgette estimated the cost of his bridge as follows:—

Cost of approaches	- - - - -	£850,000
Bridge in one span	- - - - -	400,000
		£1,250,000

(If bridge in three spans, £250,000 as against £400,000).

On the question of estimated cost Mr. Horace Jones pointed out that
Blackfriars Bridge with five spans involved an expenditure of £350,000
exclusive of approaches.

After disposing of the "Tower Bridge High Level Bridge," the City
architect proceeded to the question whether or not it would be possible
to construct a bridge on a *low* level, with openings so simple that
there should be no interference with land traffic, and so capacious in
plan and rapid in operation as not to interrupt the river traffic. With
passing references to various swing bridges (single and double pivot),
and explanations of their respective disadvantages: to a bridge with a
movable central platform to be raised and lowered before and after the
passage of large vessels, and with a word of praise for the steam ferry,
then actually working, Mr. Horace Jones laid before the Committee a
proposal for a low level bridge on the *bascule* principle. It is described
briefly as follows: The proposed bridge, having in its centre the
same height of water-way as London Bridge, viz., 29 feet, would
consist of two side spans of 190 feet each, and a centre span of 300 feet.
The roadway of the side spans would be carried by two ordinary wrought-
iron girders or by shallow lattice girders, carried by suspension chains from
the towers, with girders 35 feet apart, and cross girders between, carrying
buckled plates on which the roadway would be bedded. The centre span
of 300 feet would be bridged by two hinged platforms, forming what
is known as a "bascule" or "see-saw" bridge (bascule is the French for
see-saw). The longitudinal and cross girders and buckled plates of
the platforms were to be reduced in weight by the use of steel. Each
platform was to be suspended by eight pitched chains passing over
polygonal barrels fixed in the semi-circular arches between the towers,

and from thence to the hoisting machinery in the towers, where they would terminate in a plain chain or iron rod carrying the balance weights. The hoisting machinery could be worked by steam power, or by hydraulic apparatus, supplied by tanks fixed in the roof of the towers. The arches between the towers carrying the polygonal chain barrels were to be formed of four wrought-iron braced semi-circular arched ribs, connected transversely by four wrought-iron lattice frames, the rise of each arch in the centre to be 130 feet above Trinity high water mark, or 100 feet headway for a width of at least 150 feet.

The principal advantages claimed for this design were

First. Lowness of level, and consequently, easy gradients for the land traffic.

Second. Economy of construction in the approaches on both banks of the river, the lowness of the level allowing of direct access, and necessitating very slight alterations of the adjoining streets and properties.

Third. Occupation of less river space than a swing bridge, which, when swung open, requires a clear space equal to half the span of the bridge.

Fourth. Less interference with the tide-way or navigation of the river, there being only two towers or piers instead of three or four, as in the swing bridge schemes.

Fifth. Beauty of form. The chief features of the bridge being capable of architectural treatment, it might be rendered the most picturesque bridge on the river.

Sixth. Facility and rapidity of working by the special arrangements of machinery proposed. For instance, a ship signalled at a quarter of a mile distant, and sailing or steaming at the rate of, say, six or seven miles an hour, could pass the bridge, and the land traffic be resumed in three minutes, or if half a dozen vessels were within half a mile of the bridge, all could pass in five-and-a-half minutes.

The estimated cost given by the architect was £750,000, which was the amount named by him in his report of April 23rd, 1877. The report also contains sketches for the proposed bascule bridge, open and shut, which, however, differs in some important particulars from the present bridge spanning the Thames. The principal point of difference is with regard to the passage of pedestrians by means of an upper footway during the opening of the platforms in the central arch. There was no provision for this in the original bascule bridge sketched by Mr. Horace Jones.

The Committee closed their report by recommending the adoption of the City architect's design, and suggesting that the necessary steps should be taken for obtaining the authority of Parliament to raise upon the credit of the Bridge House Estates (subject to the existing charges thereon), the sum of £500,000, and the continuation and appropriation of the coal and wine dues to the extent of the balance required for the bridge and approaches, estimated at £250,000. This report was not adopted, and the matter appears to have lapsed for several years. In the meantime, however, the public outside, and especially the citizens, continued to agitate for a new bridge, and various petitions were presented to the Corporation. The Common Council was apparently dissatisfied with the Special Bridge or Subway Committee, and on January 24th, 1879, it transferred all outstanding references to this Committee to the Bridge House Estates Committee, which from this period was the only Committee directly responsible for the construction of Tower Bridge.

The Wharfingers' Association petitioned, early in 1879, against any proposed high level bridge such as that recommended to the Metropolitan Board of Works by the engineer to the Board, Sir Joseph Bazalgette. The wharfingers also petitioned against the payment of any City moneys by the Corporation to the Metropolitan Board of Works in aid of such a bridge. Early next year the Aldgate Wardmote presented a resolution in favour of providing means of communication between the north and south sides of the river east of London Bridge. In March following the Common Council instructed the Bridge House Estates Committee to consider whether the free opening of the Thames steam ferry would be the best means of carrying traffic across the Thames and obviate the necessity of erecting a new bridge. This was speedily followed by an order for the architect of the City to examine into the condition of the Thames steam ferry boats, the cost of working them, the value of the property, etc.

A year after, in June, 1881, the Metropolitan Board of Works invited a conference upon the subject of providing means of communication below London Bridge, their engineer being still strongly in favour of a high level bridge, as opposed to the idea finally carried out, of a low level bridge with means for the passage of large vessels. In the Concise History of the Metropolitan Board of Works, issued by that body just prior to its dissolution, the opposition of the Corporation and the Thames Conservancy Board to its Bill and the rejection of the Bill by the Select Committee of the House of Commons are referred to. "The matter," says this official record, "was again carefully considered with a view to seeing in what way the Board could secure for the inhabitants of the East-end what they required; and as the City authorities would be among the opponents of the high level bridge scheme, the Board made overtures to the Corporation with a view to an arrangement being come to which would be satisfactory to the City as well as to the districts further east. The only result of the negotiations, however, was a conclusion eventually come to by the Bridge House Estates Committee of the Corporation that the need for any bridge or tunnel did not seem sufficiently proved to justify the Corporation in taking part in the promotion of a scheme."

The conference referred to above was actually held in October, 1881. A further conference was suggested in January, 1882, in consequence of a resolution of the Wardmote of Aldgate, to the effect that it had become more necessary than ever that a bridge should be erected east of London Bridge, but this second conference does not seem to have taken place. A public meeting was held at the Mansion House on the 25th of May, and a strong protest was made against further delay in the matter of improving the means of vehicular traffic east of London Bridge.

An opportunity of easing the traffic of London presented itself in the proposal for the free working of the Thames steam ferry, submitted by the owners of the ferry in May, 1882. During the summer the Corporation considered this proposal favourably, in spite of the refusal of the Metropolitan Board of Works to aid the City in converting the Thames steam ferry into a free mode of transit. The Corporation considered it desirable that the ferry should be made free, as a means of testing the traffic across the Thames. Another plan, viz., that of a floating chain bridge between the north and south sides of the river at Greenwich, or some other suitable spot, was referred to the Bridge House Committee for consideration in November, 1882. The Committee at the same time had power to consult with other bodies.

For some months three proposals occupied the attention of the Bridge House Committee: the proposed freeing of the Thames steam ferry, the erection of a floating chain bridge, and the building of a new low level bridge east of London Bridge. During every month of the next two years the question of communication between the north and south of the Thames, east of London Bridge, occupied the attention of the Corporation. Many schemes were presented, more or less original in their character, and some extremely impracticable in working or costly in execution. Two Bills were introduced into Parliament in January, 1883, one for the Tower (duplex) Bridge, which was to be double at the middle portion and in action resembling a lock, and another for a Tower (Thames) Subway. These Bills were referred by the Court of Common Council to the Bridge House Estates Committee for consideration, and the Corporation also issued an order for ascertaining the cost of freeing the Tower Subway from toll for twelve months. In May a deputation of the Bridge House Committee visited Portsmouth and Gosport and Southampton, to examine and report upon the various floating bridges in use there. In the same month was received a petition from the owners and occupiers of property in the several parishes within the Whitechapel district and others interested in trade in that locality, praying the Court of Common Council to advocate and promote the construction of a low level bridge below London Bridge at the eastern boundary of the Tower. A similar petition was read from the Board of Works for the Whitechapel district. A third petition was presented from delegates "representing every section of the industrial classes in the east and south of London," in favour of the construction of subways under the Thames, and the Wards of Portsoken and Aldgate again petitioned the Court to promote the speedy construction of a low level bridge below London Bridge. Nor were these the only expressions of public interest in what had now become a burning question.

The Corporation, in June, 1883, consulted the Thames Conservancy Board on the expediency and advisability of having a floating bridge on the Thames at Greenwich, but this was objected to by the Board at a meeting in October. Several references having been made on the subject of Thames communications to the Coal and Corn and Finance Committee, a report was brought up in July of this year, in which that Committee expressed it as their opinion that some means of communication between the north and south of the River Thames below London Bridge was imperatively necessary and should be at once provided, seeing that the population of London east of London Bridge was nearly as large as that of Liverpool, Manchester, Birmingham and Leeds put together, and represented thirty-nine per cent. of the entire population of London. The Committee also considered that the expenses of such necessary communication should be met by a continuance of the coal dues, and recommended that the Bridge House Estates Committee should inquire and report forthwith as to the desirability of establishing and maintaining two or three steam ferries across the river, eastward of London Bridge, together with the probable cost of the same and the best places for their establishment. These several recommendations were agreed to by the Court, and the Bridge House Estates Committee at once proceeded to make the necessary inquiries. In October of this year the Bridge House Committee brought up a report recommending the Common Council to authorize them to make application to Parliament for authority to establish steam ferries. The Court agreed to this, and the Remembrancer was instructed to give the necessary notices. The Remembrancer was afterwards authorized to include in the notices power to establish a ferry from Irongate to Horselydown Stairs, the site of the present Tower Bridge. Seeing that the Corporation was bent upon trying the experiment of a ferry, the owners of the Thames steam ferry again approached the Corporation with a view to the disposal of their property. They undertook to supply a service of boats on a monthly subsidy of £1,150 guaranteed for three years. The Company was to put in order and keep in repair the two boats already existing, and build a new one, and run a boat from each side of the river every quarter of an hour free of charge within certain hours every day of the year excepting Sundays.

The Corporation was to have the option of purchasing the whole ferry premises and the property appertaining thereto, including the warehouse, for the sum of £90,000 at the expiration of the three years. The then City solicitor (Sir Thomas Nelson) reported on this proposal to the Bridge House Committee. The ferry was established by a company which had gone into liquidation and was situated a mile and a half below London Bridge. It had ceased to work for some four years, and the boats and machinery were therefore out of order. Under these circumstances the City solicitor was of opinion that it would be more economical for the Corporation at once to acquire the property at its then value. The City architect (Mr. Horace Jones), on the other hand, considered that it would be unwise for the Committee to acquire the property until its public utility had been actually proved by a three years' test.

§ 4.   The Story of the Tower Bridge.

Possibly the question of steam ferries might have been further considered, but a general feeling was prevalent that nothing short of a bridge would really solve the difficulty, and a petition from the owners and occupiers of property in the parish of St. Botolph Without Aldgate and the immediate neighbourhood for the erection of a bridge at Irongate Stairs seems to have given voice to this feeling, for a week later the Bridge House Committee was directed to consider the question of a low level bridge, with or without mechanical openings.

From January, 1884, it may be said that the question of the *means* of improved communication between the north and south banks of the lower Thames was settled. Subways, duplex bridges and floating bridges sank into the background, and though the steam ferry was considered worthy of attention for some time as a palliation of the evil, the low level bridge was regarded as essential.

About this time a definite line of action was taken in Parliament which greatly facilitated the work of the Corporation. In March, 1884, three Bills were before Parliament, referring to the crossing of the River Thames east of London Bridge, viz. :—

1. Metropolitan Board of Works (Thames Crossings) Bill.
2. Tower (Duplex) Bridge Bill, introduced by private promoters.
3. Lower Thames Steam Ferries Bill, introduced by the Corporation.

These three Bills were referred to a Select Committee of the House of Commons, who sat for twenty-five days, dealing with the whole question of Thames communications, and presented a report to Parliament on July 4th. In this report the Select Committee, after referring to the particular schemes submitted for their consideration, and reporting against the duplex bridge and the subway at Nightingale Lane, proceeded to state as follows : —" Your Committee are of opinion that two crossings are required, and should be sanctioned by Parliament : The one a low level bridge at Little Tower Hill, with two openings, each about 100 feet wide, to be spanned by a pivot swing bridge ; the other a subway at or near Shadwell, which would be central and would best meet the wants and wishes of the inhabitants east of London Bridge." After a passing reference to the swing bridge over the Tyne at Newcastle, the Select Committee concluded their report by "expressing a hope that the Corporation of the City of London may be induced to undertake this great and useful work contemporaneously with the construction of a subway at Shadwell by the Metropolitan Board of Works."

The Bridge House Estates Committee brought up a report on July 24th, 1884, expressing agreement generally with the opinions of the Select Committee of the House of Commons, and especially with the suggestion that the work should be undertaken by the Corporation of the City of London, and constructed out of the Bridge House Estates funds. Without pledging themselves to actual details, the Committee recommended as follows : "That a low level bridge, with mechanical opening or openings, be erected at Irongate Stairs, at the end of the street known as Little Tower Hill, by the Corporation, out of money to be raised upon the credit of the Bridge House Estates, and that it be referred back to your Committee to obtain a design or designs for such a bridge, together with an estimate of the cost thereof, with authority to make such inquiries, seek such practical information, and obtain such professional or other assistance as in their judgment may be necessary to enable them at an early date to submit to your

Honourable Court such a scheme as they can confidently recommend
for adoption, with a view to an application being made to Parliament
during the present year."

This report was agreed to by the Court of Common Council on the
28th July, and referred back for the Committee to obtain the necessary
designs and estimates for the proposed bridge.   A deputation of the Bridge
House Estates Committee was also authorised to proceed to Holland and
Belgium, to view the bridges with mechanical openings in those countries,
as well as the Newcastle Bridge referred to by the Parliamentary Com-
mittee.   The deputation consisted of Mr. (now Alderman) Frank Green,
Chairman of the Bridge House Estates Committee, Mr. Deputy Crispe,
Mr. George Shaw, Mr. (now Alderman) Treloar, Mr. Edward Atkinson,
Mr. Thomas Beard, Mr. John Cox, Mr. J. Sheppard Scott, Mr. George
Manners, and Mr. Frederick Dadswell, who were accompanied by the
Comptroller, Mr. J. A. Brand.   Realising the urgency of the case, they lost
no time, and started on the 16th of August for the continent.   They were
met at Brussels by Mr. F. T. Reade, a civil engineer, the architect being
prevented from accompanying the deputation by the state of his health.
After their return in September the deputation presented an interesting
report containing a short description of each bridge examined by them, and
a longer and more detailed report from Mr. Reade.   This gentleman
divided the bridges visited into five classes.   Class A included those
on the bascule principle, the chief of which was the Jan Kulten Bridge
at Rotterdam, and the Entrepôt Bridge at Koningshaven.   Only one
example of rolling bridges (class B) was viewed, viz., the bridge leading
to the Bassin aux Bois at the New Docks at Antwerp.   The most
important swing bridge (class C) was at Boom, about ten miles from
Antwerp, crossing the River Rwypel, and carrying two lines of rails of
the Antwerp and Alost line of railway.   This revolves on a centre pier,
with two equal openings.   The deputation visited another bridge of this
class at Koningshaven, and the swing bridge over the River Tyne at
Newcastle.   Class D included the Victoria single swing bridge at the
Leith Docks, near Edinburgh, and a similar bridge at Queen's Docks,
Glasgow.   A double swing bridge (class E) was viewed at Antwerp
Docks.

On the 28th October, 1884, exactly three months after they had received instructions to obtain and submit designs, the Bridge House Estates Committee brought up their report to the Court of Common Council with designs for a low level bridge with mechanical openings. The Committee had had plenty of material to deal with. For ten years a mass of reports, evidence, and other information had been accumulating, and during the last seven years as many different schemes for crossing the river from Little Tower Hill to Horselydown Stairs had been prepared for Parliament. Only one of these the Tower (high level) Bridge had been introduced by public authority (the Metropolitan Board of Works) as a free bridge for the benefit of the public, the others being promoted by companies who looked to tolls for remuneration. Each of these schemes in turn had been rejected by Select Committees of the House of Commons, the only one now holding the field being the Corporation proposal for a low level bridge with openings, on which the Bridge House Committee had been concentrating its attention.

The Committee, in their report, pointed out that ever since 1877, when the Special Bridge or Subway Committee had the matter under consideration, the site had been practically agreed upon, and they adhered to the Little Tower Hill site as being in every respect the most suitable one. The Committee had consulted the Thames Conservancy Board and hoped the Corporation scheme would receive no opposition from that quarter. The architect had had an interview with Major-General Sir Andrew Clark, K.C.M.G., C.B., R.E., surveyor-general of fortifications, during which it transpired that the Government would not oppose the general scheme, provided that certain requirements connected with the Tower were complied with. Parliamentary notices had to be given early in November, and designs were at once taken in hand by Mr. Horace Jones, the City architect, who submitted three, marked A, B and C, for the consideration of the Committee.

Design A was a proposal for a swing bridge, showing the probable effect of the piers and dolphins required, having a central opening of 250 feet, two side spans of 125 feet each, and two shorter spans to the river wall.

Design B was an elevation of the same bridge, but in a different style of architecture, designed to meet the suggestions of the War Office authorities as regards the towers and breastworks considered necessary to command the bridge, as well as its architectural appearance.

Design C was that of a bascule bridge with a centre opening of 200 feet, evolved from the design approved by the Special Bridge or Subway Committee, and submitted to the Court in the year 1878.

The Committee submitted the designs marked A and C, and recommended the C design for adoption, believing that a bridge of this construction could be more easily and speedily opened than the other. The piers would not be so large and would be only two in number instead of four, consequently much less of the waterway, viz., 80 feet only, would be occupied. Besides which, the four dolphins necessary to protect the platform of the swing bridge when opened would be wholly dispensed with ; whereas the sweep of the swing bridge would necessarily prevent the berthing of vessels within the radius of the platform on either side. No such disadvantage would attach to a lifting platform, and vessels could be berthed close alongside. The length of the proposed bridge from shore to shore would be 880 feet, and the width 50 feet between the parapets. The height above high water mark would be 29 feet, the same as the centre arch of London Bridge. There would be two piers only in the tideway, of about 40 feet each, leaving between them a clear way for the passage of vessels of 200 feet.

Availing themselves of the authority of the Court to obtain such professional assistance as might be deemed necessary, the Committee had submitted the designs to Mr. John Wolfe Barry, the eminent engineer.

The approaches to the bridge on the north would commence near the northern end of Little Tower Hill, and have a gradient of about 1 in 70; and on the south side they would have a gradient not exceeding 1 in 40, commencing at Tooley Street, which had recently been widened and improved by the Metropolitan Board of Works.

They also reported that the architect estimated the cost of the bridge at £750,000, an amount which was not beyond the resources of the Bridge House Estates.

It was given in evidence before a Select Committee of the House of Commons that not more than twenty-three vessels on the average passed

Irongate Stairs daily, and of ten days in March, 1884, the average was only 14·3 per day.

This in effect constituted the report and recommendation of the Bridge House Committee. An appendix was added giving a detailed account of the continental visit and another setting forth in full the report of Mr. Horace Jones, supplemented by a letter from Mr. J. Wolfe Barry and the sketches before referred to.

Mr. Horace Jones, the City architect, referred to his three designs in the following terms :—

A is a view treated somewhat in an Italian character, looking eastward and showing the probable effect of the piers and dolphins required for a "swing bridge" of 250 feet opening in the centre. The length of the bridge may be taken at, say, 880 feet from the north land pier to the south land pier ; the piers in the river will be two small ones of, say, 20 feet each, and two others, to form the pivots to swing the bridge on, 60 feet each, making the total width of pier 160 feet, consequently leaving at high water mark 720 feet of water-way. The bridge would consist of, say, a roadway of four lines of traffic (36 feet) and two footpaths of 7 feet each, making a total width of 50 feet between the parapets. The gradient in the centre would be 1 in 100, 1 in 70 on the north side and 1 in 40 on the south side. Some inconvenience to the immediate occupiers or riparian owners east and west of the bridge may be feared, as the swing of the bridge between the dolphins which will have to be erected to protect the bridge when open, will be about 310 feet, or say an extreme length of 340 or 350 feet actually occupied by the swing of the bridge. These, I am aware, are serious points, and will require grave consideration. The height from high water mark to the riverside of the bridge will be 29 feet, the same, in fact, as now exists in the centre of London Bridge.

Sketch B is an elevation which has been made for the purpose of meeting the expression of certain views which appear to be held by the War Office authorities, who expressly said that as military authorities they were indisposed to allow any interference with the boundaries of the Tower ; but considering the importance of the question as a matter of general public convenience, they would not object to the views of the City in occupying a certain portion of the Tower land, provided that something like the architecture of the Tower is kept to on the north side, and also certain military constructions, such as towers and breastworks, so as to have a command of the bridge. In plan or sketch B something of this character is endeavoured to be retained in the upper stories of the "look out house," or gazebo, necessary for signalling and working the hydraulic apparatus by which the bridge is to be worked. You will see by the sketch that the centre opening is 250 feet wide, and the side spans 125 feet each, and when the bridge is open the passage between the piers will be as facile for steam or sailing vessels as the present fairway between the barge berthings.

Sketch C shows a "bascule" bridge evolved from the one I had the honour of laying before you some five or six years ago. Apart from the question of appearance and convenience in the passage of vessels, it will render the construction of our road and approaches lighter than in the former bridges, as we should be able to obtain a gradient of 1 in 40 on the south side to the centre of the present level in Tooley Street without any interference with the present level of that street; this would of course give a considerable saving both in compensation and in work. It would be the same length as previously stated, viz., 880 feet; the waterway would be obstructed by two piers only of, say, 40 feet each, leaving between them a clear way of 200 feet in the centre; the waterway would therefore be 800 feet at high water mark, instead of 720 feet as given by the swing bridge; and indeed I am inclined to think that the 40 feet width of piers might be somewhat reduced. I am not, however, at present prepared to positively assert this. The width of bridge might be made the same, viz., 50 feet between the parapets, and the gradient need never exceed 1 in 40. The time occupied in raising and lowering the bridge would also be in its favour, as against a swing bridge, but as both might have the duration of each operation counted by seconds, I will not press much upon this. I would further add that the foot traffic need not be interrupted even when the bridge is open for the passage of vessels—staircases must be constructed for the service of the bridge, and they can, as well as passenger lifts, be so constructed as to serve the public. The convenience to the occupiers or riparian owners, east or west, having nothing before them to interfere with the approach to their wharves, will be an additional advantage, and small craft could pass underneath with greater safety and convenience, the danger of the bridge suddenly swinging round and over them being avoided. The wider piers and dolphins would cause considerable delay in construction, which would also be avoided in this bridge; the height to underside of bridge from high water mark would be the same, viz., 29 feet, and when open the height to underside of arch would be about 125 feet, which in my opinion would be ample.

Mr. Horace Jones mentions that he had consulted Mr. John Wolfe Barry, whose letter he appended, and concluded by roughly estimating the cost of the bridge and approaches at £750,000. The letter referred to in the architect's report, signed by Mr. Wolfe Barry, is appended:—

23, DELAHAY STREET,
WESTMINSTER, S.W.,
October 17th, 1884.

MY DEAR SIR,

TOWER BRIDGE.

I have given the subject of the Tower Bridge as much consideration as the time which has been at my disposal since you did me the honour of consulting me would allow.

I have agreed with you the centre line and section shown on the plan, and need not further allude to them.

With respect to the opening portion of the bridge, I would recommend that the fairway between the tiers of shipping should be kept clear when the bridge is open, and that no centre pier should be permitted.

With regard to the mode of opening the bridge, I think that either of the suggested plans shown on your sketches is practicable.

A swing bridge would cause a certain amount of inconvenience to the berthing of vessels in its immediate vicinity, and would require dolphins in the river to protect the bridge when open. It would thus during revolution, and when open for river traffic, occupy more of the river than a "bascule" or lifting bridge.

A "bascule" or lifting bridge would perhaps save some small amount of time in the passage of vessels ; it would render the alteration of the level of Tooley Street unnecessary, and would admit of a footway served by hydraulic lifts being practicable from shore to shore, when the bridge was open for river traffic.

Further, I see no difficulty, if the latter system be adopted, in spanning the whole of the side openings between the piers on each side of the fairway and the river banks in one span. This would render the construction of side piers unnecessary, and would be a convenience to the side channels.

For the above reasons I think this bascule or lifting system of opening the centre span should not lightly be set aside, but should be thoroughly investigated, as well as the problems involved by a swing bridge. For this investigation there will be ample time, as the Parliamentary notices can, I believe, be so framed as to admit of either system being adopted.

I have not forgotten that another system of opening by means of a draw or sliding bridge might be adopted ; but considering all the points involved in the present question, I think it will be better for you to confine your attention to the proposals above mentioned.

I would urge that no hasty decision should be come to in adopting one or other mode of opening, as there are many important questions of an engineering nature to be considered, for which consideration time is necessary.

I quite agree with you in the impossibility of making any estimate of the cost at the present moment, but no doubt an approximate estimate might be ready shortly.

I may perhaps be permitted to say that any of the three designs shown in the sketches would in my judgment be an ornament to the Port of London.

My dear Sir,
Yours very faithfully,

Horace Jones, Esq.,
    Guildhall.
                                            J. WOLFE BARRY.

The Court of Common Council unanimously adopted the recommendations of the Bridge House Committee, and the Remembrancer was authorized to take steps to promote a Bill in Parliament for the construction of a low level bridge.

It having become well known, through the public press and otherwise, that the Corporation not only had the subject of a new bridge under consideration, but had actually agreed to its erection, and had directed the Remembrancer to take steps to promote a Bill in Parliament, many letters were received by the Corporation from parishes interested in the new traffic-way, warmly expressing thanks for the prompt attention given by the City to their petitions and resolutions.

The Bill for the erection of a bridge over the Thames was rapidly prepared. It was referred to a Committee of the House of Commons, who sat for nineteen days and received a large amount of valuable evidence, not only dealing with the traffic of the river, but at the same time demonstrating the absolute necessity for further bridge accommodation. The architectural, structural and engineering details of the bridge, as well as its working, were carefully gone into, and the Committee passed the Bill without any alteration on these points. The Bill was nevertheless strongly opposed by the wharfingers, who pleaded that danger and delay might be caused to their trading vessels by the erection of a bridge. The third reading of the Bill in the Commons having been passed, it was referred to a Select Committee of the House of Lords, whose first sitting took place on July 17th. The Lords were called upon to determine if the wharfingers' pleas were just, and if just what compensation should be made to them for possible depreciation in the value of their businesses and properties by reason of the bridge. It was eventually decided that a clause should be inserted in the Bill, giving the owners and occupiers of particular riverside premises defined in a schedule the right of appeal to an arbitrator in case of any loss arising from the new bridge, the arbitrator assessing the compensation for the particular wharves affected, provided such compensation did not exceed two years' net rateable value of each of the wharves. The compensation also was limited to the south side of the river, and no compensation was to be claimed until four years after the opening of the bridge. In view of the fact that the City itself owned some of the premises, some portion of the compensation, it was pointed out, would return to the Corporation as landlords.

The last legislative stage was reached on August 14th, 1885, when "an Act to empower the Corporation of London to construct a bridge over the river Thames near the Tower of London, with approaches thereto, and for other purposes," received the Royal assent. In the following September the Common Council authorised the Bridge House Estates Committee to carry into effect and execution the Tower Bridge Act of 1885. The City architect (Mr. Horace Jones) and Mr. John Wolfe Barry, engineer, had been appointed to superintend the construction of the bridge, and the actual works were begun on April 22nd, 1886. The contract for the first portion of the bridge, viz., the abutments on each side of the river and the two piers of the bridge from their foundations up to a height of 4 feet above Trinity high water mark, was given to Mr. John Jackson, of

Victoria Chambers, Westminster, for the sum of £131,344, that being the lowest tender.

On Monday, June 21st, the memorial stone of the new Tower Bridge was laid by H.R.H. the Prince of Wales, on behalf of Her Majesty the Queen. In addition to the members and officers of the Corporation, invitations were sent to members of the Houses of Lords and Commons, and to all the official and leading men connected with the City of London. Upwards of 200 visitors from India and the Colonies, who had come over to the Colonial and Indian Exhibition, were invited to be present, and a tent was constructed to accommodate between 1,500 and 1,600 guests. The band of the Coldstream Guards was stationed at the south end of the pavilion, and a choir from the Guildhall School of Music, under the direction of Mr. Weist Hill, sang selections before the commencement of the ceremony, which took place at four o'clock in the afternoon.

His Royal Highness the Prince of Wales was accompanied by their Royal Highnesses the Princess of Wales, the Prince Albert Victor, and the Princesses Louise, Victoria and Maud of Wales. A company's escort of the 2nd Life Guards accompanied His Royal Highness from Marlborough House to the Tower. On his arrival at the pavilion the Prince was received by the Lord Mayor, with the Sheriffs of London and Middlesex, the Bridge House Estates Committee, and the officers of the Corporation. The Bishop of London and the Secretary of State for the Home Department awaited the arrival of the Prince of Wales at the dais, where the Recorder read the following address to His Royal Highness :—

"We, the Lord Mayor, Aldermen, and Commons of the City of London, in Common Council assembled, heartily and gratefully welcome the presence of your Royal Highness on behalf of Her Most Gracious Majesty the Queen upon an occasion so interesting, and in its object so important to the commercial interest of this vast Metropolis.

"The Corporation of London has possessed for centuries estates charged with the maintenance of London Bridge. These estates were partly bestowed by generous citizens, and partly derived from gifts made at the Chapel of St. Thomas à Becket on London Bridge, for the maintenance of the bridge.

"By the careful husbanding and management of these estates, the Corporation has been enabled during the present century to rebuild, entirely free of cost to the ratepayers, London Bridge and Blackfriars Bridge, and to purchase and free from toll Southwark Bridge.

"These obligations being provided for, the Committee charged with the management of the Bridge House Estates brought up to the Court, by the hand of their chairman, Mr. Frank Green, in 1884, a full and exhaustive report, with plans, recommending that application be made to Parliament for powers to construct a new bridge across the River Thames from the Tower; which was agreed to.

"In the Session of 1885, the same Committee, under the chairmanship of Mr. Thomas Beard, successfully promoted a Bill in Parliament authorising the construction of a bridge, to inaugurate which, in the name of Her Majesty the Queen, your Royal Highness so graciously attends to-day.

"Its completion within the space of four years, at a cost of £750,000, will supply a paramount need that has been sorely felt by dwellers and workers on the north and south sides of the Thames below London Bridge, and at the same time will greatly relieve the congested traffic across that ancient and famous thoroughfare.

"In conclusion, we desire to express, on the first day of the fiftieth year of Her Majesty's happy and prosperous reign, our unswerving loyalty and devotion to Her Majesty the Queen, and to heartily thank your Royal Highness for the important part you have been pleased to undertake in the great work before us, enhanced as it is, to our intense gratification, by the graceful presence of Her Royal Highness the Princess of Wales, to whom, with your Royal Highness, we wish long life and all prosperity and happiness."

To which His Royal Highness made the following reply:—

"Gentlemen,

"It gives the Princess of Wales and myself sincere pleasure to be permitted, on behalf of the Queen, my dear mother, to lay the first stone of the new Tower Bridge, and in her name we thank you for your loyal address, and assure you of her interest in this great undertaking.

"All must allow that this work, when completed, will be one of great public utility and general convenience, as tending materially to relieve the congested traffic across this noble river.

"We shall always retain in our remembrance this important ceremony.

"We cordially thank you for the very hearty welcome which you have accorded to us, and we will not fail to communicate to the Queen the sentiments of affectionate attachment which you have expressed."

The stone having been "well and truly" laid by the Prince of Wales, the Bishop of London offered a short prayer, and the auspicious event was announced by the firing of a salute from the Tower guns. The chairman of the Bridge House Estates Committee presented to the Princess of Wales the emblem of the Bridge House Estates set in diamonds, which was graciously accepted. After the usual presentations the proceedings were brought to a close with the National Anthem sung by the choir of the Guildhall School of Music. The City architect, Mr. Horace Jones, shortly afterwards received the honour of knighthood.

The following is a copy of the inscription on the memorial stone : —

THIS MEMORIAL STONE

WAS LAID BY

H.R.H. ALBERT EDWARD PRINCE OF WALES, K.G.,

ON BEHALF OF HER MAJESTY QUEEN VICTORIA,

ON MONDAY, THE 21ST JUNE, 1886,

IN THE 50TH YEAR OF HER MAJESTY'S LONG, HAPPY, AND PROSPEROUS REIGN.

THE RIGHT HON. JOHN STAPLES, Lord Mayor
DAVID EVANS, ESQ^{RE} Alderman ⎫
THO^S CLARKE, ESQ^{RE}   ⎬ Sheriffs.
EDWARD ATKINSON, ESQ^{RE} Chairman of the Bridge House Estates Committee.
HORACE JONES, ESQ^{RE} City Architect.
JOHN WOLFE BARRY, ESQ^{RE} Engineer.

The Corporation of London (Tower Bridge) Act, 1885 (48 and 49 Vic., cap. cxcv), empowered the Corporation to construct the bridge within four years from the passing of the Act. At the same time it authorised the Corporation to borrow, on the credit of the Bridge House Estates, the sum of £750,000 and such further sums as might be necessary. Owing, however, to the necessity which arose for alteration of the levels of the southern approach to the bridge, and for taking additional property, it became impossible to complete the bridge within the time specified, and an extension of time was granted by the Act of 1889 until the 12th of August, 1893. The time was further enlarged to the 14th of August, 1894, some weeks before the expiration of which the Tower Bridge was completed and opened to the public. The official programme of the ceremonial on this occasion will be found in the Appendix.

It should be mentioned that in addition to the designs submitted to the Corporation and referred to above, there have been other designs for a bridge across the lower Thames, some of which have attracted considerable notice. Even as early as 1813 Mr. James Walker, F.R.S., and Sir Samuel Browne proposed to erect a high level suspension bridge at the Tower, the centre span to be 145 feet above Trinity high water level. There were to be three spans in all, 600 feet each in the clear.

During the present century the Corporation have expended on new bridges across the Thames, out of the Bridge House Estates, no less a sum than £2,489,057, made up as follows :

London Bridge and its immediate approaches	£715,246
Blackfriars Bridge	506,289
Southwark Bridge	218,868
Peg's Hole (Stratford)	3,500
Tower Bridge (exact cost not yet ascertained)	1,045,154

These bridges are under the control and maintenance of the Corporation, and it is a very remarkable instance of civic care, prudence and integrity, that the revenues of the Bridge House Estates, originating in the generosity of private citizens, should have been so used during a number of centuries as to produce such magnificent results.

THE TOWER BRIDGE, 13th JUNE, 1894.

CHAPTER III.

Description of the Tower Bridge,

ITS DESIGN AND CONSTRUCTION.

BY

JOHN WOLFE BARRY, C.B., M.INST.C.E.,

ENGINEER OF THE BRIDGE.

THE problem to be solved in the design of the Tower Bridge was one of no small difficulty, for it was necessary to reconcile the requirements of the land traffic with the very important interests of the trade of the Upper Pool. This part of the river is always crowded with craft of various kinds, and it was this fact that made the "bascule" system so desirable. Any opening bridge revolving horizontally would have occupied so large an area of the river as to be very undesirable from many important points of view, whereas a bridge revolving in a vertical plane, not only occupies the minimum of space in the river, but also at an early stage of the process of opening affords a clear passage for ships in the central part of the waterway, increasing in width rapidly as the operation of opening is continued.

The mode in which the traffic of the Pool is conducted prescribed the general arrangement of the spans of the bridge. Sea-going vessels of all kinds are moored head and stern in two parallel lines in the Upper Pool, on each side of the centre line of the river, leaving a central channel from 200 to 250 feet wide free for the passage of vessels up and down the river, and this space is frequently contracted by barges and small craft lying alongside the larger vessels, to a width of from 160 to 180 feet. The spaces in the river occupied by the large vessels on each side of the free central channel are called tiers, and as vessels lie in the tiers two or sometimes three abreast, with barges alongside them, it will be seen that if the piers of a bridge were made alignable with the tiers there would be no obstruction to navigation, and little to the flow of water, by two piers of a width not greater than that of the tiers. On the landward side of each of the tiers channels are preserved for the passage of vessels to and from the wharves, and it was of course necessary that these side channels should not be obstructed by any pier of the bridge. Thus the mode in which the river traffic has for many years adjusted itself, made it evident that a bridge with a clear central opening of from 160 to 200 feet, and two side openings of about 280 or 300 feet, would meet all requirements, and that there could be no objection to piers wide enough to accommodate a counter-balance, seeing that the width of two vessels lying in the tiers would be more than the width necessary for such an extension of the moving girders into the piers as would provide for a sufficient counterpoise.

With these few words on the principles that governed the main features of the Tower Bridge, we will proceed to consider the details of the structure generally.

It is wished that the description which follows should not be regarded as an engineering paper upon the bridge, nor as one which would be suitable to a body of experts. Such a paper would overrun the limits of space available, and would, while requiring a very large number of detailed drawings to make it intelligible, be unsuitable for any but strictly engineering records. The description is written with a view of giving such particulars as will enable a reader to form a general conception of the design of the bridge, and of the various considerations which determined its mode of execution, with only such an amount of technical detail as appears indispensable under the above conditions.

GENERAL DESCRIPTION OF THE TOWER BRIDGE.

The Act of Parliament prescribed the leading dimensions of the Tower Bridge to be as follows : —

(1) A central opening span of 200 feet clear width, with a height of 135 feet above Trinity high water when open for vessels with high masts, and a height of 29 feet when closed. (It may be mentioned in passing that the central span has been made 6 inches higher when closed than was stipulated, and is, as executed, of the same height as

the centre arch of London Bridge which is 29½ feet above Trinity high water, and that it is 5 feet higher when open than was prescribed by Parliament).

(2) The size of the piers to be 185 feet in length and 70 feet in width.

(3) The length of each of the two side spans to be 270 feet in the clear.

The Act also defined the utmost permissible size of the temporary stagings in the river.

The Conservators of the Thames, who very properly considered chiefly the importance of the river traffic, procured the insertion in the Act of

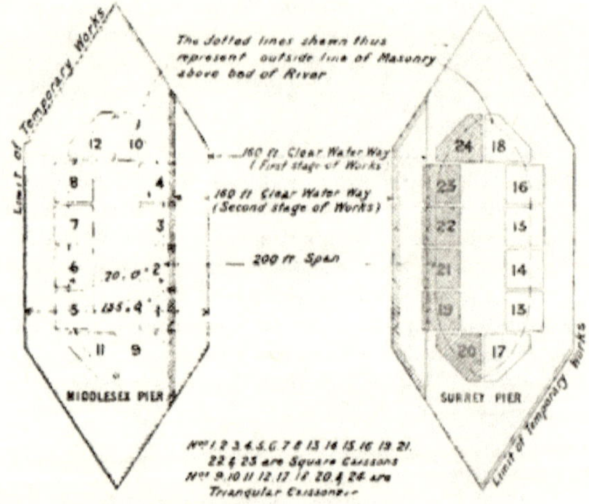

FIG. A. PLAN TO SHOW LIMIT OF TEMPORARY WORKS.

Parliament of a clause obliging the Corporation to maintain at all times during the construction of the bridge a clear waterway of 160 feet in width, and this necessity occasioned much delay in the construction of the permanent piers, as the opening defined was too wide to permit of both piers being constructed simultaneously. The plan (Fig. A) shows the limits of the temporary works as laid down by Parliament. The outer lines round each pier are the limits of the temporary stagings, and it will be

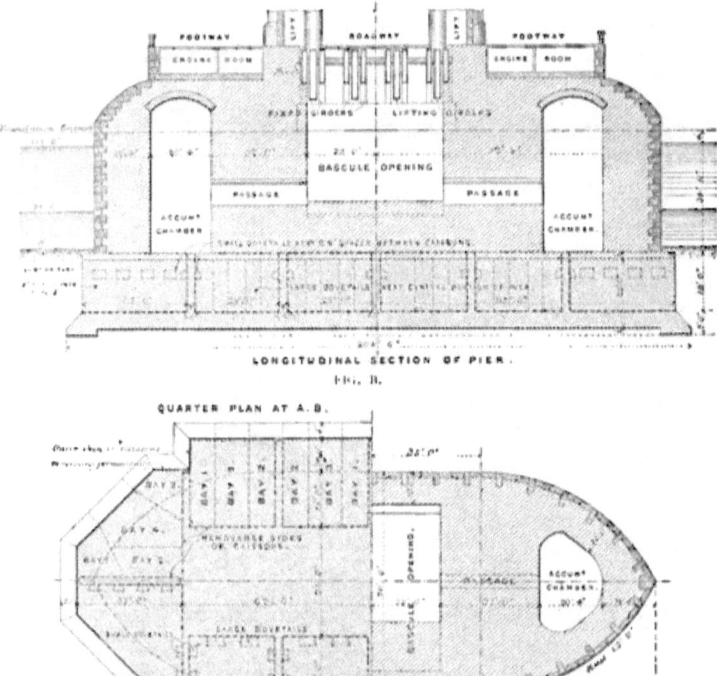

LONGITUDINAL SECTION OF PIER.

FIG. B.

QUARTER PLAN AT A. B.

QUARTER PLAN AT C.D.   HALF PLAN AT E.F.

FIG. C.

seen that, in order to give a navigable width at all times of 160 feet, there could be only one staging at a time of the full width required for building the piers.

The Government authorities gave every facility for the execution of the works, and, to enable them to be carried out without interfering with very important wharf property, allowed a small part of the Tower Ditch to be occupied by a portion of the north approach. If this concession had not been made the cost of the land for the undertaking would have been almost prohibitory. It was stipulated in return that the design of the bridge should be made to accord with the architecture of the Tower, and at one time it was intended that the new works should be made suitable for the mounting of guns and for military occupation. The latter idea was afterwards to a great extent discarded.

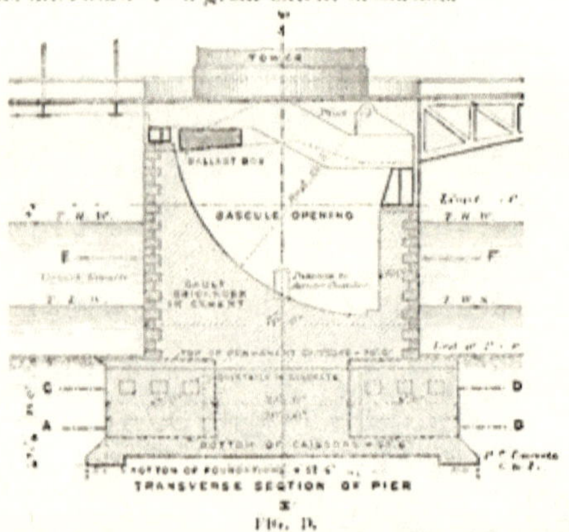

Fig. D.

The piers of the Tower Bridge are essentially different from the piers of an ordinary bridge, inasmuch as they have to contain the counterpoise and machinery of the opening span, as well as to support the towers which carry the overhead girders across the opening span and the suspension chains of the fixed spans. They are thus very complex structures, as will be seen by the illustrations (Figs. B, C, and D). Their form in plan (Fig. C) may be described as a square of 70 feet elongated by cutwaters at each end, bringing the total length to 185 feet 4 inches. The depth from the roadway level to the London clay, on which the foundations rest, is 92 feet, or 60 feet below Trinity high water.

The form of the piers up to the level of the roadway, which is
32 feet above Trinity high water, may first be considered. They each
contain (1) a large cavity to receive the landward end and counterbalance
weight of one leaf of the opening span; (2) two large chambers for the
hydraulic accumulators; (3) two chambers for the hydraulic engines which
actuate the opening span; and (4) two long tunnels, one for receiving the
main pivot shaft on which the leaf of the opening span revolves, and the
other for the pinion shafts by which the power is transmitted to the opening
span from the hydraulic engines.

FIG. 1.—BASCULE BRIDGE ACROSS A DUTCH CANAL.

A diagram (Fig. S, page 197) will explain the method of actuating the
opening span. The old bascule bridges of Holland had (Fig. E) their
counterbalance above the roadway level, mounted on posts at the abutments, and attached to the bridge by chains or ropes. The dimensions of
the Tower Bridge forbade such an arrangement of an overhead counterweight, and the counterbalance is there applied, as shown in Fig. S, directly
to a prolongation of the girders of the opening span. These girders turn
on the main pivot, behind which a space, or cavity, has been provided to
permit of the movement up and down of the landward ends of the girders

and the counterweight. This space, which is called the bascule chamber or opening, is in the form of a quadrant, and its leading dimensions are 50 feet from north to south, 44 feet from east to west; it is 50 feet in height next the central or opening span, diminishing to nothing next the landward or fixed span of the bridge. The two machinery chambers are each 35 feet by 30 feet, and 10 feet high, and the two chambers for accommodating the accumulators are each 30 feet by 20 feet 4 inches, and are 50 feet in height, extending from below the floor of the machinery chamber to within 26 feet of the bottom of the foundations.

Before describing the mode in which the substructures of the piers were constructed, it will be best shortly to describe the general arrangement of the remainder of the fixed portion of the bridge.

The mode adopted for spanning the landward openings is by suspension chains, which, in this case, are stiffened. The chains are anchored in the ground at each end of the bridge, and are united by horizontal ties across the central opening at a high level (Fig. X, page 205). These ties are carried by two narrow bridges 10 feet in width, which are available as foot bridges when the bascule span is open for the passage of vessels. The foot bridges are 140 feet above Trinity high water, and as their supports stand back 15 feet from the face of the piers, their clear span is 230 feet. Access is given to them by hydraulic lifts and by commodious staircases in the towers.

Above the landings at the tops of the stairs, and on which the foot passengers land from the lifts, come the roofs of the towers, the crestings on the tops of which are 206 feet above the roadway level, or 298 feet from the bottom of the foundations.

The leading dimensions of the structure having now been given, it is proposed to describe (1) the mode in which the piers were constructed up to roadway level; (2) the details of the opening span and machinery; (3) the details of the fixed superstructure, namely, the towers, the suspension chains, and the overhead footways; (4) the mode of erecting the superstructure.

THE MODE OF CONSTRUCTING THE SUBSTRUCTURE OF THE PIERS.

Iron caissons, strutted with strong timbers, were used in excavating the bed of the river and building the foundations of the piers. During these operations the external pressure of the water and earth surrounding the caissons was very great, as there is a depth of 32 feet of water at high tide at this part of the river, and the caissons had to be carried about 21 feet into the bed of the river to secure a good foundation. The caissons were boxes of wrought iron, without either top or bottom, and with the bottom edges made sharp and strong (Fig. F) so as to

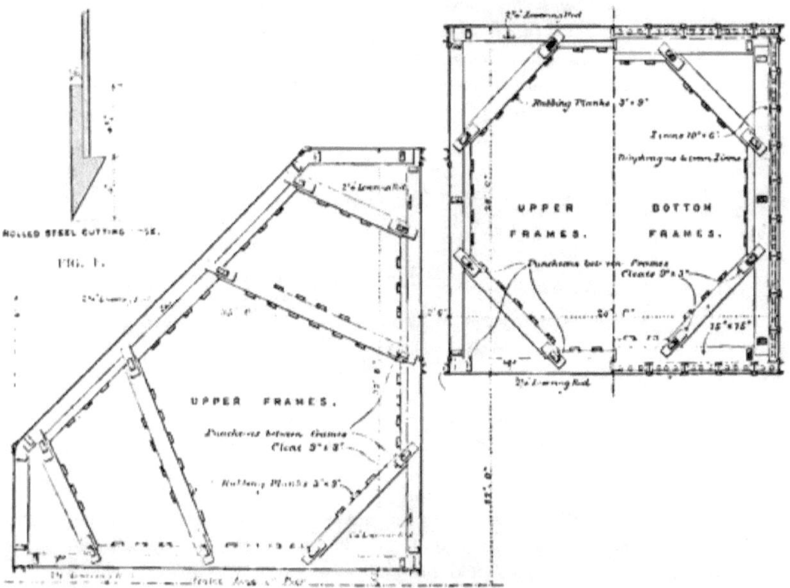

FIG. G.   SQUARE AND TRIANGULAR CAISSONS IN THEIR RELATIVE POSITIONS AT END OF PIER.

easily penetrate the ground. There are twelve caissons for each pier, as will be understood from Fig. A. Those about the central parts of the pier are 28 feet square in plan, and those near the cutwaters are triangular in plan, the dimensions being 35 feet by 33 feet 8 inches. Fig. G shows a square caisson and a triangular caisson in plan with their timbering and other details. The bottom part of the caisson having to be sunk deep into the bed of the river could not be removed on the completion of the pier, and was thus called the permanent caisson. The purpose of the upper part of the caisson was merely to exclude water during the process of building the pier, and it could be removed when the brickwork and masonry were finished. This part was thus called the temporary caisson.

The description of the mode of sinking one caisson will apply more or less to all, though, of course, the circumstances attending the various caissons required some differences of treatment. The temporary timber staging for the pier having been constructed with pile-work in the river,

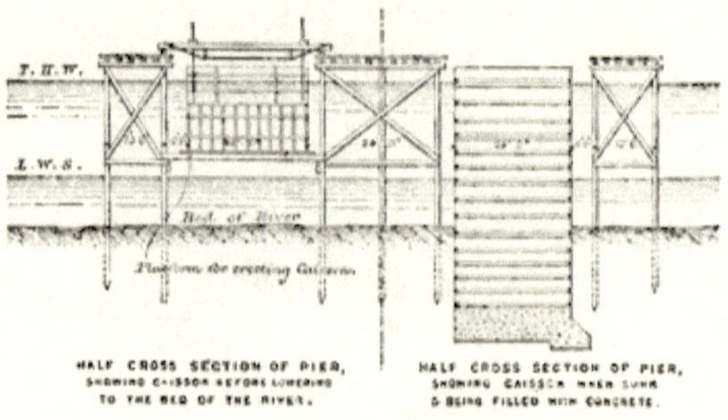

FIG. II.

the next operation was to erect the permanent caisson upon the staging. The permanent caisson was 19 feet in height, divided horizontally into two lengths. It was erected on timber supports, which were slightly above low water mark (Fig. II), where it was rivetted together and firmly strutted inside with strong timbers 14 inches square. It was then lifted slightly by four powerful screws attached to four rods, from which was slung the weight of the caisson and the timbering in it. The timber supports were removed, and the caisson was lowered by the screws on to the bed of the river, which had previously been levelled by divers.

After the permanent caisson reached the ground various lengths of temporary caisson were added to it till the top of the temporary caisson came above the level of high water. The junction between the permanent and temporary caissons was made with india-rubber, as shown in Fig. I.

Divers working inside the caisson excavated first the gravel and then the upper part of the clay forming the bed of the river, and as they dug away the soil, which was hauled up by a crane and taken away in barges, the caisson gradually sank until at length its bottom edge penetrated some 5 to 10 feet into the solid London clay.

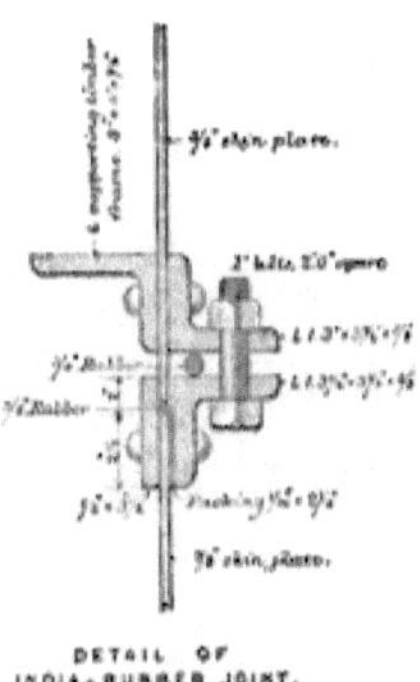

DETAIL OF INDIA-RUBBER JOINT.

FIG. I.

London clay is a firm, water-tight stratification, and when the above-mentioned depth was reached it was safe to pump out the water, which up to this time remained in the caisson, and rose and fell with the tide through sluices in the sides. The water having been pumped out, navvies proceeded to the bottom of the caisson and dug out the clay in the dry.

Additional lengths of temporary caisson were added as the caisson sank, so that at last each caisson was a box of iron, 57 feet high and of the dimensions above stated, in which the preparation of the foundations could be commenced. A detailed view of one of the completed caissons is given in Fig. K.

It is of great importance in sinking caissons or cylinders, that they should be controlled from above and be prevented from sinking unevenly. It is comparatively easy to prevent a caisson from going wrong (as is the case with many animate subjects as well as inanimate) by timely control, but it is a very different thing to put the matter right when a wrong course has been pronouncedly taken. This control was given to the caissons by the screws and rods to which allusion has been made, and which were lengthened from time to time as the caisson descended into the bed of the river and prevented any irregularity of movement.

London clay being peculiarly hard and uniform in texture, advantage was taken of this circumstance to increase the area of the foundations by

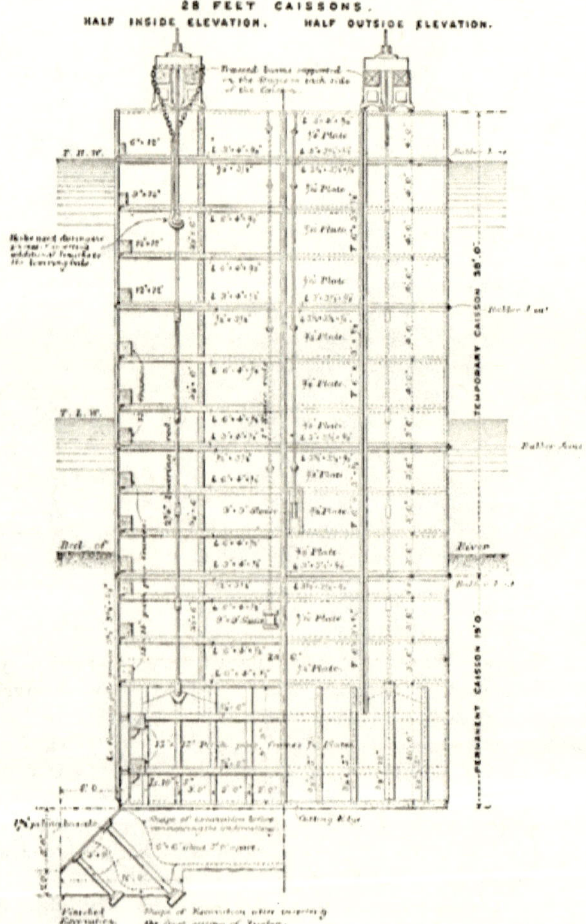

FIG. K.   COMPLETE CAISSON WITH TIMBERING AND SUSPENSION RODS.

digging out sideways or undercutting below the bottom edge of the caisson,
as shown at the bottom of Fig. K.   The caisson
having been controlled from the first by the
suspending rods and screws, its descent any further
than was desired was easily arrested by the rods
when the bottom of the caisson was 20 feet below
the bed of the river.   The clay was then excavated
7 feet deeper than the bottom of the caisson, and
outwards beyond the cutting edge for a distance
of 5 feet on three of the four sides of the caisson.
In this way not only was the area of the foundations

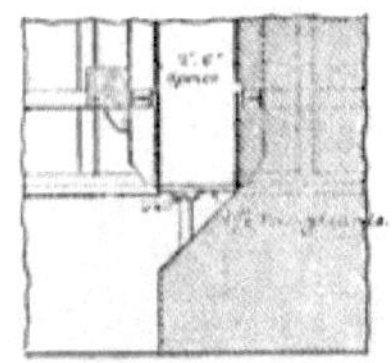

FIG. L.

of the pier enlarged, but as the sideways excavations adjoined similar
excavations from the next caissons (Fig. L.), the whole foundation
was made continuous.   The whole of the permanent caissons, with the
spaces between them, were then completely filled with concrete, upon

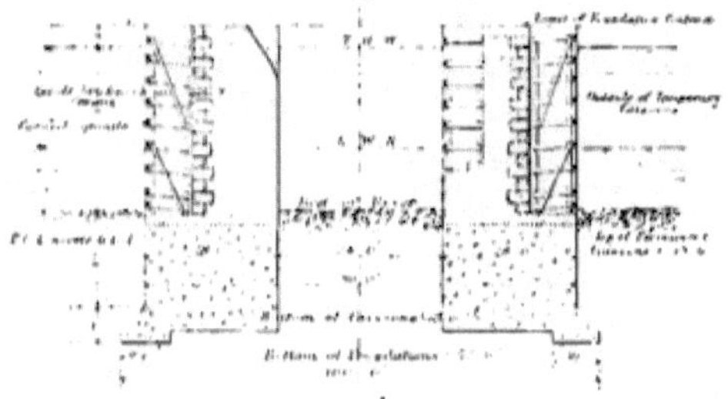

FIG. M.   CROSS SECTION OF PIER SHOWING OUTSIDE WALL COMPLETED.

which the brickwork and masonry were commenced in the temporary
caisson, and carried up to 4 feet above Trinity high water, as shown
in Fig. M.

It was not desirable to build isolated portions of the brickwork and
masonry, even if they were joined together afterwards.   Accordingly,
the temporary caissons were so designed as to admit of their sides being
removed (Fig. C) and of the whole area enclosed by their front and
back plates being thrown together to permit of continuous building.

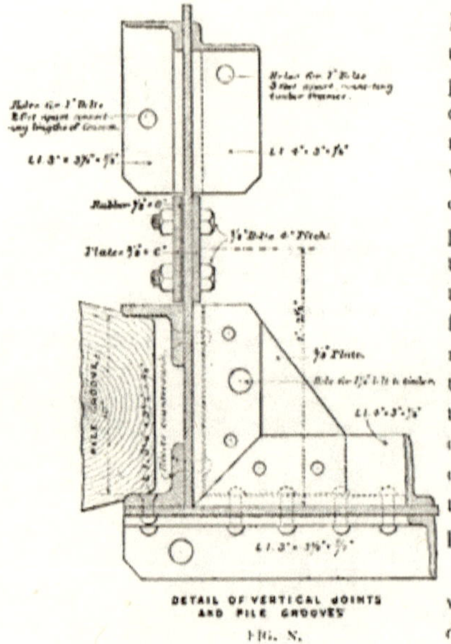

For this purpose the corners of the caissons were united by timber piles, which were driven in a groove on each caisson (Fig. N), and when these had been driven and made water-tight (as to which no difficulty occurred), the sides of the temporary caissons were removed. In this way the outside portions of the piers were built, and eventually formed a continuous ring of a strong masonry wall, water-tight and able to resist the external pressure of the water (Fig. O). The foundations of the central portion of the pier enclosed by the outside walls were then excavated and the pier completed.

The abutments of the bridge were built within ordinary cofferdams, and, though formidable in size and depth, presented no new features of construction such as have been explained with regard to the piers.

The work of the foundations was troublesome and tedious, owing to the isolation of the piers, and still more to the great amount of river traffic, rendering the berthing of barges difficult. The substructure thus occupied a considerably longer time than was anticipated.

The view Fig. P gives an idea of the appearance of the works during the construction of the piers.

THE OPENING SPAN.

The stipulated dimensions of the opening span have been already given as providing, when the bridge is open for ships, a clear waterway of 200 feet in width, with a clear height throughout the 200 feet of 135 feet (which has been increased in construction to 140 feet) from

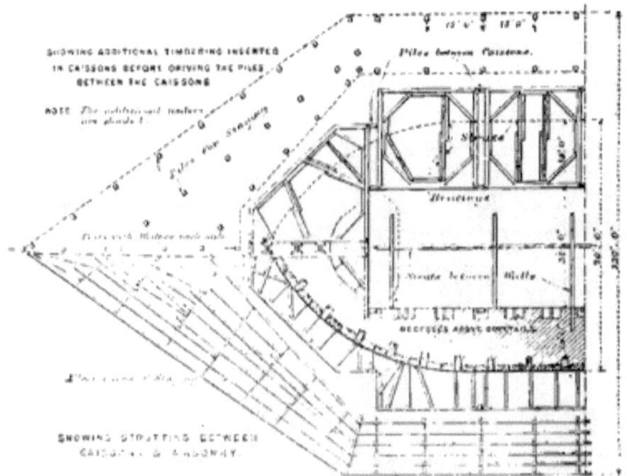

FIG. O. HALF PLAN OF PIER AT DIFFERENT PERIODS OF CONSTRUCTION.

FIG. P. VIEW OF THE FOUNDATIONS IN PROGRESS.

Trinity high water mark.   These dimensions constitute the largest opening bridge in the world; the next largest opening bridge is, it is believed, at Newcastle, where there are two separate spans of 100 feet each.

The opening span of the Tower Bridge consists, as already explained, of two leaves, each turning on a horizontal pivot of solid forged steel. This pivot, which rests on live rollers, is 1 foot 9 inches in diameter, and weighs 25 tons.   Each leaf is formed with four main longitudinal girders 13 feet 6 inches apart from centre to centre, which, together, provide for a clear width of bridge between the parapets of 50 feet.   This width is divided into 32 feet for a roadway (which is sufficient for four lines of

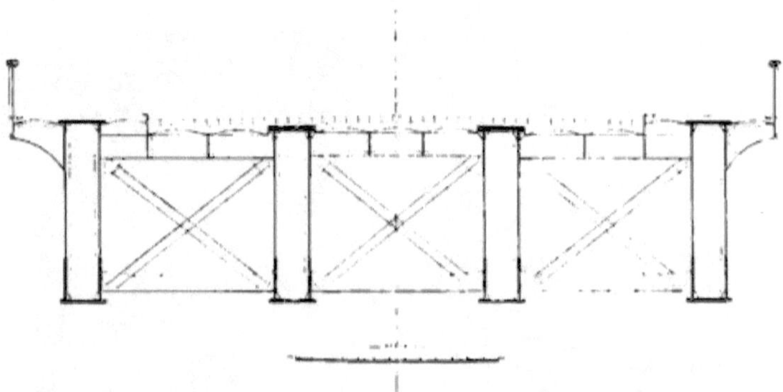

FIG. Q.   CROSS SECTION OF LEAF OF OPENING SPAN.

road traffic) and for two footpaths each 9 feet wide.   The arrangement is shown in cross section in Fig. Q.   The spaces between the longitudinal girders are filled with cross girders and roadway plates, on which are laid the wood pavement of the roadway and footpaths.

The total length of the moving girders which form the semi-span, and which rest on each pier, is 162 feet 3 inches (Fig. R).   They revolve on the main pivot, which is 12 feet 9 inches back from the face of the pier. Thus the distance from the centre of the main pivot to the end of the girders, at the centre of the span, is 112 feet 9 inches, and to the end of the girders in the other direction is 49 feet 6 inches.   The centre of gravity of the part over the river is 48 feet from the centre of the main pivot, and the estimated weight of this portion of the semi-span is 424 tons. A counterbalance box is attached to the landward ends of the girders, and is filled with 422 tons of iron and lead ballast. The centre of gravity of this portion of the moving girders together with the counterbalance box and ballast is 32 feet 9 inches from the centre of the main pivot, and the total weight landward of the main pivot is 621 tons. Thus the total weight of each leaf of the opening span resting on the main pivot when the bridge is being moved, or on the resting blocks when the movement is completed, is the sum of the two weights given above, or 1,045 tons.* The pier has,

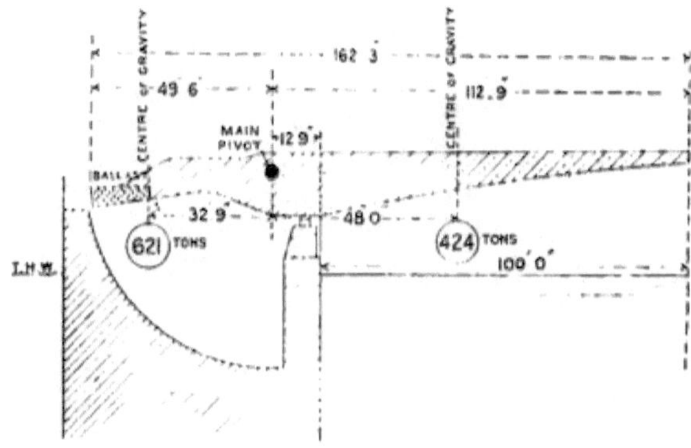

FIG. R. DIAGRAM OF WEIGHTS OF ONE BASCULE LEAF.

therefore, to carry on its riverward face a very considerable load, which is distributed by a longitudinal and several cross girders.

The two outside girders of each leaf have at their counterbalanced ends a quadrant (Fig. S), on the periphery of which are fixed teeth, and these teeth engage with similar teeth on revolving pinions which are actuated by the hydraulic machinery. It will thus be seen that when the pinions are turned round the quadrants are made to revolve on their centres, and consequently the whole of each leaf of the opening span is made to rise or fall. It may be mentioned that there are two distinct pinions to each

---

* The weights above given were the estimated weights. They have been slightly modified in execution.

quadrant, making four pinions to each leaf, and that any one of the four
is strong enough to actuate and control the whole leaf.

It will be observed that the landward ends of the moving girders are
bent downwards and extend backwards into the bascule chamber in the pier,
so as to carry the counterbalance box; but it is, of course, necessary that

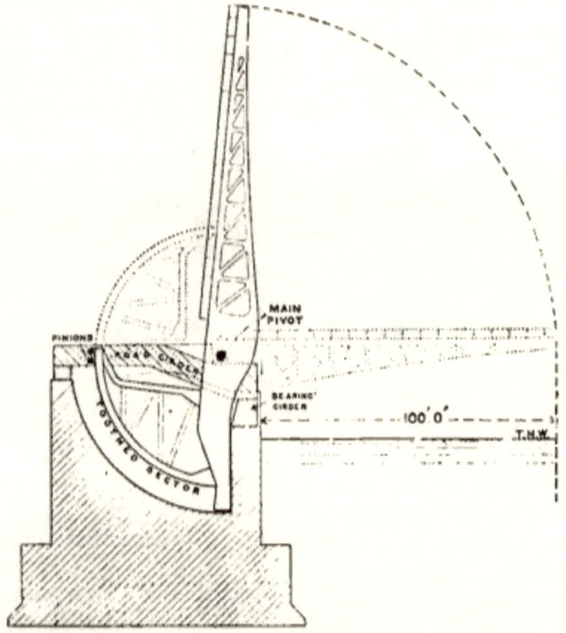

FIG. 8.   DIAGRAM OF BASCULE TO SHOW QUADRANT OR SECTOR.

the road and footpaths should extend continuously across the pier.   This is
effected by eight fixed longitudinal girders, which carry the roadway over
the bascule chamber, and between which the landward ends of the
moving girders can rise and fall.   Where the moving roadway over the
central span adjoins the fixed roadway over the bascule chamber there

must be, of course, a cross slit or joint. This space is covered by a hinged flap, which rises and falls automatically with the movement of the moving girders.

Before leaving the subject of the opening span, it is proposed to give a short account of the actuating machinery in its main features. It will be, of course, impossible to describe it within the available space in any minute detail.

For those who may not be acquainted with the leading principles of the application of water under pressure to machinery in general, a short elementary explanation of the subject may be useful. First of all, a pump is required, powerful enough to pump water under great pressure which in the present instance amounts to about 850 lbs. on every square inch. This pressure is nothing unusual, but its magnitude will be appreciated when it is remembered that in the boiler of a locomotive engine the steam pressure is usually not more than about one-fifth of the above amount.

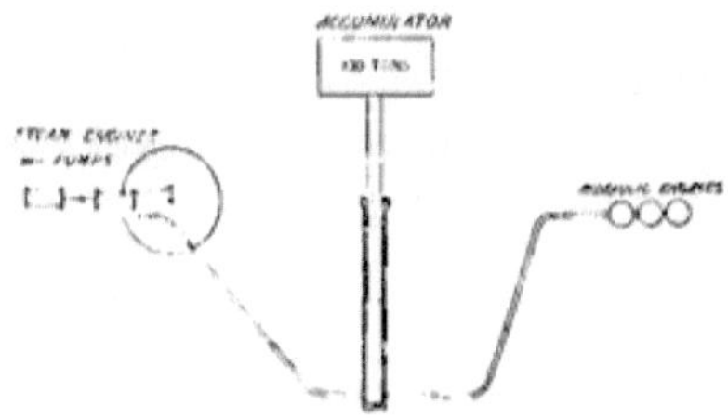

FIG. T. DIAGRAM OF APPLICATION OF HYDRAULIC POWER.

A very important feature of hydraulic machinery has to be explained, and that is the accumulator, the object of which is (Fig. T), as its name suggests, to accumulate or to store up power, and this is effected as follows. The origin of the power is the steam engine actuating a pump, and if hydraulic machinery were always working and always requiring the same amount of power an accumulator would be of comparatively little use, as the pump could pump the water direct to the hydraulic engines, to be used there in a continuous effort. But such is not the requirement, for in almost every application of hydraulic power the machinery is not called upon for a continuous effort, but, as it were, for spasmodic efforts lasting over short periods, and the accumulators are of the utmost utility in storing up the power provided by the pump in order to give it out at a greater speed than the pump, though working continuously, would provide.

To carry out these principles the accumulator is a large cylinder, in which fits a long plunger, on the top of which are placed weights, which bring a heavy pressure such as that above mentioned on every square inch of the area of the cylinder. The steam pumps pump water into the accumulator with that pressure, and as it is a principle of hydraulics that any pressure applied to water in a closed vessel is communicated to the whole of the water in that vessel, the pump, though much smaller than the large plunger of the accumulator, raises it with its superincumbent weight though of course proportionately slowly.

The pipes which convey the water to work the hydraulic engines are in communication with the cylinder of the accumulator, and this being of great internal capacity can supply high pressure water with great rapidity to work the hydraulic engines for their spasmodic efforts. In the meantime the pumps are working away to re-supply the accumulator. The water pressure being so high per square inch, enables the pistons and pipes of hydraulic machinery to be comparatively small, and as the water can be conveyed anywhere in pipes of suitable strength, the power produced by the pump can be applied at any desired place.

The steam pumping engines which generate the power at the Tower Bridge, and produce the pressure on the water, are of the horizontal tandem compound surface condensing type. There are two pairs of these engines, each pair being of about 360 indicated horse power, and having two high pressure cylinders, each 19¾ inches diameter and 38 inches stroke, and two low pressure cylinders, each 37 inches diameter and 38 inches stroke. The air and circulating pumps are worked directly from the main engines. There are four boilers of the Lancashire type, each 7 feet 6 inches diameter and 30 feet long, working at a pressure of 85 lbs. per square inch.

The pumps are on the Surrey side of the river, and are placed in archways under the south approach. The high pressure water is brought thence by pipes along the Surrey fixed span, up the Surrey tower, across the high level foot bridge, and down the Middlesex tower. Return pipes convey the water when it has exerted its pressure at the hydraulic engines, which are fixed below the footway on each pier—back again to the pumps at the steam engines, where it is again subjected to pressure and made ready for work again.

At the Tower Bridge there are six accumulators, viz., two near the pumps on the Surrey side of the river, 20 inches in diameter with 35 feet stroke, and two on each pier, 22 inches in diameter with 18 feet stroke. Their capacity is ample for the most liberal demands of the hydraulic engines.

It will not be possible to describe in any detail the hydraulic engines themselves by which motion is imparted to the bascule leaves. It will be sufficient to say that there are two pairs of engines on each pier, and that their leading principle is that of reciprocating cylinder engines.

Each pair consists of one larger and one smaller engine, the plungers of the larger engine being 8½ inches in diameter and 2 feet 3 inches stroke, and of the smaller 7½ inches in diameter and 2 feet stroke. All the engines have three cylinders, which are fixed on the bed plates, the plungers being fitted with connecting rods as in an ordinary steam engine. The valves and connections are arranged so that either one of each pair of engines can be run alone or the two together; the engines which are not doing actual work being nevertheless in motion, and ready to come into operation if required in case of any accident to the engine which is actually doing the work. The power of the engines is communicated by means of gearing to a pair of steel shafts, ranging in diameter from 14 inches to 11½ inches, extending across the whole width of the bridge, and fitted with forged steel pinions which gear into the teeth on the quadrants on the rear end of the bascule girders. The teeth are of cast steel, and their pitch is 6 inches. The gearing is fitted with powerful brakes, which would come into action automatically in the event of the hydraulic pressure falling below a certain limit, so that the bridge cannot get out of hand in case of any accident to the supply pipes, which, however, are in duplicate throughout.

When the Tower Bridge was being discussed in Parliament, the disaster to the Tay Bridge was fresh in the minds of many, and some alarm was expressed lest the machinery might not be strong enough to control the opening span in heavy winds. The Board of Trade had reported with regard to the Tay Bridge, that provision should be made in all future structures for a wind pressure of 56 pounds per square foot, and though this is, perhaps, an excessive estimate, even for the wind in such an exposed place as the Firth of Tay, and is much more excessive in the comparatively protected position of the Tower Bridge, it was considered right to provide, not only for the extreme pressure of 56 pounds per square foot, but also to provide the machinery of this strength in duplicate on each pier. Thus the machinery is equal to twice the requirements of the Board of Trade. An ordinarily strong wind, however, will not give a pressure exceeding about 17 pounds per square foot, and therefore the hydraulic engines are arranged in pairs, one engine of each pair exerting a power equal to a 17 pounds wind and the other equal to a 39 pounds wind, the two together being equal to the extravagant pressure of a wind of 56 pounds. On each pier the duplicate pair of engines follow up the work of the first pair, and provide against breakdowns.

When the two leaves of the opening span are brought together, four long conical bolts, actuated by hydraulic machinery, fixed on one leaf and shooting into sockets in the other leaf, complete the union of the two leaves. These locking bolts are drawn in and out by direct acting hydraulic cylinders.

Hydraulic cylinders are provided for working the resting blocks on which the girders rest when the bridge is open for traffic, and hydraulic buffers for limiting the range of the bridge, both in opening and closing, are fixed in the bascule chamber and to the girders which carry the roadway over that chamber.

Signals are provided by semaphores by day and signal lamps by night to show ships whether the bridge is open or shut. By night when the bridge is open for ships, four green lights will be shown in both directions, and when it is shut against ships four red lights will be similarly exhibited. By day similar intimation is afforded by semaphore arms on the same posts as those which carry the signal lamps. During foggy weather a gong will be used in specified ways.

All the machinery of the opening span is worked from cabins on the piers, in which there are levers like those in a railway signal box, so interlocked one with the other, and with the signals, that all the proper movements must follow in the arranged order.

The time required for the actual movement of the opening span from a position of rest horizontally to a position of rest vertically is estimated at about one and a half minutes. To this must be added the time necessary for stopping the road traffic and clearing the bridge, and withdrawing the bolts. This may take, perhaps, some one and a half minutes more, and we then have to add the time for the passage of a ship and the lowering of the bridge. The time of one and a half minutes for opening or shutting the bridge gives a mean circumferential speed at the extremity of each leaf of two feet per second, which is a moderate speed for an opening bridge.

One other part of the machinery remains to be mentioned. This is that of the passenger lifts between the roadway level and the high level foot bridge. There are two lifts, 13 feet by 6 feet, and 9 feet high, in each tower, which are raised and lowered by an ordinary

FIG. C. SIR H. JONES'S DESIGN OF A BASCULE BRIDGE (SHUT AGAINST SHIPS).

hydraulic ram with chain gearing, and are capable of carrying about twenty-five passengers. Each ascent or descent is through a height of 110 feet, and will occupy about one and a half minutes, including the delays of opening and shutting the doors.

Each lift is suspended by six wire ropes, four in connection with the lifting cylinders and two in connection with the counterweight which balances the weight of the lift. In addition to the ordinary precaution of safety apparatus in connection with the attachment of the ropes to the lift, the whole of the machinery is in duplicate, each cylinder being fitted with its own ropes, multiplying sheaves, etc., independent of the other. One cylinder only is in actual operation, the water in the other cylinder merely passing through it, but the whole arrangement of valves, connections, etc., is such that at any time the idle cylinder will be brought into operation in case of any accident to the cylinder which is doing the work.

THE FIXED SUPERSTRUCTURE.

The fixed parts of the superstructure of the Tower Bridge consist, as has been said, of two shore spans, each of 270 feet, and of a central high level span of 230 feet. The fixed bridge is of the suspension form of construction, and the chains are carried on lofty towers on each pier and on lower towers on each abutment.

When an opening bridge was first proposed there was some outcry by

FIG. V. SIR H. JONES'S DESIGN OF A BASCULE BRIDGE (OPEN FOR SHIPS).

æsthetical people lest it should ruin the picturesqueness of the Tower of London by hideous girder erections, and it seemed to be the universal wish that this bridge should be in harmony architecturally with the Tower.

To carry out these views various architectural studies were made, and it was originally intended by Sir Horace Jones, the City architect, that the towers should be of brickwork in a feudal style of architecture (Figs. U and V), and that the bridge should be raised and lowered by chains somewhat like the drawbridge of a Crusader's castle. Subsequently, Sir Horace Jones proposed a combination of brick and stone, with towers similar to those in the view Fig. W on page 204.

The ideas were in this condition when the writer was appointed engineer to the scheme, with Sir Horace Jones as architect, and the Corporation went to Parliament for powers to make the bridge. It was seen that any arched form of construction across a span to be used by masted ships was inadmissible, and that whatever headway was given should be absolutely free of obstruction throughout the whole width of the span. Sir Horace Jones unfortunately died in 1887, when the foundations had not made much progress, and up to that time none of the architectural designs had proceeded further than such sketches and studies as were barely sufficient to enable an approximate estimate to be made of the cost. Since the death of Sir Horace Jones, the general architectural features of the Parliamentary sketch designs have been preserved, but it will be

FIG. W.   DESIGN SUBMITTED TO PARLIAMENT.

seen that the structure as erected differs largely therefrom, both in treatment and material.

The width, and consequently the weight, of the bridge was increased by the requirements of Parliament, and the span of the central opening was enlarged from 160 feet, as originally intended, to 200 feet. At the same time the provision of lifts and stairs to accommodate foot passengers when the bridge was open was felt to be a necessity.

In this way it became apparent that it would not be possible to support the weight of the bridge on towers wholly of masonry, as in the first designs, unless they were made of great size and unnecessary weight. It was consequently requisite that the main supports should be of iron or steel, which could, however, be surrounded by masonry, so as to retain the architectural character of the whole structure.

It was clear that in any event a large part of the steelwork of the

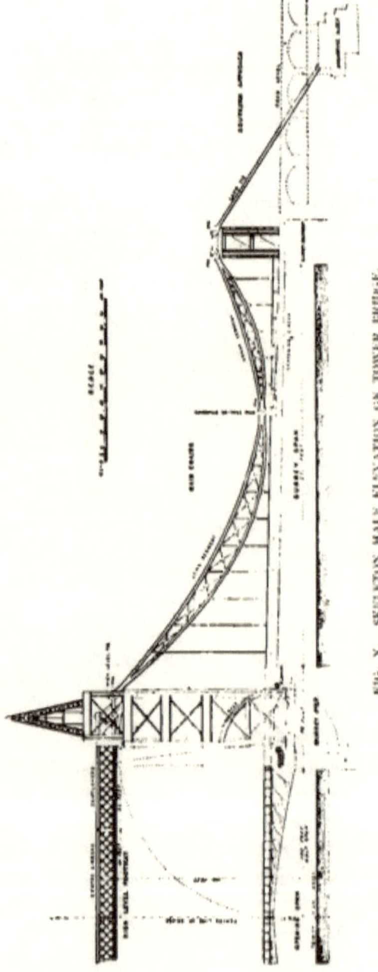

FIG. X. SKELETON HALF ELEVATION OF TOWER BRIDGE.

towers must be enclosed in some material, for the moving quadrants project upwards some forty feet from the level of the roadway, while the stairs and lifts also required protection from the weather. It thus became a question of surrounding the towers either with cast iron panelling or with stone, and eventually a granite facing, with Portland stone dressings, was adopted.

Æsthetically speaking, stone seems better than cast iron, which would equally hide the constructive features, and practically speaking it is also better, when it is considered that there is no mode so satisfactory for preserving iron or steel from corrosion as embedding it in brickwork, concrete or masonry. Careful provision has been made in all parts for expansion and contraction of the two materials, and though there have been great extremes of heat and cold since the masonry has been built, no effects resulting from any difference of temperature have been observed.

The Fig. X. which is a half elevation of the steelwork of the bridge, shows the general arrangement of the towers, which have been since enclosed with masonry and brickwork, and may be described as being steel skeletons clothed with stone.

It is to be feared some purists will say that the lamp of truth has been sadly neglected in this combination of materials, and that the architects of classical or mediæval times would not have sanctioned such an arrangement as a complex structure of steel surrounded by stone.

One reason may be that the architects of those ages did not know much about iron or steel. Perhaps if they had been acquainted with their capabilities they might have been as ready to employ them as they were to back up stone-faced walls with brick, and to hide the constructive features of their buildings, as Sir Christopher Wren did when he used a brick cone to support the internal and external domes of St. Paul's.

However all this may be, "needs must when Parliament drives," and if the appearance of the Tower Bridge is approved, we may forget that the towers have skeletons as much concealed as that of the human body, of which we do not think when we contemplate examples of manly or feminine beauty.

Returning, however, to the details of construction. The skeleton of each tower consists of four wrought steel pillars (Fig. Y), octagonal in plan, built up of rivetted plates. The pillars start from wide spreading bases, and extend upwards to the suspension chains, which they support. They are united by horizontal girders and many diagonal bracings, to which it is not necessary here to refer in detail. The chains are carried on the abutments by similar but lower pillars. All these and other particulars appear in Fig. X.

Between the pillars are spaces for the public stairs and the passenger lifts, and for the quadrants of the opening span when in their upward position. When all these necessary things are accommodated, it will be seen that there is very little room left in the towers for the first forty feet of their height, that is to say, up to the level of the archway over the road.

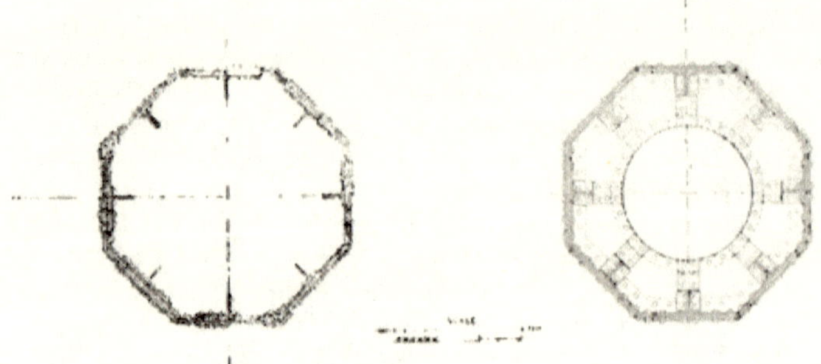

FIG. Y. PLANS OF MAIN PILLARS.

The horizontal girders in the towers, above the archway, carry various floors to provide landings from the public stairs and rooms for the police and staff, or for other purposes.

On the tops of the octagonal pillars rest a series of rollers which will allow the chains so to move as to accommodate themselves to changes of temperature and to unequal distribution of the road traffic.

The arrangements of the rollers are peculiar (Figs. Z and AA). The amount of space available for their reception on the tops of the steel octagonal pillars is limited, while the weight which they have to support is very large, being estimated when the bridge is fully loaded at 1,000 tons. It was thus necessary that the weight should be equally distributed over the whole series of rollers, and that there should be no possibility of a concentration of weight on any one or two rollers. This is effected by an arrangement by which the weight brought on the top of the system is first carried by two blocks, thus ensuring equal division between them, then the weight so divided is sub-divided between two plates and the weight on each plate is again sub-divided between two rollers.

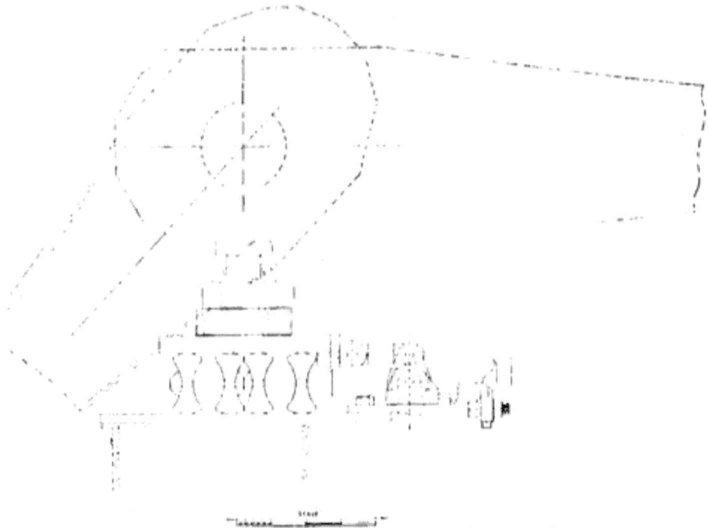

FIG. 2. ARRANGEMENT OF THE ROLLERS ON THE TOWERS ON THE PIERS.

The main chains, which are 60 feet 6 inches apart from centre to centre, extend from the rollers on the piers to other rollers on each abutment, and support the fixed spans of the bridge by rods suspended from the bottom of the chains.

It may be asked why are these structures, which look like girders, called chains? They are, in fact, chains stiffened to prevent deflection, and the object of the form is to distribute the local loads due to passing traffic, which, in the case of an ordinary suspension bridge, depress each part of the chain as the load passes, and consequently distort the platform of the bridge. By making the chain, as it were, double, and bracing it with iron triangulations, these local deflections are avoided.

The ends of the chains on the abutments and on the towers are united by large pins to the ties. The ties on the abutments are carried down into

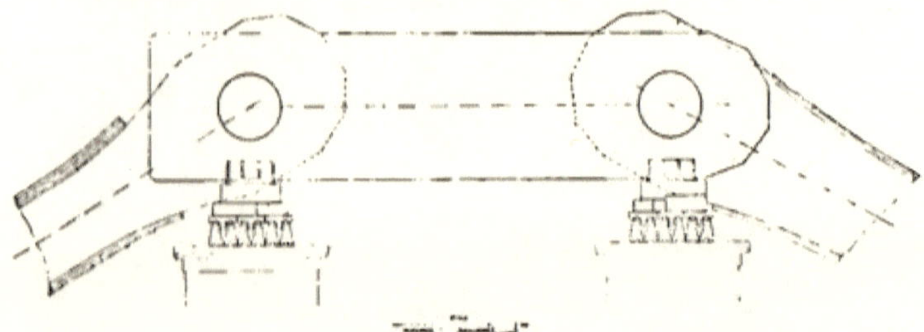

FIG. AA. ARRANGEMENT OF THE ROLLERS ON THE TOWERS ON THE ABUTMENTS.

the ground below the approaches, and are there united to anchorage girders, which rest against very heavy blocks of concrete, and are abundantly adequate to resist the pull of the chains. The ties at the high level between the towers are for the purpose of uniting the upper ends of the

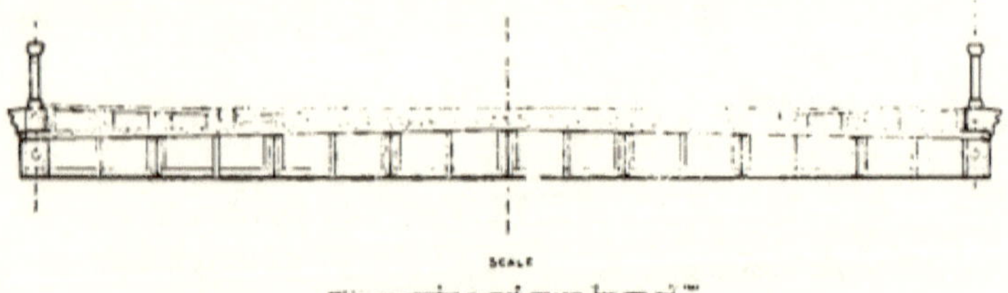

FIG. BB. CROSS SECTION OF PLATFORM OF SUSPENSION SPANS.

two chains, and by this means the stress on the chains is conveyed from anchorage to anchorage.

The platform of the fixed spans of the bridge is formed of cross girders, which extend transversely from side to side, their ends being immediately under the chains, to which they are suspended by solid

FIG. CC. PROGRESS OF TOWER ON PIER IN RIVER.

steel rods. Between the cross girders are short longitudinal girders, and on these rest corrugated steel plates, which carry the paving and footways. The arrangements are indicated in the Fig. BB. The total width between the parapets on the fixed spans of the bridge and on the approaches is 60 feet, which is divided into 36 feet for the vehicular traffic and into two pathways each 12 feet wide. It may be mentioned in passing that London Bridge is 54 feet wide between the parapets.

FIG. BB. PROGRESS OF HIGH LEVEL BRIDGE.

The total weight of steel and iron in the Tower Bridge amounts to nearly 12,000 tons.

THE ERECTION OF THE BRIDGE.

The erection of the superstructure of the bridge has been effected without any considerable difficulty. Temporary stagings of pile work were erected in the river and formed piers, upon which wrought iron horizontal girders were erected, which supported timber beams and planking, thus forming temporary bridges communicating from the shores to each pier.

Less difficulty was experienced than was expected in driving the pile work either round the permanent piers or to form the supports of the temporary bridge, and but little serious damage was caused to it during the time of the erection of the bridge by collisions with it of river craft, which from time to time occurred. Access being thus given from the shores, the next thing to be done was to erect the pillars, girders and bracing forming the steel framework of the abutment and river towers. All the work had been put

FIG. FF. PROGRESS OF ERECTION OF MAIN CHAINS.

together at the works of Messrs. Sir W. Arrol & Co., at Glasgow, and was brought thence in small pieces to be rivetted together at the bridge. The view (Fig. CC) shows this work in progress at one of the river towers.

The next work taken in hand was the erection of the high level footway bridges between the towers. These bridges are cantilevers for a distance from each tower of 55 feet, and are girders for the remaining space of 120 feet between the ends of the cantilevers. They were erected, however, by temporary expedients entirely as cantilevers, piece by piece from the tops of the towers, and without scaffolding from below, for the whole of the semi-span of 115 feet till they met over the centre of the river. Their progress from week to week, as they advanced towards each other, was watched with much interest by the public from London Bridge. A view (Fig. DD) shows the cantilevers a short time before they met.

The chains were erected in their position by means of scaffolds and trestles resting on the temporary bridge. The succeeding views (Figs. EE and FF) show this work in progress. Cranes on stages travelling along the

FIG. FF.   GENERAL VIEW OF PROGRESS OF ERECTION OF MAIN CHAINS.

temporary wooden bridge served to place the various parts of the chain on the trestles, where they were rivetted together in their permanent positions. In the meantime the land ties from the anchorages had been brought up to the tops of the abutment towers, and the long horizontal ties which are carried by the high level bridges had been erected and rivetted in their places. The holes for the connecting pins at the ends of the ties and at the junctions of the short and long segments of the chains were then bored finally and the pins inserted, thus forming a through connection from the

anchorage on the north side of the river to the corresponding anchorage on
the southern side.

Another interesting part of the work was the erection of the fixed
roadway girders across the bascule chamber and the placing of the moving
girders in their position. The fixed girders were first erected on the
temporary bridge, and moved from thence into their places over the bascule
chamber. The portions of the moving girders which would eventually be

FIG. 66.   MOVING GIRDERS IN PROGRESS.

landward of the main pivot and 10 feet riverwards of it were similarly
erected on the temporary bridge, from whence they were launched forward
and then placed between the fixed girders in a vertical position. The main
pivot could now be threaded through the moving girders and the revolving
bearings adjusted. A sufficient length of the moving girders to reach
about 40 feet over the central span of the bridge was then erected vertically,
with the accompanying cross girders and bracing, after which the quadrants
to carry the teeth by which the moving span was to be actuated were

erected in their places. The teeth were bolted on the quadrants, and to ensure an accurate fit between them and the pinions, which are turned by the hydraulic engines, which were not then in position, the moving girders were revolved by temporary means, and exact measurements taken. The view (Fig. GG) shows this work in progress. The regulations of the Act of Parliament rendered it necessary to confine operations in the first instance to a length of 40 feet only of a semi-span, so as not to reduce the free

FIG. HH. VIEW OF THE BRIDGE IN AUTUMN OF 1892.

passage for vessels through the central opening during the process of adjustment to less than 160 feet. When the adjustment was completed the remaining portions of the moving girders were erected in their vertical position, and they were not lowered again till the hydraulic machinery and the whole of the structure of each semi-span was finished.

The succeeding view (Fig. HH) shows the general appearance which the bridge will present when opened for the passage of sea-going vessels. It will be observed that the tops of the towers are incomplete, and that part

FF

of the temporary staging in the river, on which the steelwork of the side spans was erected, is still standing.

It is gratifying to record that the loss of human life during the construction of the bridge has not, considering the magnitude and nature of the work, been great. In all, eight men have met with fatal accidents, and at least one of these accidents was the result of a fit.

THE APPROACHES.

The northern approach to the bridge is constructed partly on a viaduct of brick piers and arches, faced with stone, and partly by means of retaining walls, and extends from Tower Hill, opposite the Royal Mint, to the northern abutment, a distance of 330 yards. The ground on which these works stand was acquired from Government, and comprised the glacis and part of the eastern ditch of the Tower. An entrance to the Tower property from the east is afforded by a wide archway beneath the approach at its southern end. Some of the arches of the viaduct adjoining this entrance are used for a guard room, and others for stores for the fortress and for the bridge. Most of the northern approach is level, and there is a gradient of 1 in 60 on the remainder, extending across the north shore span to the northern pier of the bridge. The southern approach stands wholly on property acquired from private owners, and extends from Tooley Street to the southern abutment, a distance of 280 yards. It is partly constructed on a viaduct near the bridge, and under the arches of the viaduct are placed the engine and boiler houses, with the coal stores, for the hydraulic pumping engines. The rest of the southern approach is upheld by retaining walls, built so as to form cellarage for houses to be built on each side of the approach. The gradient of the southern approach is, throughout its length, 1 in 40, and this gradient extends across the south span to the southern pier of the bridge. From the piers the inclines are continued to the centre of the river by gradients of 1 in 75, on both leaves of the opening span.

COMMUNICATION BETWEEN EXISTING THOROUGHFARES AND THE TOWER BRIDGE.

The approach to the bridge on the north side of the river is connected directly with the southern end of the Minories, where that important street, which runs north and south, joins wide thoroughfares extending in all directions, but the access from the districts south of the river is not at present so satisfactory. The approach constructed by the Corporation extends from the bridge to Tooley Street, which is an important street running east and west in Bermondsey, but there is no good thoroughfare in a southerly direction from the junction of the approach with Tooley Street.

The London County Council undertook to make a wide street extending from the Old Kent Road and Bricklayers' Arms Station to Tooley Street, but up to the present time nothing has been done, except to bring into Parliament bills which have been abortive, from the fact that the Council had included in them the principle of what is called betterment. It is much to be hoped that this greatly needed southern approach will be made expeditiously, as it cannot be doubted that, though the heavy traffic of Tooley Street will be served by the present arrangement, much of the utility of the Tower Bridge will remain unrealised until a direct north and south thoroughfare for traffic is opened up. The Corporation have performed their part of the enterprise, and it is to be regretted that the London County Council are wholly in arrear with their share of the undertaking.

CONCLUSION.

The accommodation of the interests of the road and river traffic at the site of the Tower Bridge has presented many difficulties, but it is hoped that the bridge which has been erected to a great extent solves the problem. Being a low level bridge the total rise of the road traffic is not great, and the gradients of the approaches are short and easy. The river traffic has ample accommodation in the width and height of the spans, and the machinery for opening the bridge for the passage of ships will be rapid in its action. Lastly, there are arrangements for the continual accommodation of foot traffic.

The sea-going ships which pass above the site of the Tower Bridge, and for which the central span will have to be opened, are estimated to number, on an average, seventeen daily. They pass by chiefly at or near the time of high water, and it may well be arranged that several may pass one behind the other. The number of sea-going ships in this part of the river does not show any tendency to growth, but, on the contrary, such traffic will rather, it is thought, gravitate to the docks down stream as time goes on, independently of any consideration connected with the bridge.

Some disappointment may occasionally be felt when vehicular traffic is stopped by the opening of the bridge, but it may be hoped that no serious delays will occur either to sea-going ships or to vehicular traffic, as the periods during which the opening span will be raised, though sufficient for the accommodation of the river traffic, will not be of frequent occurrence or of long duration. The Tower Bridge will, it is thought, fairly compromise all the difficulties of the case, but if the road traffic becomes of greater importance, and the sea-going river traffic grows less, the fate of the bridge may possibly be to become a fixed bridge. How soon this may happen no one can tell. It is able to fulfil its duties either as an opening or as a fixed bridge.

The cost of the bridge, with its approaches, and including the cost of the property purchased, will amount to about a million sterling, and the whole of the expense will be defrayed out of the funds carefully husbanded and administered by the Bridge House Estates Committee. Londoners will thus be presented, without the charge of one penny on the rates, with a free bridge. The expense of working the bridge, which will be very considerable from the quantity of machinery comprised within it, will also be paid by the Corporation.

The writer is very glad to take this opportunity to record how much he is indebted to many gentlemen who have assisted him in the carrying out of the work, and how much the undertaking generally has benefitted from their cordial co-operation. It is impossible to refer to more than a few by name, but first and most important of all, he would desire to mention his partner, Mr. H. M. Brunel, who has supervised the whole of the complicated calculations and details of the structure, and has taken a very active share from first to last in the superintendence of the work. Afterwards follow the resident engineer, Mr. E. W. Cruttwell, who has been in most efficient control of the works from their commencement ; Mr. A. Fyson, who had the duty of the preparation of the detailed working drawings and the calculations of engineering matters ; and Mr. G. D. Stevenson, who has acted as architectural assistant and has had charge of the drawings of the masonry and other similar work of the superstructure. In connection with this subject the writer cannot but express his great regret that the work was, so soon after its commencement, deprived of the architectural knowledge and experience of Sir Horace Jones, and that he did not live to see the mode in which his conception of a large bascule bridge across the Thames has been realized.

The chief contractors who have been employed in the construction of the bridge are as follows : Mr. John Jackson and Mr. William Webster, who made the substructure and approaches ; Sir William Arrol and Co., to whom the steelwork of the superstructure was entrusted ; Messrs. Perry and Co., who carried out the masonry ; and lastly, but by no means least, the firm of Sir W. G. Armstrong, Mitchell and Co., who have executed the hydraulic machinery, which, it is believed, is without rival in size and power.

The time of construction (eight years) has seemed long, but it may be some comfort to those who are impatient to remember that old London Bridge was thirty-three years in building, old Westminster Bridge eleven and three-quarter years, and new London Bridge seven and a half years, and that the Tower Bridge is no ordinary bridge, and in no ordinary position. The structure and its machinery are full of the most elaborate and complicated work of all kinds.

In drawing this short description of the works to a conclusion, a hope may perhaps be expressed that the Tower Bridge will be considered to be not unworthy of the Corporation of the greatest city of ancient or modern times.

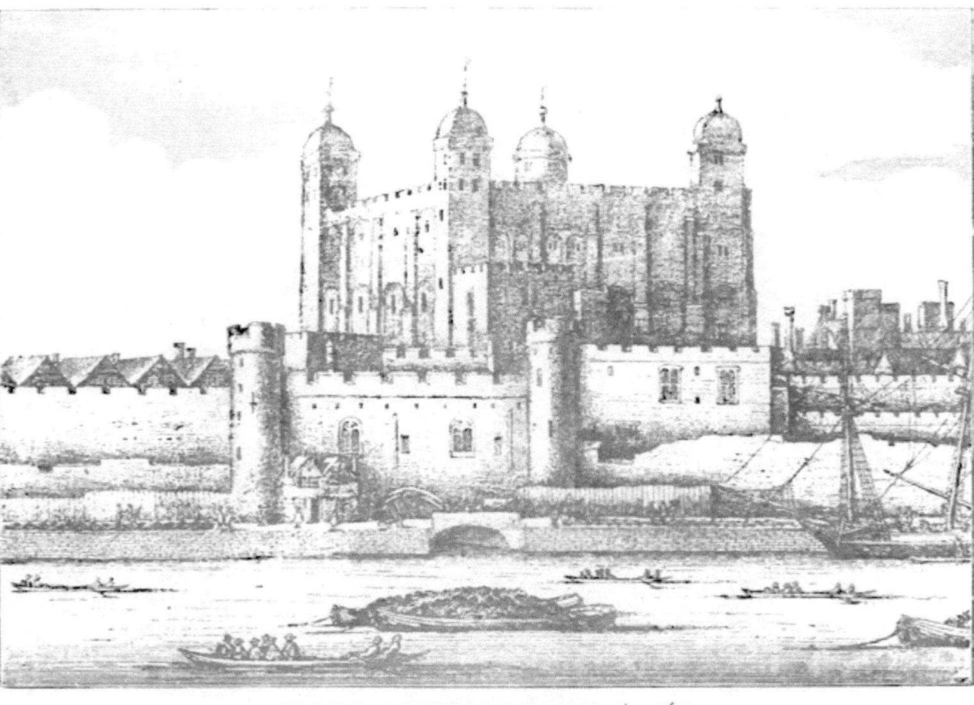

THE TOWER OF LONDON, FROM THE RIVER, *circa* 1650.

CHAPTER IV.

The City, the Tower, and the River.

BY

PHILIP NORMAN, F.S.A.

IT must have occurred to most people interested in the history of the City to ask themselves why the particular site which it occupies was so marvellously suited for the development of commercial prosperity. The answer would be that it grew up on the bank of a splendid navigable river, within easy distance of the Continent, and just where that river happened to be narrower than for some distance above or below, and could, therefore, be most easily bridged over. It was not always so; the river once opened out into a broad lagoon, and ages elapsed before it was controlled within its present limits. On the comparatively high ground close to the northern edge of this lagoon, a Celtic camp or village may have grown up in very remote times, and as civilization increased, even before the conquest by the Romans, some trade may have been carried on here: but this is mere conjecture.

Concerning Roman London various statements have come down to us, some of which are rather puzzling. At first it seems to have been an open town, for when Boadicea revolted, the Roman general did not attempt to defend it; she destroyed the buildings and killed many of the inhabitants. The next settlement here was a military one, perhaps little more than a fort to protect a ferry across the Thames. The Romans also occupied Southwark; and it is a curious fact that Ptolemy, who lived in the reigns of Hadrian, Trajan, and Antoninus Pius, places Londinium on the south side of the Thames. The level of all towns has a tendency to be raised by the gradual accumulation of débris. Now that the foundations of new buildings in the City are taken down to a great depth, we come upon successive layers of relics, until sometimes indeed the primæval soil is reached. A fine collection of such relics is appropriately housed in the Guildhall Museum. If it were possible adequately to search the bed and the banks of the Thames, we should doubtless find that a rich hoard of antiquarian treasures lies hidden there, but of course this is quite out of the question, and it is only on rare occasions that something of interest comes to light. We may name as examples of very different dates, palæolithic implements from the drift at Erith, Northfleet, Richmond, and Wandsworth; a polished greenstone celt and neolithic flint flakes from the Thames in London; a bone spear-head from Dowgate, and perforated bone pins from Barge Yard. In Roman remains the Museum is rich, but not many come from the Thames. Among mediæval relics the Guildhall collection of pilgrims' signs is of unique interest, containing as it does more than 250 specimens, and these are almost exclusively from the river or its banks. The courses of the old Fleet River and the Walbrook have also been productive; the Romans seem to have been fond of building along the banks of the latter. We should add that, in dredging for the foundations of the Tower Bridge, one of the vertebræ of a whale and some less interesting relics were found.

The Romans no doubt helped to alter very much the character of the Thames, and to make it far more navigable, by embankments in the lower reaches; something of the sort had perhaps been begun before their time. Subsequent embanking, drainage, and gradual reclamation of land did the rest. They also left an important legacy to those who came after, in the strong wall of defence marking the final limits of their city, which, though several times renewed, was still in a sense almost intact till the time of the Great Fire. The condition of London for some years after the advent of the Saxons is more or less of a mystery. At first perhaps it lay desolate and almost uninhabited, though surely some Britons must have lingered there. Be this as it may, in the early part of the seventh century we find it described as an important town, the metropolis of the East Saxons, with trade by land and sea. The Danes indeed saw its true value, and made persistent and partly successful efforts to secure it. Alfred drove them out and rebuilt its walls. Canute's siege, some years afterwards, has been rendered famous by a very remarkable incident. He dug a ditch or canal on the Southwark side of the river (the course of which has been much disputed), in order that he might drag his ships above bridge—for by this time there must have been a wooden bridge—and more completely blockade the town. The plan seems to have failed, though eventually he became master not only of London but of the kingdom.

We pass on to the time immediately after the Norman Conquest, when an encroachment was made on the old City walls, which marks an important era in our history. We are proud of that splendid old fortress, the Tower of London, but we are apt to forget the special circumstances to which it owes its existence. When, having crossed the Thames, the Conqueror marched on London, it is said that before entering it he ordered a camp to be formed which should command the City. No doubt, one of his earliest acts was to fix upon the site most suited for a permanent citadel. William was crowned in 1066, and immediately afterwards, from his camp at Barking, he superintended the laying out of the new works. At first, says Mr. G. T. Clark, a leading authority, they no doubt consisted of a deep ditch and strong palisade only. The Norman castle which replaced this temporary fort, was begun by Gundulf, Bishop of Rochester, under William's direction, about the year 1078, at the south-eastern corner of the City wall, probably just outside the external ditch, and close to the river bank. For the sake of getting a good foundation, the actual structure would, it is thought, have been on undisturbed ground; but to make room for its defensive outworks, a breach appears to have been made in the old wall, the two flanking towers nearest the Thames being removed. The great fortress served a double purpose—to protect London, and also to overawe it; if necessary, to cut off its supplies and reduce it to subjection. At the same time, William encroached as little as possible on the limits of the City; the greater part of the enclosure was outside the line of the old wall, and while the Tower liberties extend some distance eastward, on the opposite side they include very little ground. As years went on, the Tower came to fulfil many purposes; in the words of Stow, it was "a citadel to defend or command the City; a royal palace for assemblies or treaties; a prison of State for the most dangerous offenders; the only place of coinage for all England; the armoury for warlike provision; the treasury of the ornaments and jewels of the Crown; and general conserver of the most ancient records of the King's Courts of Justice at Westminster." For some of these functions it is still used, and it still bears itself bravely, undwarfed by the great structure to which it has given a name, the one a unique survival of a state of society which has passed away, the other a wonderful proof of modern enterprise and science.

Among the various records of the Tower which have come down to us, none are more interesting to a Londoner than those which throw light on the relations, often strained, between it and the City, and to this subject we intend to devote a few pages. The office of Constable or Governor of the Tower was made by William, hereditary. Geoffrey, grandson of Geoffrey de Mandeville, the companion of the Conqueror, was third hereditary Constable, and created Earl of Essex by King Stephen. He afterwards espoused the cause of the Empress, and though besieged by the citizens, held his own for a long time, and even sallied forth and took the Bishop of London prisoner at Fulham. The King at last got possession of his person by a stratagem, and compelled him to give up the stronghold, which then seems to have been regarded as almost impregnable, though the wet ditch had not been added. There is no doubt that in those early days, and long afterwards, the Tower and its Governors were apt to be odious to Londoners, always jealous of any interference with their rights, and if occasion arose they were ready enough to attack it. When Richard Cœur de Lion went to fight in the Holy Land, he placed the Tower under the charge of Longchamp, Bishop of Ely, who strengthened the defences, and made a deep ditch which he tried to fill with water from the Thames, an attempt in which he failed. These works caused certain encroachments on Tower Hill, and on property belonging to Trinity Church, East Smithfield, and to St. Katherine's Hospital, and no doubt raised the apprehensions of the citizens. In the struggle which shortly ensued between Prince John and the Bishop, they declared against Longchamp, and blockaded the fortress by land and water. Again, in the reign of Henry III the Londoners showed their dislike to any increase of the Tower defences. The King, who often used it as his residence, was careful to strengthen the outworks, on which the citizens expostulated, and the King tried to appease them. The next year, namely in 1240, a stone gate and wall

which had been completed on the west side fell down suddenly, no doubt
owing to the badness of the foundations. They were at once re-built, but
soon afterwards fell down again; this second fall being attributed to the
supernatural intervention of St. Thomas the Martyr. We are told by
Matthew Paris that "the citizens of London were nothing sorry, for they
were threatened that the said wall and bulwarks were built to the end
that if any of them would contend for the liberties of the City they might
be imprisoned." Edward I completed various defences begun by his
father, and made new fortifications to the west. Mr. Bayley considers
that these were the last additions to the Tower which, from a military
point of view, would be considered of importance. Some of the works were
flimsy enough; thus we read that in 1316 the Mayor and Commonalty
of London were fined for pulling down a mud wall outside the Tower,
which had been built by Henry III. and which, as they doubtless
thought, encroached upon their liberties.

In the reign of Edward II stirring events took place at the Tower, in
which the citizens played a bold part. In 1326 he demanded a supply of
men and money from them. Their reply was that "they would at all times
revere the Sovereign Lord the King, the Queen, and the Prince their son,
the indubitable heir to the Crown, and shut their gates against and to the
utmost of their power resist all Foreigners and Traitors," but "they were
not willing to march out and fight unless, according to their ancient
privileges, they could return home the same day before sunset." The King
does not appear to have enforced his demand; in October of that year he
retired to the west, leaving his son, John of Eltham, with the Constable, Sir
John de Weston, in the Tower, and Walter Stapleton, Bishop of Exeter, in
command of the City. The citizens, who were opposed to Edward and in
sympathy with his Queen, suddenly rose, seized the Bishop, and beheaded
him in Cheapside; and the next day accidentally meeting John de Weston,
the Constable, they took from him the keys of the Tower, and possessed
themselves of that fortress, when they discharged the prisoners, turned out
the officials, and appointed others under John of Eltham, whom they made
for the time nominal guardian of the City. Next year the King was seized
in Wales, and the Queen, with her elder son Prince Edward, attended by
many of the chief nobles and prelates, entered London, and were received

by the citizens with great joy and rich presents. Edward III spent much time at the Tower, and had it carefully repaired and garrisoned. In 1337 the Sheriffs of London were compelled to pay £40 out of the farm of the City, to be spent "on the great Tower," then in a bad state. The Sheriffs of Kent, Surrey, and Sussex, also contributed to the work. After this reign the importance of the Tower for military purposes seems to have declined, but the old fortress continued from time to time to be the scene of desperate deeds which profoundly affected Londoners. In the popular risings of Wat Tyler and Jack Cade, the feeling of the moneyed class was no doubt strongly on the side of order. The fight with Lord Scales in 1460 was a very different affair; London threw in her lot against the adherent of King Henry: the Tower, his headquarters, was besieged by land, and great guns were brought to bear on it from the opposite bank of the Thames, while Scales incessantly plied the City with his ordnance and with small arms, destroying houses, and killing men women and children. The garrison had to yield from lack of provisions, and its chief was slain ignominiously, when trying to escape in a boat, for the purpose of taking sanctuary at Westminster.

In times of peace two Courts of Justice were held at the Tower; there were public entries of citizens within the precincts, to attend them. Thus we learn from Liber Albus, that when in the reign of Henry III the King held his Court of Common Pleas there, the Aldermen and citizens met at the Church of Allhallows Barking, and thence proceeded to the Tower, "first sending from the church six or more of the most serious, honourable, and discreet Aldermen, for the purpose of saluting and welcoming the King, his Council, Justiciaries, etc. begging that the citizens may safely appear before them in the said Tower, saving all their liberties and customs unto the Mayor and all other citizens." In 1285 the Lord Treasurer summoned the Mayor, Aldermen and citizens to the Tower, to render an account how the peace of the City had been kept; but Gregory de Rokesley, the Mayor, for the honour of the City, refusing to attend in that capacity, laid aside his insignia of office at Barking Church, delivered the City seal to Stephen Aswy or Asly, and then repaired to the Tower as a private gentleman. In consequence he and some of the chief citizens were thrown into prison, and the Mayoralty was suspended, the government of the City being in the hands of custodes till the year 1298.

Here, perhaps, we may not unfittingly say a few words with regard to the relations between the citizens and the head official of the Tower, during the earlier period of its history. We have seen that the first Constables transmitted their office from father to son, but this had ceased to be the case in the reign of Henry II. The person selected was usually a man of rank and military skill; Bayley quotes records proving that in the time of Henry III. he was called indiscriminately "Constable of London," "Constable of the Sea," and "Constable of the Honor of the Tower." By a charter of 26 Edward I. the Mayor was to be presented to him in the absence of the Barons of the Exchequer and the King, and at long intervals Lord Mayors have been so presented—when the plague was raging, or when a Lord Mayor happened to die in office—occasional friction resulting therefrom. The Sheriffs could also be thus presented to the Constable. Besides having the custody of the fortress, he was endowed with arbitrary rights and privileges, such as that of preventing merchants and others from leaving the Port of London, allowing men having royal licence to export prohibited commodities, taking security that owners of vessels should not traffic with hostile countries, the prevention of forestalling, and the power to restrain ships of the Cinque Ports from conveying grain out of the kingdom. There is in existence an account of John de Crumbwell, Constable of the Tower between 1 and 14 Edward II. which shows that he received many additions to his salary. Here are a few instances: Rent for herbage on Tower Hill and from persons who dried skins in East Smithfield, within the Tower Liberty. For boats called "Stalebotes," belonging to the inhabitants of London, fishing in the Thames between the Tower and the sea for fish called "sprots," 6s. 8d., and for the boat of every stranger fishing there, 8s. From every ship carrying herrings from Yarmouth to London, and from every foreign merchant bringing herrings, 12d.; and 2d. from each person going and returning by the Thames on a pilgrimage to St. James's Shrine.* In a previous reign

* This was the shrine of St. James of Compostella in Galicia. In 1427 numerous vessels were fitted out under permit from the King, for pilgrims journeying thither.

the Constable had stopped various ships loaded with corn and taken possession of their cargoes, the price of which he fixed at his pleasure. This had caused a great outburst of wrath on the part of the citizens. It was finally arranged that if at any time he required corn for the King or the inhabitants of the Tower, he should be supplied at 2*d.* per quarter cheaper than the price fixed by the Mayor.

Under the Plantagenet Kings, a frequent source of trouble was the right claimed by Constables of the Tower to set kiddles, or weirs fitted with nets, in any part of the Thames, Lea or Medway, or to issue licences allowing others to set them. In the reign of Henry III the Sheriff of London, Jordan de Coventre, went with a body of armed men to Yantlet Creek, near Rochester, carried off thirty kiddles and took several prisoners. There was an appeal; the case was brought before the King and tried at his palace at Kennington. The judges upheld the Sheriff, the prisoners were fined, and the captured nets publicly burned in Cheapside. A manuscript of 4 Richard II shows that the Constable's yearly salary was then £100; he also got large fees from prisoners. All swans coming through London Bridge became his property; the owners of all swans nesting beneath the bridge paid him a cygnet out of every nest. In a patent issued two years afterwards, the King granted to Sir Thomas Murrieux, Constable of the Tower, various other privileges and emoluments; for instance, from every ship laden with wines coming from Bordeaux or elsewhere, one flagon before the mast and another flagon behind the mast. Every ship or other vessel, deserted by her crew and floating between London and Gravesend, was to become his property; also all oxen, cows, pigs and sheep falling from the bridge into the river, or all such animals swimming through the middle of the bridge to the Tower which the Constable's servants should take. These claims met with strenuous opposition from the citizens, who looked upon them as infringements of their ancient rights, granted by former Kings, especially by a charter of Edward III, dated March 6th, in the first year of his reign. The claims, however, were afterwards confirmed to the Constables by Parliament, and we are told that the contention did not finally cease "till James I annulled the grants that had been made to the chief officers of the Tower and restored the City to its ancient franchises."

Another frequently recurring difficulty was the limitation of the Tower Liberties, spaces of ground bordering on the Tower, to which was attached the right to be subject to no jurisdiction but that of the Tower itself. These Liberties are not to be confused with the Tower Hamlets, a far larger district. Tower Hill was always a difficulty; on this spot for centuries there stood a scaffold and gallows, kept at the charge of the City, for the execution of those who were delivered by writ to the Sheriffs. In the fifth year of the reign of Edward IV, the King's officers set up a scaffold and gallows here, on which account the Mayor and citizens complained. The King, no doubt anxious to be popular with those who had supported him loyally, in reply issued a proclamation acknowledging the City's right to Tower Hill. He added that the erection of the gallows was not done by his command, and was not to be taken as a precedent for future infringement of the City privileges. As late as the year 1595, when Sir John Spencer, the Lord Mayor, had occasion to suppress a tumultuous meeting of apprentices, and in so doing encroached on disputed ground, there was almost a conflict between the citizens and the Tower officials. No doubt it was to avoid the recurrence of such scenes that the old custom of walking the bounds of the Tower Liberties arose. This is still observed every third year. After service at the Chapel of St. Peter ad Vincula in the Tower, a procession is formed, including the Major of the Tower, the Chaplain, and other Tower officers, the Yeoman Porter (Chief Warder) with the Tower Liberty mace, and the Yeoman Gaoler with his axe of office, the school-children with white wands, and other residents in the Tower. The procession then visits all the boundaries of the Liberties, and the marks thereof, consisting of a broad arrow, are beaten by the children with their wands. How completely ancient rivalries have passed away is proved, if proof were needed, by the fact that the pass-word of the Tower for each day in every three months is quarterly sent to the Lord Mayor under the Sovereign's sign manual, and enables him at any time of the day or night, even though the guard is set, to pass through the gates to see the person in command, or for any other public duty.

Not only as a fortress, but as a prison, has the Tower been used to coerce and overawe the City. Many a leading citizen has there paid the penalty of over zeal or a determination, at all costs, to do what he

considered his duty. Witness the imprisonment and death by hanging of
Sir Nicholas Brembre, a great supporter of Richard II. Less tragic was
the fate of the Sheriffs who, having in 1542 committed George Ferrers, M.P.
for Plymouth, to the Compter in Bread Street, and afterwards been parties
to an assault on the Serjeant-at-Arms who came to release him, were
brought up at the Bar of the House of Commons for breach of privilege,
and committed to the Tower, with one of their clerks, who was
placed in a room grimly called of "Little Ease." In the troubled reign
of Charles I citizens suffered with the rest. They were bound to take
sides, and Sir Richard Gurney, elected Lord Mayor in 1641, happened
to be a zealous Royalist. When the King, in June, 1642, issued an order
forbidding the proclamation of the Parliament's militia ordinance, Gurney
had it publicly read in the City. For this he was impeached by Parliament,
put out of his office, committed to the Tower, and condemned to be kept
there during the pleasure of the two Houses. He remained in the Tower
almost till his death in October, 1647. Lloyd, in his " Memoirs of Excellent
Personages," asserts that Sir Richard lost £40,000 by his loyalty, and that
he refused to pay £5,000, for which sum he might have obtained his release.

Before the death of Gurney, another brave Lord Mayor, Sir John
Gayer, paid the penalty of opposing those who could enforce their demands.
He was committed to the Tower, with four Aldermen, for high treason in
aiding and abetting a tumult against the ordinance passed by Parliament on
July 23rd, 1647, for compulsory service in the militia. Though this ordinance
was almost immediately annulled, they were kept in prison till June,
1648. Gayer died in the following year. He had been a traveller, and
left £200 to the parish of St. Katherine Cree to pay for an annual sermon
on the 14th of October, now called the " Lion Sermon," which commemorates a romantic event in his life. The story runs, that he was once lost
in a desert of Arabia, where a lion passed without hurting him, in consequence of his prayers and vows of charity. In April, 1649, a Lord Mayor
was again so unfortunate as to find his way into the Tower prison. Sir
Abraham Reynardson, who then held office, having refused to obey the
order of Parliament to proclaim in the City the abolition of monarchy in
Great Britain and Ireland, was degraded from his mayoralty, fined £2,000,
and committed to the Tower for two months. In 1682 the Sheriffs

Pilkington and Shute and Alderman Cornish were imprisoned there, nominally for being concerned in a riot, really because they took the popular side as opposed to the King. A curious incident marked the proceedings which led up to this event. Sir John Moore, anxious to serve the Court, was induced to exercise the Lord Mayor's privilege, which had long been in abeyance, of nominating one of the Sheriffs for the following year, by drinking to a fellow-citizen at the Bridge House feast on the 18th of May. The person so nominated was Dudley North, brother to the Lord Chief Justice, who was also of the King's party, which eventually gained the day.

The prominent citizens who in the latter half of last century suffered durance in the Tower, were perhaps not unwilling to pose as martyrs at a cheap price, for by this time there was not likely to be much risk. The first of these in point of time, and the master-spirit, was the witty and licentious John Wilkes, who, not yet Lord Mayor of London, was committed to the Tower in 1763 for his share in the periodical known as the *North Briton*. Eight years later, Lord Mayor Brass Crosby and Alderman Oliver, both members of Parliament, found their way into the same place, imprisoned for acting with Wilkes as champions of the City against Parliament, the dispute being as to the right of publishing reports of debates, which they upheld, and which had always been denied by the House. When the masses became aware of this high-handed action of Parliament, excitement rose to fever-heat. In a *London Chronicle* it is recorded that between April 1st and 5th "the populace amused themselves by conveying to Tower Hill certain stuffed figures, representing some of the leading political characters, and with due solemnity their heads were chopped off, amid the exulting shouts of the multitude." The House had shrunk from a new contest with Wilkes, who in point of fact was the chief offender. The imprisoned members were released on the prorogation of Parliament, when the Aldermen and Court of Common Council, in their robes, preceded by the City Marshal and his deputy, went to the Tower to conduct Lord Mayor Crosby and Alderman Oliver to the Mansion House in the state coach, and fifty-three carriages followed in the train. On the prisoners being brought to the Tower gate by the officers of the fortress, "they were saluted by a discharge of twenty-one pieces of cannon belonging to the Honourable Artillery Company, and received by the people with the greatest acclamations, which were continued all the way to the Mansion House." "The great end of the contest," says Mr. Orridge, "was obtained. From that day to the present the House of Commons has never ventured to assail the liberty of the Press or to prevent the publication of the Parliamentary debates."

In one respect the Londoners of to-day seem much to resemble their forefathers, that is in their love of shows and processions, but unfortunately they have less chance of indulging their taste. How infinitely picturesque and fantastic must have been those of mediæval London. Imagine, for instance, the coronation festivities of Richard II. The King, clad in white robes, issued from the gates of the Tower, accompanied by a multitude of nobles, knights and squires. The streets through which he passed were hung with rich drapery ; the conduits ran with wine ; in all the chief thoroughfares pageants were shown. That in Cheapside was a castle with four towers, from two sides of which "the wine ran forth abundantlie, and at the top stood a golden angel holding a crown, so contrived that when the King came near, he bowed down and presented it to him. In each of the towers was a beautiful virgin, in stature and age like to the King, apparelled in white vestures, the which blew in the King's face leaves of gold and flowers of gold counterfeit." On the approach of the cavalcade the damsels took golden cups, and filling them with wine at the spouts of the castle, presented them to the King and his nobles. Another famous occasion was that of 1390, when the same monarch held a tournament for four days at Smithfield, which was proclaimed throughout France and Germany, the English challenging all comers. On the appointed day there came forth from the Tower of London, to the delight of expectant thousands, a cavalcade headed, says Froissart, by "three score coursers apparelled for the jousts, and on every one an esquire of honour, riding a soft pace ; and then issued out three score ladies of honour, mounted on fair palfreys, riding on one side richly apparelled, and every lady led a knight with a chain of silver, which knights were apparelled to joust ; and thus they came riding along the streets of London, with great number of trumpets and other minstrels, and so came to Smithfield, where the King and Queen and many ladies were ready, in chambers richly adorned, to see the jousts."

Riding was, from the Conquest until late in Tudor times, the one comparatively rapid means of progression by land, the roads being almost impassable for wheeled vehicles, which were indeed of the most primitive kind until the introduction of coaches, about the middle of the 16th century. Great personages unable to ride, were conveyed in chairs or litters. The young Isabella, second wife of Richard II, seems to have used a horse litter; and in 1422 the infant son of Henry V was carried in state from the Tower through the City, on his mother's lap in an open chair, to Westminster, where his right to the crown was recognised by Parliament. The ancient kings on state occasions made it a matter of policy, one might almost say of religion, to show themselves in the streets with all the splendour possible, and thus to arouse the loyalty of the mass of the citizens. In a manuscript called the "Liber Regalis" it is laid down that, "the day before the coronation the King shall come from the Tower of London to his Palace at Westminster, through the midst of the City, mounted on a horse, handsomely habited and bareheaded in the sight of all the people *(in cultu decentissimo equitabit, capite denudato)*."

Henry IV, who no doubt was most anxious to court popularity, carried out the old fashion with unusual splendour. On Saturday, October 11th, 1399, before coronation, he went from the Palace at Westminster to the Tower, with a great number of attendants and forty-six esquires, who were to be made knights on the following morning. Froissart—an eye witness, who loved to record quaint details—makes special note of the rather surprising fact, that here each esquire had his separate chamber and his bath which he used overnight, this being no doubt part of the ceremony. The next morning they were all knighted in a mass, and received as presents, rich costumes; and after dinner the future King went from the Tower to Westminster, bareheaded, gorgeously attired, and mounted on a beautiful courser. He was accompanied by the Prince his son, six dukes, six earls, eight barons, eight or nine hundred knights; "and in this manner they made through London, where all the citizens and Companies, with their ensigns and different devices, met and conveyed the Duke to Westminster. Their number amounted to full 6,000 horsemen; and that day, as well as the next also, were nine branches of fountains in the Cheap, which ran both red and white wine." On Monday he was crowned with the utmost ceremony, and afterwards feasted in the Great Hall. Again, before the coronation of Edward IV, we read how he came from his Palace of Shene (now Richmond), and was met at Lambeth by the Mayor and Aldermen in their finest robes, and attended by 400 citizens on horseback, all in green, richly accoutred, by whom he was conducted to the Tower. Thence, two days afterwards, he rode in state to Westminster, and was solemnly crowned at St. Peter's.

Though, however, our earlier monarchs preferred the streets for state ceremonials, they were no doubt constantly using the Thames as a highway, the Tower of London, Westminster and Greenwich being natural points of departure. On the river front there was more than one means of access to the place first mentioned. The most important was that under St. Thomas's Tower, more commonly named or misnamed Traitors' Gate, the channel of which traversed Tower quay and communicated with the main ditch. Traitors' Gate seems to have been kept exclusively for prisoners, who by water could be conveyed more secretly, and with less chance of a rescue, than by land; it was under the arch so clearly shown in our most interesting coloured view, that those unfortunates were hurried. Mr. Clark is convinced that this was the gateway which, with part of the adjacent curtain, twice fell in the reign of Henry III. No doubt much against the wishes of the citizens, it was completed a third time, and successfully, either before his death or by his son Edward. The stairs where royal personages generally came on shore lay beneath the Byward Gate and Belfry, with passage by bridge and postern through the Byward Tower, into what was called Water Lane. The Galleyman Stairs, seldom used, lay under the Cradle Tower, whence there was an entrance to the royal quarters. It was doubtless at the Queen's Stairs, close to the Byward Tower, that Elizabeth of York was landed in 1487, before her coronation, which Henry VII delayed as long as he could, from what motive it is hard to determine. She came from Greenwich attended by the Mayor, Sheriffs and Aldermen, and members of the City Guilds in their barges, "freshly furnished with banners and streamers of silk", was received by her husband at the Tower, and the next day, after dinner, proceeded through the City to Westminster, in a litter hung with cloth of gold, meeting on her way many fine pageants.

Perhaps the most gorgeous water procession of Tudor times was that which took place in response to the order of Henry VIII, who, already married to Anne Boleyn, had determined that she should be publicly crowned at Westminster. The citizens were proud of her descent from a Lord Mayor, and vied with each other in doing her honour. Hall, in his Chronicle, has left a picturesque account of the ceremonies on this occasion, from which we quote at some length, as it serves to illustrate, not only a royal, but a civic procession of the highest class. It seems that after the King's command had been received, the Lord Mayor called a meeting of the Common Council, and it was arranged that his Company (the Haberdashers') should prepare "a barge for the Batchelors,* with a wafter and a foyst† garnished with banners and streamers, likewyse as they use to dooe when the Maior is presented at Westminster, on the morrow after St. Symon and St. Jude. Also all other craftes were commaunded to prepare barges, and to garnishe them, not alonely with their banners accustomed, but also to decke them with targettes by the side of the barges, and so set vp all suche semely banners and bannerettes as they had in their halles, or could gete mete to furnishe their sayd barges; and every barge to have mynstrelsie. Accordyng to which commaundementes great preparacion was made for all thynges necessary for suche a noble triumph." At the appointed time the Mayor and his brethren, all in scarlet, such as were knights having collars of esses, and the others good chains, assembled with the Common Council at St. Mary's Hill, and descended to their barge, which was garnished with many goodly banners and streamers, and richly covered. In this barge "wer shalmes shaglushes and divers other instrumentes whiche continually made goodly armony." After the Mayor and his brethren had gone on board, and arranged the procession, which numbered no less than fifty barges of City Companies, they started in the following order. First, before the Mayor's barge, was

---

* The "Batchelors" were chosen every year, from the same Company as the Mayor (but not of the Livery). They served on festive occasions to wait on the Mayor; being in number according to the Company he belonged to, generally from 60 to 100; they had a barge set apart for them in all processions. In royal pageants there was also sometimes a Batchelors' barge appropriated to the younger sons of the nobility.

† The foyst was a vessel usually hired for the day, in addition to the barges of the several Companies which attended the Lord Mayor. Among the accounts of the Merchant Taylors' Company, there is an agreement for the hiring of a foyst in 1561: "It is aggreed and concluded with Thomas Ewen and Nicholas Hollonby that they shall provide a foyste of xviij or xx tonne to be furnysshed with xvj peces of ordenaunces called bassys— and to shoot of all the said peces of ordenaunces the said daye vj times." This was for Sir W. Harper's pageant.

a foyst or wafter full of ordnance, in which was a great dragon continually moving and casting wild-fire; and round about the foyst stood terrible monsters and wild men casting fire and making hideous noises. Next, at a good distance, came the Lord Mayor's barge, on whose right hand was the Batchelors' barge, "in the whiche were trumpettes and divers other melodious instrumentes. The deckes of the sayd barge and the toppe castles were hanged with riche cloth of golde and silke. At the foreship and the sterne were two great banners riche beaten with the armes of the kinge and quene, and on the toppe castle also was a long stremer newly beaten with the sayd armes. The sides of the barge were sette full of flagges and banners of the devises of the Company of Haberdashers and Marchauntes Adventurers, and the cordes were hanged with innumerable penselles, havyng litle belles at y endes, whiche made a goodly noyse and a goodly sight, waveryng in the wynde. On the left hand of the Maior was another foyst, in the which was a mount, and on the same stode a white fawcon crowned, upon a rote of golde, environed with white roses and red, whiche was the Quenes devise: about whiche mount satte virgyns singyng and plaiyng swetely." The various guilds followed, "every Company havyng melodye in his barge by himselfe and goodly garnished with banners, and some with silke, some with arras and riche carpettes." At Greenwich they anchored "makyng great melody." At three o'clock the Queen, apparelled in rich cloth of gold, entered her barge accompanied by divers gentlewomen, and the citizens set forward in order, their minstrelsy continually playing, and the Batchelors' barge going on the Queen's right hand, which she took great pleasure to behold. About the Queen's barge were many noblemen, as the Duke of Suffolk, the Marquis Dorset, the Earl of Wiltshire her father, the Earls of Arundel, Derby, Rutland, Worcester, Huntingdon, Sussex, Oxford, and many bishops and noblemen, every one in his barge, a goodly sight to behold. "She, thus beyng accompanied, rowed towarde the Tower; and in the meane time the shippes whiche were commaunded to lye on the shore for lettyng of the barges, shotte divers peales of gunnes, and ere she landed, there was a mervailous shotte out of the Tower, as ever was harde there. And at her landyng there met with her the Lord Chamberlain with the officers of armes, and brought her to the Kyng, which received her with lovyng countenance at the Posterne by the water syde and kyssed her; and then she turned backe again and thanked the Maior and the citezens with many goodly wordes, and so entred into the Tower. After which entry the citezens all this while hoved before the Tower makyng great melody, and went not alande, for none wer assigned to land but the Maior, the Recorder and two Aldermen. But for to speake of the people that stode on every shore to beholde the sight, he that sawe it will not beleve it." This was the hour of Anne's triumph, when her dreams of ambition were being realized. Her next visit, three years later, was to the prison, not to the palace, and it ended with her life on Tower Green. Surely the King must have had some qualms of conscience or must have regretted at least one change for the worse, when, in 1540, he and his plain bride, Anne of Cleves, passed the Tower as they went by water from Greenwich to Westminster, with all the chief citizens in attendance, many of whom had no doubt been present on the previous occasion.

In those days it was an easy matter to organise a fine water procession or what the old writers called "a fluminous pageant," the Lord Mayor's barge and those of the great City Companies being at short notice available. It was not always so, for like the Kings, the earlier Mayors had always ridden to Westminster after they had been chosen, to have their elections confirmed. It was Sir John Norman, in 1453, who first changed the custom. He caused a stately barge to be built at his own expense, and was rowed thither on the usual anniversary, attended by members of the chief guilds who had imitated his example. This so delighted the London watermen that they wrote a ballad in his praise, beginning,

> "Row thy boat, Norman, row to thy leman."

Some barges were no doubt hired for the occasion. In the accounts of the Merchant Taylors' Company for 1453-4 are such items as this:— "Barge hire to Greenwich for the Master and others, going to meet the King and Queene to the feste of St. John, 4s." The late Mr. F. W. Fairholt, who described many civic pageants by land and water, has proved from the books of the Grocers' Company that there were water processions at least nineteen years earlier. It is, perhaps, worth while here to note that until the year 1711, when a new state coach was built for the Lord Mayor, the civic cavalcade continued to pass to and from the waterside on horseback.

Centuries before the first of the grand water processions, citizens were continually using the river for purposes of business and pleasure. They all lived within easy distance of its banks, and it was associated with their daily lives. A monk of the 12th century—Fitzstephen, biographer of Becket—has left a singularly graphic account of the London of his day. He dwells lovingly on the athletic amusements to which the sons of citizens were devoted; one of their games was a sort of water quintain, which he describes as follows:* "In the Easter holidays they play at a game resembling a naval engagement. A target is firmly fixed to the trunk of a tree which is fixed in the middle of the river, and in the prow of a boat driven along by oars and the current stands a young man, who is to strike the target with his lance; if, in hitting it, he break his lance, and keep his position unmoved, he gains his point, and attains his desire; but if his lance be not shivered by the blow, he is tumbled into the river, and his boat passes by, driven along by its own motion. Two boats, however, are placed there, one on each side of the target, and in them a number of young men to take up the striker when he first emerges from the stream, or when

"A second time he rises from the wave."

On the bridge, and in balconies on the banks of the river, stand the spectators.

"—— well disposed to laugh."

In the year 1253 some of the King's servants came into the City to play a game of quintain on the river, when they ridiculed certain citizens, who fell upon and beat them, for which offence a fine was inflicted on the Corporation of no less a sum than 1,000 marks. Stow tells us how, in the summer season, he had seen men rowed in wherries "with staves in their hands flat at the fore-end, running one against another, and for the most part one or both overthrown and well ducked." There is a drawing of water quintain, and another of a water joust, in an illuminated book at the British Museum. Howell in his "Londinopolis" (1657) says : "There was in former times a sport used upon the Thames, which is now DISCONTINUED; it was for two wherries to row, and run one against the other, with staves in their hands flat at the fore-end; which kind of recreation is much practiced amongst the gondolas of Venice."

* The translation is by Mr. W. J. Thoms, from his edition of "Stow's Survey, 1876."

But it was to the river as a means of every-day communication for all, from the highest to the lowest, that we have, as is natural, the most frequent reference among the older writers. Here the poet, Gower, met King Richard II, as it were by chance; what a delightful sketch of the scene has been handed down to us. He relates that—

> "In Thames when it was flowing,
> As I by boate came rowing,
> So as fortune her time set,
> My liege lord perchance I met,
> And so befel, as I came nigh,
> Out of my boat, when he me sygh,
> He bade me come into his barge."

The King then invited him to an audience and asked him to write "some new thinge," the "Confessio Amantis" being the result of the interview. We frequently find in old records evidence of the use to which the Thames was put by Kings and great people for the affairs of every-day life. Thus the "Privy Purse Expenses of Henry VIII" contain many notes of money paid for boats and barges to and from his different palaces. The men who propelled them were probably for the most part his servants. There was also a large number of watermen in the service of the nobility, some of whom occasionally took fares, if we may judge by the following extract from Clarendon, vol. I, p. 72, which relates to the year 1637: "A waterman belonging to a man of quality, having a squabble with a citizen about his fare, showed his badge, the crest of the Earl, his master, which happened to be a swan, and thence insisted on better treatment from the citizen, but the other carelessly replied that 'He did not trouble himself about that goose.' For this offence he was summoned before the Marshal's Court, was fined and imprisoned, until he paid considerable damages for having opprobriously defamed the nobleman's crest." But the largest and most important class employed on the Thames were the professional watermen, who plied publicly for hire. Many of these men volunteered and did good service at the time of the Spanish Armada. Stow says that when he wrote "there were probably 2,000 wherries, whereby at least 3,000 men found employment"; and Taylor, who "flourished" but a few years later, makes the astonishing statement that "the number of watermen and those that lived and were maintained by them, and by the only labour of the oar and scull, betwixt the bridge of Windsor and Gravesend, could not be fewer than 40,000." This same John Taylor, the Water-Poet, was a remarkable character in his way—a Thames waterman, who had a talent for doggrel, and has left us writings which, though of small literary finish, are distinctly valuable as pictures of a most interesting time. He was a contemporary of Shakespeare, and knowing Southwark well, may have ferried him from Blackfriars to the Bankside. Later he was living near St. Saviour's Church. The river being to him a source of livelihood, he naturally praised it with his whole heart:—

> " But noble Thames, whilst I can hold a pen,
> I will divulge thy glory unto men :
> Thou in the morning, when my coin is scant,
> Before the evening dost supply my want."*

His great grievance was the advent of the coaches, which interfered with his business. In a prose tract, published in 1623, he says: "I do not inveigh against any coaches that belong to persons of worth and quality, but only against the caterpillar swarm of hirelings. They have undone my poor trade whereof I am a member; and though I look for no reformation, yet I expect the benefit of an old proverb, 'Give the losers leave to speak.'" In a pamphlet called "An Arrant Thief," he gives the approximate date of the introduction of these vehicles which so raised his ire :

> " When Queen Elizabeth came to the crown,
> A coach in England then was scarcely known ;
> Then 'twas as rare to see one, as to spy
> A tradesman that had never told a lie."

At one time the Water-Poet held the office of collector of perquisites for the Lieutenants of the Tower, from all ships importing wine into the Thames ; probably one of the claims before mentioned, which were granted to Sir Thomas Murrieux by Richard II. In his "Farewell to the Tower Bottles," he gives us his experiences when thus employed. In spite of Taylor's gloomy forebodings, the river almost throughout the 17th century must have been in its glory as a thoroughfare. Howell, in 1657, declared that it was unequalled, "if regard be had to those forests of masts which are perpetually upon her, the variety of smaller

---

* "The Praise of Hempseed, with the voyage of Mr. Roger Bird and the writer hereof in a boat of brown paper, from London to Quinborough in Kent, etc., etc.' 1620-23.

wooden bottoms playing up and down, the stately palaces that are built upon both sides of her banks so thick, which made divers foreign ambassadors affirm that the most glorious sight in the world, take water and land together, was to come upon a high tide from Gravesend, and shoot the bridge to Westminster.

But every phase of human life is changed by time or passes away. As the City grew crowded and great nobles migrated west, these stately palaces with their grounds were sold or let for building. Street communication was improved; coal wharves took the place of trim gardens. The river, contaminated by sewage, ceased to merit the epithet "silver" so often applied to it. The Watermen's Company in vain opposed the building of Westminster and Blackfriars Bridges. Nevertheless, a couple of generations ago the Thames watermen still prospered, and preserved something of the characteristics which distinguished them in the olden time. They were an independent class, used a phraseology more pointed than polite, and were much addicted to rough banter. Boswell records that Dr. Johnson on one occasion paid them back with success in their own coin, when they tried to ridicule him. Thames watermen received licenses from the Lord Mayor, the Thames Conservancy being formerly in the hands of the Corporation; their fares were regulated by a published rate of charges. There were also tilt boats for conveying goods to and fro between London and Gravesend. The introduction of steam has entirely changed the character of the traffic on the river. We see little now of the

> " Jolly young waterman
> Who at Blackfriars Bridge used for to ply,
> Who feathered his oars with such skill and dexterity,
> Winning each heart and delighting each eye."

But the Watermen's Company, founded, it would seem, in the time of Henry VIII, still holds its own, and does useful work. None but freemen of the Company can follow their occupation between Teddington Lock and Lower Hope Point, five miles below Gravesend. Each year we are reminded of a past state of society by the race rowed on the 1st of August among six young watermen just out of their apprenticeship, for Doggett's Coat and Badge, from the Old Swan, London Bridge, to Cadogan Pier, which is near the site of the Old Swan, Chelsea, now destroyed.

During the first half of this century water processions on the Thames were still comparatively common.   One of the grandest and most impressive ever held, was that on the 8th of January, 1806, the day before the funeral of Lord Nelson, when the body of the dead hero was brought by water from Greenwich Hospital to Whitehall.   Prominent on that occasion were the barges of the Lord Mayor and of the City Companies, and minute guns were fired from the Tower of London.   Eight years afterwards a more cheerful journey was planned for the entertainment of the allied sovereigns who were here to celebrate the restoration of peace.   They went in state from Whitehall Stairs to Woolwich, where they were taken over the Arsenal: the Lord Mayor and Aldermen, with the City barges, joined them off London Bridge.   The last procession on the river in which Royalty took part, was that on October 30th, 1849, when the new Coal Exchange was opened.   Her Majesty had consented to come by water, and to conduct the ceremonies in person. A row of steamers was moored along the whole of the north side of the Thames, from Whitehall to London Bridge; and a row of coal lighters on the south side; a space of 100 feet being left clear for the procession. The Queen, unfortunately, was indisposed, and could not be present.   Her place was taken by Prince Albert, who, with the Prince of Wales and the Princess Royal, at half past twelve left Whitehall Stairs in the Royal barge, a gorgeous structure, built for Frederick Prince of Wales, father of George III.   It was rowed by twenty-seven watermen in rich livery, and was under the command of Lord Adolphus FitzClarence.   The Lord Mayor's barge, with its quaint gilded poop, and those of the Superintendent of Woolwich Dockyard, the Commander-in-Chief at the Nore, the Admiralty, and the Trinity House were also present.   The Royal party landed at Custom House Quay.

In course of time the civic water processions became obsolete.   The last took place when Mr. Alderman Finnis was chosen Lord Mayor in 1856.   After the passing of the Thames Conservancy Act there was no further use for the Lord Mayor's state barge, and in 1860 she was sold by auction at Messrs. Searle's, then on the Surrey side of Westminster Bridge, for £105.   The "Maria Wood," named after the eldest daughter of Sir Matthew Wood, Lord Mayor in 1816, passed long ago into private hands, but until quite recently has from time to time been used for water parties. One or two of the City Companies' barges are now moored on the river at Oxford, being used by college boat clubs, but they have been patched up and altered "out of all knowledge." The Queen's state barge for the river is still in existence, and she still has her Bargemaster, and her picturesque Watermen, though like Othello, they find their "occupation gone."

Before the carrying out of the main drainage scheme, there is no doubt that the Thames had got into a very filthy condition. When we are willing to pay the price, this scheme will no doubt be perfected; meanwhile the river, always beautiful, has ceased to offend our olfactory nerves, and it may fairly lay claim to its full share in the ceremonial at the opening of the Tower Bridge. Perhaps some day water pageants may again come into fashion. They would indeed have a splendid background to show them off, for Spenser and Herrick never saw anything equal, in its way, to the picturesque "effects" produced by our smoke-laden atmosphere; a truth which is being brought home to us by the admirable pictures of several living artists. In one respect, however, the most ardent admirer of modern life must admit that we are at a disadvantage compared with our ancestors. Fancy being able to catch salmon at Chelsea, or to fish with success for the humbler roach in the neighbourhood of London Bridge. There was indeed a time when the fish supply from the river was of great importance to Londoners, and great pains were taken in order to keep it up. We have seen how the citizens fought successfully against the right claimed by Tower authorities of placing kiddles in the Thames. In the year 1405, Sir John Wodecock, Mayor, being informed that a great number of weirs had been erected, to the destruction of the young fry and the damage of navigation, caused all such weirs to be removed and the nets burnt, from Staines to the mouth of the Medway. Again, Sir Thomas Pullison, in 1584, made a close time for the different kinds of fish, and similar regulations were enforced again and again in the course of the 17th and 18th centuries.

A list of Thames fish, still frequenting the river within the jurisdiction of the City in 1772, is enough to make one's mouth water. Strange to say, in this list there is no mention of the salmon, which were even then plentiful. One or two instances of famous takes in comparatively recent times, will bear us out. It is recorded that on June 7th, 1749, forty-seven large salmon were caught below Richmond, in two draughts of the net, which lowered the price of these fish at Billingsgate from 1*s.* to 6*d.* per pound. Again, in July, 1766, a hundred and thirty salmon taken in the Thames in one day, were sent to market. In 1758 a fisherman named Pocock caught a sturgeon, and gave it to the Lord Mayor, as had been customary with those taken below bridge; any from above bridge being reserved for the table of the King or Lord High Admiral. We are glad to see that a sturgeon has been again caught in the Thames, this time off Erith, on the 12th of June, 1894; a proof that recent efforts to purify the water have been to a great extent successful. It weighed 280 lbs., and was duly presented to the Lord Mayor. In the early part of the 18th century a waterman named John Reeves, who plied at Essex stairs, got a comfortable livelihood by taking anglers in his boat. He used to watch for the shoals of roach which settled at favourite spots in the river, and thus provided good sport for those who employed him. His patrons gave him a waterman's coat and a silver badge, having on it a likeness of himself in his boat, with an angler. Punt fishing for roach off the starlings of London Bridge was a common amusement of City folk. Even now, to remind us of that time, there are fishing tackle shops in the small piece of Crooked Lane which still remains. Mr. Goldham, of Billingsgate, who gave evidence before a parliamentary committee in 1828, when the Thames fishery was almost a thing of the past, affirmed that about 1810 he had known ten salmon and 3,000 smelts taken at one haul in the river towards Wandsworth, and not fewer than 3,000 Thames salmon brought to market in the season.

If, however, as far as most of us are aware, our present fish supply derived from the Thames in the neighbourhood of the City is confined to whitebait at Greenwich, we have, in Billingsgate, perhaps the best supplied fish market in the world, and an interesting survival of old London. According to Brompton's Chronicle, tolls were paid here for ships even in the time of King Ethelbert. Billingsgate and Queenhithe were once the chief City wharves for the landing, not only of fish, but of various commodities, Queenhithe being at first the more important, but it was gradually outstripped owing to the difficult passage of London Bridge. In the year 1282 an order was sent by Edward I to the Serjeants of Billingsgate and Queenhithe, that all boats were to be moored on the City side at night, and that their names were to be recorded; and fifteen years afterwards there was a similar order, but this time it was addressed to the Warden of Queenhithe and the Warden of the "portus" of Billingsgate. During the next reign, a letter was addressed to the Mayor and Corporation for the safe keeping of the City, wherein Billingsgate is mentioned among the quays facing the Thames which are to be well and stoutly "betrached," that is fitted with battlements. In 1370 (44 Edward III) "the Mayor, Aldermen and Commonalty" being given to understand "that certain galleys, with a multitude of armed men therein, were lying off the Foreland of Tenet," apparently with the intention of coming to London, "to destroy the people of that City," it was ordered, "that every night in future, so long as there should be need, watch should be kept between the Tower of London and Byllyngesgate, with forty men-at-arms and sixty archers; which watch the men of the trades underwritten agreed to keep in succession as follows: On Tuesday the Drapers and the Tailors; on Wednesday the Mercers and the Apothecaries; on Thursday the Fishmongers and the Butchers; on Friday the Pelterers and the Vintners; on Saturday the Goldsmiths and the Saddlers; on Sunday the Ironmongers, the Armourers and the Cutlers; on Monday the Tawyers, the Spurriers, the Bowyers and the Girdlers."

John Lydgate, the Bury monk, in his poem called "London Lackpenny," written perhaps at the beginning of the 15th century, while humorously complaining of the disadvantages of an empty purse in the metropolis, thus relates his attempt to leave London by water:

> "Then hyed I me to Belynsgate,
> And one cryed, 'Hoo, go we hence?'
> I prayd a barge man for God's sake
> That he wold spare me my expence:
> Thou scapst not here, q° he, under ii pence;
> I lyst not yet bestowed my almes dede;
> Thus lackyng mony I cold not spede."

For sober facts, we have the following description by Stow a couple of centuries later:—"Billingsgate is at this present a large water-gate, port, or harborough for ships and boats commonly arriving there with fish both fresh and salt, shell-fishes, salt, oranges, onions and other fruits and roots, wheat, rye and grain of divers sorts for the service of the City and the parts of the realm adjoining. This gate is now more frequented than of old time, when the Queene's-hithe was used, and the drawbridge of timber was then to be raised or drawn up for passage of ships with tops thither." At this time we may assume that it had somewhat the appearance given it in Antony van den Wyngaerde's view—a dock with a gabled building at the back, having an arcade beneath, and by the water-side a tower. In 1699 Billingsgate was declared "a free and open market for all sorts of fish." Until the year 1850 there was a considerable dock or creek running up in the direction of Lower Thames Street. This dock was then to a great extent filled in, and the market, a picturesque collection

BILLINGSGATE MARKET.

of wooden sheds and houses, was re-built from the designs of Mr. J. B. Bunning, the City architect. It was soon found to be too small for the increased trade, and in 1874-77 was again re-built by Mr. Horace Jones, the then City architect, the area being nearly doubled. The advent of railways has completely changed the character of the wholesale fish trade, an enormous quantity of fish being now brought to Billingsgate by land. No doubt the proverbial dialect of the place has also been considerably modified.

In the beautiful coloured view of Old London Bridge and the Tower, reproduced for this volume, which seems to have considerable topographic accuracy, an important building is shown between the two, the part of it nearest the river having gables and a cloister or arcade, while that on the land side is castellated. It is an open question whether this is intended for Billingsgate, or for the original Custom House, "new built" in 1383 by John Chircheman, afterwards Sheriff, "to serve for tronage or weighing of wools in the port of London." Several writers have stated that in Queen Elizabeth's reign a new Custom House, on the same site, was erected. Be this as it may, the print by Barth[s] Howlett, purporting to represent the Custom House of her time, shows gables and a square turreted structure not unlike that in our view. It was burnt down in the Great Fire, re-built by Wren at a cost of £10,000, again burnt (during his lifetime) in 1718, re-built by Ripley, and destroyed a third time by fire in 1814. A new Custom House was then erected by David Laing on the present site, close to Billingsgate; there had before been nine or ten quays between them, all the previous Custom Houses having stood considerably nearer the Tower. Unfortunately the piling gave way almost immediately. In 1825 the centre had to be taken down, the foundations were re-laid, and the present front towards the river was built from the designs of Sir Robert Smirke, R.A. The ancient Customs were chiefly payable on the export of native products, such as wool and leather. The duties levied on foreign commodities were at first called "prisage." Until the end of Queen Elizabeth's reign the revenue derived from Customs was comparatively small. In 1599 she farmed them to one Thomas Smith for £29,000 a year. Smith, however, was said to have gained upwards of £10,000 by the contract. The "Long Room" has been a prominent feature in successive Custom Houses. J. Macky, in his "Journey through England," 1722, remarks on it as follows:— "In the long room it's a pretty pleasure to see the multitude of payments made there in a morning. I heard Count Tallard say, that nothing gave him so true and great an idea of the richness and grandeur of this nation as this, when he saw it after the peace of Ryswick."

Our pleasant task is almost over. We have told what we could, in the space allotted to us, of the Tower, the City and the River; let us cross over to the opposite bank and say a few words about the district now called Horselydown, with which our stupendous Tower Bridge has connected us. Even in historic times the neighbourhood must have been very marshy, reclaimed little by little.   It is recorded that in 1326 (19 Edward II) there was a great breach in the bank of the Thames between Bermondsey and Greenwich, to the detriment of landowners; when Adam de Brom, William de Leycestre, and others, were ordered to view the damage and to obtain payment for repair from those on whose lands it began, and from others who were bound to contribute.   In 1380 (3 Richard II) Robert Belknap and Nicholas Hering were appointed Commissioners for repairing the banks between Greenwich and London Bridge; and in 5 Henry V there was a Commission for the banks between Deptford Strand and Bermondsey, "to act according to the custom of the marsh and the law and custom of the realm." The particular open space to which the name Horselydown was applied, became no doubt a grazing ground for horses and cattle. It belonged to the Abbey of Bermondsey. Corner, a great local authority, tells us that it was within the Lordship of the Manor of Southwark, surrendered to Henry VIII with the other possessions of the Abbey. It was leased for a time by the Parish of St. Olave, and since 1581 has belonged to the Governors of St. Olave's Grammar School. In a Paston letter dated 1456, it is called "Horshigh-down." This letter appears to be written from the house of the famous Sir John Fastolf, in Stoney Lane, Tooley Street, hard by; where, be it remembered, he was living at the time of Jack Cade's insurrection. According to popular report he had garrisoned it with old soldiers from Normandy, in order to resist Cade's progress. When the rebel leader was encamped at Blackheath, Fastolf sent his servant, Payn, thither as a spy. Payn's identity was discovered, and his master denounced, but under certain conditions he was allowed to return to Fastolf, and to warn him of Cade's approach. The knight then prudently returned to the Tower of London. Sir John's dwelling in Stoney Lane must have been almost a palace, for Cicely, mother of the Duke of York, afterwards Edward IV, with her family, stayed here on one occasion. He owned much property in the neighbourhood, part of which afterwards came, by bequest, into the hands of Magdalen College, Oxford. This connection is shown in Magdalen

Street and Maudlin Lane, the Morgan's Lane of the present day. In a list of Sir John Fastolf's Southwark property, preserved at Magdalen College, mention is made of the "High Bere House." It is shown in Braun and Hogenberg's map of 1572 as a considerable enclosure on the river bank, nearly opposite to, and a little east of, the Tower, and was referred to in some Chancery proceedings of 14 Edward IV as the "High Biere howse and gardyn lately known as ffastolfes." Centuries before there had been a place about here called "The Rosary," which belonged to a family named Dunlegh, two of whom were returned as Members of Parliament for Southwark in the reign of Edward I. Still further east was the Liberty of St. John; "the Prior of the Hospital of St. John of Jerusalem held, in the reign of Edward I, three watermills, three acres of land, one acre of meadow and twenty acres of pasture at Horsedowne (*sic*) in Southwark." The site of their manor house is covered by Messrs. Courage's brewery at the corner of Shad Thames.

There is a picture by Hoefnagle, apparently dated 1590, belonging to the Marquess of Salisbury, and exhibited at the Tudor Exhibition not long since, which shows us a fête of some kind at Horselydown or its immediate neighbourhood. Fair Street is still in existence to remind us that fairs were at one time held here. The artist's point of view in this picture, is about half a mile from the river, nearly opposite to the Tower. The meaning of the foreground scene has not been clearly explained; from a comparison of maps and views, the writer believes that the most important incident is in truth a procession from the old Church of St. Mary Magdalen, Bermondsey. But what concerns us is that the whole Horselydown district is shown, to the river bank, and some of the details are most instructive; for instance, close at hand a hawking party sallies forth on horseback; archers are practising in the middle distance; by the river shipbuilding is being carried on; a road to the left leads down to the river, possibly to a ferry. Those archers were no doubt practising on the parish ground, for here in the reign of Edward VI were butts for the parishioners of St. Olave's. In Newcourt's map of 1658 a fringe of houses has appeared along the river bank, but there is still an open space marked "Horsy Downe," and adjoining it a large enclosure, the "Artillery Yard," elsewhere called the "Martial Yard," where Southwark train-bands used to be exercised, and which was clearly the successor of the archery ground. An armoury or artillery house was built here in the year 1639, and afterwards used as a polling place for the Southwark elections. In 1725 it was turned into a workhouse for the parish, and was finally demolished about the year 1836. Artillery Lane keeps up the memory of what has been. The parish of St. Olave having greatly increased in population, the parish of St. John, Horselydown, was cut off from it in 1733, and the new parish Church was built on part of the Artillery ground. Since then the story of Horselydown has been without special interest ; the place which once, for aught we know, pre-historic man may have traversed in his rude canoe, where horses and cattle grazed, and where great men have had their dwellings, has long since become an important industrial centre. We earnestly hope that the improvements, which cannot fail to result from the opening of the Tower Bridge, will bring to it a new epoch of ever increasing prosperity.

APPENDIX.

1. Wardens of London Bridge.[1]

This list is complete from 1381 (excepting the lacuna 1446–1458), being taken from the Wardens' Accounts. The imperfect list of Wardens before that date has been obtained from deeds and other sources. Time has not permitted the preparation of more than a few brief notes. The references to wills are taken chiefly from Dr. Sharpe's "Calendar of the Husting Wills."

1176–1205	Peter de Colechurch.	1284	Richard Knotte, Thomas Cross.[4]
1205	Brother Wasce.	1287–92	Thomas Crosse, Edmund Horn.
1213	Geoffrey and Martin.	1293	Richard Knotte, Thomas Crosse.
1223	Henry de Sancto Albano, William de Alemannia.	1294	Thomas Crosse, Edmund Horne.[5]
1233	Serle Mercer, William de Alemannia.	1298	John le Benere, Thomas Romein. John le Benere, William Jordan.[6]
1237	Robert Capellanus, Serle Mercer.	1299–30	John le Benere, William Jordan.
1240	Michael Tovy.	1301	Gilbert Cross.[7]
1243	Michael Tovy.	1302–3	John le Benere, William Jordan.
1248	Robert de Basing,[2] Michael Tovy.[3]	1304	Gilbert Cross.
1254	Michael Tovy.	1306	Gilbert Cross, Sir Robert Wethersete.
1256	Michael Tovy, Stephen de Ostregate.	1311	John Burton. Thomas Apprentice or Prentice, John de Wymondham.
1265	Robert de Cornhull.	1314	Thomas Prentice, John de Wymondham.
1271	James de Sancto Magno, Frasby St. Gregory.		Thomas Prentice, John de Wymondham.[8]
1272	James [de Sancto Magno].	1315	Henry de Gloucester,[9] Anketyn de Gisors.[10]
1273	James de Sancto Magno, Frasby St. Gregory.		
1274–75	Brother Stephen de Fulburn.		

[1] The following names of Wardens appear in deeds of the 13th century, but the exact dates of their Wardenships are not known, viz.:—Benedict Sipwrighte, Thomas de Chelke and Gregory de Rok' Rokesle?].

[2] Robert de Basinge, Alderman of Candlewick Ward in 1285.

[3] Michael Tovy was at the same time Mayor of London.

[4] Thomas Cross, Alderman, and in 1288 a Sheriff, will enrolled 1298, his wife Margery. Son of John Cross, fishmonger, whose will is dated 1294.

[5] Edmund Horne was appointed guardian to the children of Walter le Blund in 1291. His will was enrolled in 1296, whereby he left property to his wife Margaret. Certain debts were remitted to the executors of both Crosse and Horne, the Wardens for 1294.

[6] William Jordan, by his will, dated 1304, left property to his wife Avice, and 6s. to London Bridge.

[7] Gilbert Cross, fishmonger.

[8] Prentice and Wymondham were removed from their office in 1315.

[9] Will dated 30 November, 1332, whereby he left rents for the maintenance of chantries for twelve years, property to his children, and rents in various parishes to London Bridge.

[10] Alderman of Aldgate Ward in 1319.

1319	Matthew de Essex,[1] Robert Yon.[2]	1352	Henry Vanner,[13] John le Chandler. Henry Vanner, John de Hatfeld.
1320–21	John Vivian,[3] John Sterre.		
1322	Robert Pipherst, John Sterre. John Sterre, Roger atte Vigne.[4]		
1323	John Sterre, Roger atte Vigne.	1357–62	Richard Bacoun,[14] John le Hatfeld.
1326–27	John Sterre, Roger de Ely.[5]		
1332–35	Anketyn de Gisors, Robert Swote.[6]	1368–78	John de Coggeshale,[15] Henry Yevele.[16]
1337	Henry Cros.[7]	1381	John Hoo, Henry Yevele.
1339	Alan Gylle, John Lovekyn.[8]	1382–87	John Hoo [Henry Yevele].
1342	Alan Gylle, John Lovekyn.	1388–92	Henry Yevel, William Waddesworth.[17]
1344–45	Alan Gylle, John Gille.[9]		
1348–49	Alan Gille, John de Hardynham.[10]	1399	Henry Yevel, John Clifford.
1350	John Lyttle,[11] James Andrue.[12]	1401	William Chichely,[18] Thomas (?) Tenyele.

[1] Apothecary. Will enrolled in 1325, whereby he left property in Cordwainer Street to Margaret, his wife.

[2] Fishmonger. His will enrolled in 1321.

[3] Cordwainer. His will enrolled in 1321.

[4] The will of a Roger Vyne leaving property in London and Manningtree, dated 1348.

[5] A fishmonger. Will dated 1349. He left considerable property to his children. His son, Roger de Ely, was a canon of Newark.

[6] A fishmonger. He left money in 1355 to the Carmelites, the Friars Minors, the Preaching Friars, and Augustine Friars, also to the fabric of St. Paul's Cathedral and to London Bridge.

[7] Will dated 13 October, 1348.

[8] Mayor in 1348, 1358, 1365 and 1366.

[9] Master of the Works of the Bridge.

[10] A clerk. Was removed from his office 2 November, 1350. Will enrolled in 1352.

[11] A fishmonger. A long list exists of the goods delivered to him and his co-Warden by the previous Wardens (see p. 200). A John Little was Sheriff in 1354.

[12] He was in the first Common Council (representing Dowgate Ward) in 1347, and was an Alderman in 1370 on the election of Walworth as Mayor. His will dated 1374.

[13] A vintner. By his will, dated 1354, he left bequests to the fabric of St. Paul's Cathedral, to London Bridge, and to the chaplains of St. Thomas on London Bridge.

[14] A fishmonger. He was called to the first Common Council in 1347 to represent Bridge Ward. He left property to the value of 100 marks for the works of London Bridge.

[15] Cordwainer or ropemaker. He was left lands and tenements in Colman Street by Stephen de Amiens, 1348; also by John Tornegold, merchant, in 1377. By his will, dated 1385, he left bequests to every anchorite in the city, to every Lazar house within two miles, to prisoners in Newgate, etc. Under certain circumstances his property was to go to the Lord Mayor and Commonalty and the Wardens of London Bridge for the repair of the same.

[16] Vevele or Ventele, "mason," citizen and freeman of the City of London, and parishioner of the Church of St. Magnus at London Bridge. He was one of the masons' representatives to regulate trade in 1356, and in 1380 was chosen one of the four to supervise the building of a tower on each side of the Thames to protect the shipping. As in the will of Coggeshale, under certain conditions his money was to go to the use of London Bridge for the maintenance of two chantry priests.

[17] In 1383 William Waddesworth, pepperer, received property by the will of Felicia Pentry. And by his will, dated 1403, William Waddesworth, grocer, left this same property to his children, sisters and others.

[18] A grocer, of Higham Ferrers, Northampton. By his will he left certain property to his wife and the rest to a college at Higham Ferrers, founded by Henry Chichele. He was Sheriff in 1409 and Alderman in 1415, when thanks were publicly given by the Lord Mayor and Corporation for the victory at Agincourt. He was also present at Whittington's third election to the Mayoralty, 1418.

1404	William Sevenoke,[1] John Whatele.[2]	1473–74	Edward Stone, Henry Bumstede.
1405–16	Henry Julyan,[3] John Whatele.	1474–75	Peter Caldecote, William Galle.
1416	John Whatele alone.[4]	1475–76	William Gall, Edward Stone.
1416–18	John Whatele, William Weston.[5]	1476–85	William Gall, Henry Bumstede.
1418–20	William Weston, Nicholas James.	1485–87	William Galle, Symond Harrys.
1420–21	William Weston, Richard Stile.	1487–90	Symond Harrys, John Tuttesham.
1421–33	Robert Colbroke, William Trimnell.	1490–92	Symond Harrys, Cristofer Elyot.
1433–38	Thomas Badby,[6] William Wetenhale.[7]	1492–93	Thomas Bullysdon, Robert Weston.
1438–40	Thomas Badby, Richard Lovelas.	1493–95	Symond Harrys, Cristofer Elyot.
1440–45	Thomas Cook,[8] John Herst.[9]	1495–97	Cristofer Elyot, Symond Harryes.
1458[10]–59	Thomas Davy, Peter Aldfold.[11]	1497–1500	Cristofer Elyot, Edwarde Fenkyll.
1459–67	Peter Aldfold, Peter Caldecote.[12]	1500–1	William Hotte, Edward Grene.
1467–68	Peter Caldecote, Richard Frome.	1501–9	William Maryner, Cristofer Eliot.
1468–70	Peter Caldecote, Peter Aldford.	1509–11	William Maryner, Thomas Myles.
1470–73	Edward Stone, Peter Caldecote.		

[1] Grocer. Four wills of his are enrolled—December, 1426; June, 1432; July, 1432 (2), leaving property to the Churches of St. Martin Ludgate, St. Dunstan toward the Tower, and the convent and hospital of St. Mary, Bishopsgate. By the will of a certain William Burton, it appears that William Sevenoke left another will (not enrolled in the Husting) in which he bequeathed five marks a year towards the payment of "some honest man, not in holy orders, to teach poor children," and also "ten shillings yearly to each of thirteen poor men and women." The school was founded at Sevenoaks, in Kent, and has since been re-constructed under the Endowed Schools Act. The almshouses still exist. He was Sheriff in 1413, Alderman in 1415, and Mayor in 1419.

[2] A mercer. Buried at St. Mary Abchurchbury. By his will, dated 1425, he left a house for the maintenance of a chantry in the Church of St. Christopher.

[3] He received property through his wife Elena, daughter of John Shalyngford, draper.

[4] John Whatele was the sole Warden from 31 October to 5 December, 1416.

[5] William Weston and Johanna, his wife, received the reversion of a tenement near "Mullyngshoppe," Cornhill, in 1396.

[6] A Thomas de Baddeby, grocer, possibly the father of this man, left property in Aldgate in 1398. Will dated 1397.

[7] William Wetenhale, grocer, left property in the parish of St. Mary Woolchurch, and St. Pancras, also a bequest to the "Wardens of the Mistery of Grocery of the City of London, in trust for pious and charitable uses," 14 February, 1455.

[8] Described as Senior.

[9] A skinner. He left two wills, one only enrolled in the Husting. Careful directions are left that from a certain house the windows and lattices, cupboards, etc., are not to be moved, but are all to go to the maintenance of a chantry in St. Stephen's, Walbrook. In default the bequest is to go to the maintenance and use of London Bridge.

[10] The volume of the Bridge House Accounts for 1445 to 1458 is lost, so that the list of Wardens cannot be given for this period.

[11] Aldfold or Aldford.

[12] Or Caleot.

1511–12	Thomas Myles, John Hyll.[1]	1593–94	Richard Denman.
1512–22	Symond Ryce, William Campyon.[2]	1594–1615	Richard Denman, John Hall.
		1615–18	John Hall, John Langley.
1522–24	Symond Ryse, Thomas Carter.	1618–25	John Langley, Richard Foxe.
1524–29	William Campion, Thomas Carter.	1625–31	Daniel Hille,[11] Humphrey Hall.
		1631–36	John Potter,[12] David Bourne.
1529–30	Thomas Carter, Thomas Crull.	1636–42	John Hawes, Noadiah (sic) Rawlin.
1530–40	Thomas Crull, Robert Draper.		
1540–47	Robert Draper,[3] Andrew Woodcoke.	1642–43	John Hawes.
		1643–45	Francis Kirbie, Henry Allen.
1547–48	Andrew Woodcoke, John Sturgeon.[4]	1645–55	Francis Kirby, Nicholas Claggett.
1548–57	Andrew Woodcok, Thomas Maynard.[5]	1655–59	Francis Kirby, Nathaniell Hall.
1557–58	Richard Bearde, William Chambers.	1659–61	Francis Kirby, Robert Hussey.[13]
1558–67	William Draper,[6] Robert Esshington.	1661–69	Robert Hussey, Anthony Scarlet.[14]
1567–68	Robert Esshington, Thomas Bates.[7]	1669–77	William Rutland,[15] William Allott.[16]
1568–74	Thomas Bates, John Randalle.[8]	1677–78	Francis Parson, Richard Brackley.
1574–85	Thomas Bates, Robert Aske.[9]	1678–79	Richard Brackley, John Sexton.
1585–88	Robert Aske, James Gonnelde.[10]	1679–80	John Sexton, Matthew Sheppard.
1588–92	James Gonnelde, Thomas Ware.[11]	1680–82	John Sexton, Richard Brackley.
1592–93	James Gonnelde, Richarde Denman.	1682–84	Richard Brackley, William Togham.

[1] John Hill, grocer, took the place of William Mariner, deceased, on 20 April, 1512.

[2] Symond Ryce, mercer, and William Campyon, grocer, had associated with them on 22 September, 1518, Nicholas Warley, goldsmith, and Thomas Carter, draper.

[3] A goldsmith. There was a Draper family well known in Camberwell, and a certain Robert Draper was Page of the Jewel Office to Henry VIII.

[4] Sturgeon left a piece of land in Finsbury Fields and another near Newgate, known as "graye fryers," to the Lord Mayor and citizens of London; also an annuity of 40s. to the Church of St. Benedict, Gracechurche. Woodcoke and Sturgeon were called "Keepers" for the first time. Haberdasher.

[5] Maynard *loco* Sturgeon, elected governor of Merchant Adventurers' Co.

[6] Died in the following year.

[7] Elected 15 January, *loco* Draper deceased.

[8] Both Haberdashers. Randalle elected *loco* Esslington deceased.

[9] Goldsmith. 8 July, *loco* John Randall deceased.

[10] Stationer. 4 February, *loco* Thomas Bates.

[11] Fishmonger. He left a messuage in Thames Street to the Fishmongers' Company. He was to be buried near "Bersabe," his last wife. By a second will he left money for an annual dinner to the Fishmongers' Company, and twenty-four pence a week to be given to poor people.

[12] Richard Hilles left to his "nephewe," Daniel Hilles, houses in the parish of St. Botolph's, to be held in trust for him till the decease of his son Gerson. 1587.

[13] To 28 June. His widow is mentioned in a will enrolled 1647.

[14] Robert Hussey, Salter.

[15] Anthony Scarlet, Grocer.

[16] William Rutland, Leatherseller.

[17] William Allott, Merchant Taylor.

1684–88	Richard Brackley, Thomas Nicholas.
1688–96	Thomas Nicholas, Isaac Puller.
1696–98	Isaac Puller, George Sittwell.
1698–1702	George Sittwell, Thomas Crane.
1702–9	George Sittwell, John Pitt.
1709–17	John Pitt, Robert Swann.
1717–18	Robert Swann.
1718–24	Robert Swann, Henry Owen.
1724–25	Henry Owen.
1725–26	Henry Owen, Matthew Suablin.
1726–27	Matthew Suablin.
1727–28	Matthew Suablin, John Webb.
1728–29	John Webb.
1729–34	John Webb, John Lund.
1734–40	John Lund, Thomas Hyde.
1740–44	Thomas Hyde, Thomas Piddington.
1744–46	Thomas Piddington, William Mingay.
1746–50	Thomas Piddington, John Grant.
1750–58	John Grant, Hugh Rossiter.
1758–59	John Grant, Hugh Rossiter.
1759–60	John Grant, William Smith.
1760–61	William Smith, John Grant.
1761–62	William Smith, Edmund Stevens.
1762–64	William Smith, John Shewell.
1764–65	John Shewell, John Clarke.
1765–66	John Shewell, John Nicholls.
1766–72	John Shewell, John Tovey.
1772–75	John Shewell, Thomas Borwick.
1775–79	Thomas Borwick, John Townsend.
1779–81	John Townsend, David Buffer.
1781–83	John Buffer, R. Haslefoot Garrard.
1783–84	John Buffer, Joseph Dixon.
1784–87	John Dixon, John Burbank.
1787–92	John Burbank, Joseph Speck.
1792–96	Joseph Speck, John Redhead.
1796–1801	Joseph Speck, John William Galabin.
1801–5	J. W. Galabin, Samuel Marriott.
1805–7	J. W. Galabin, Joseph Wells.
1807–20	J. W. Galabin, Richard Yeoward.
1820–24	J. W. Galabin, Richard Thodey.
1824–25	J. W. Galabin, Lewis Lewis.
1825–31	Lewis Lewis, William Gillman.
1831–41	Lewis Lewis, Joseph Walson.
1841–49	Joseph Walson, David Gibbs.
1849–54	David Gibbs, George Ledger.
1854–55	George Ledger, Charles James.
1855–64	Charles James, Thomas Plant Rose.
1864–77	Thomas Plant Rose, Edward Ledger.
1877–82	Thomas Plant Rose, William Henry Kemm.
1882–94	William Henry Kemm, John Beckwith Towse.

2. The Oath of the Wardens of the Bridge.

6 Edward II. This oath is entered with documents of this date but of
a much later hand, probably Henry VII.

Juramentum custodum Pontis London.

Ye shal swer that ye shall wel and lawfully serve the Cite of London in the offis of the Warden of the Brigge of the same Cite and what so evere ye have in your warde towchyng the goodes or profit of the same Brigge, be hit in londis, rentes, tenements, or comodites to the same Brigge perteynyng, savely and surly ye shal kepe hit to the use and profit therof. And the same Brigge and the londis and rentis ther to perteynyng trewly ye shal repeyr and susteyne. And alle the profites and avauntages that ye may ther to do after your wit diligently ye shal do and reasonably encrece.   And harme to the Brigge londes, rentes, ne tenementes a bove seid ye shall non do ner in as myche as in yow is suffre to be do but be your power ye shall lette hit other ellis to the mayr and aldermen of the same Cite for the tyme beyng in all haste that ye dewly may ye shal do wityng.   And ye shal make no byldyng of newe rentes or tenements above seid withowte lycence, assent, and consent of the mayr aldermen and comyn councell of the seid Cite.   And all the ston, tymber, yryn, and led and other necessaris to the use of the seid Brigge londes and tenements thereof nedeful ye shal bye or do bye at the lowest pris that ye can or may, withowte eny encrece or wynnyng to your use or profit in eny wise.   And in these thyngis a bove seid and in alle other thyngis that longith to the wardens of the Brigge of London and to the londes, rentes, and tenements, therto perteynyng for to do, wel and lawfully ye shall do.   And in your acownte be for the auditours be the seid Cite assignyd holly with owte concelement of eny of alle the profites commodities or avauntages thereof receyvid or comyng ye shall your sill charge and non unlawfull a lowaunce aske as God yow helpe and Alle Seyntes.

3. Abstract of earliest extant Wardens' Account,
1381-2.

John Hoo and Henry Yevele, Wardens of London Bridge from the twenty-ninth day of September, the feast of St. Michael the Archangel, in the fifth year of the reign of King Richard the Second after the Conquest to the same feast then next following in the sixth year of the reign of the King aforesaid.

Arrears from the last account 22*l.* 1*d.*

Rents and farms :   The same render account of 380*l.* 16*s.* 4*d.* received from the rents of tenements in London and Southwark, and of 12*l.* from the rent of twenty [fishmongers] standing under the Wall of the Friars Minors, London, and 30*l.* 3*s.* 2*d.* from quitrents in London and Southwark, and 33*l.* 11*s.* 10*d.* from the farm of manors and lands at Lewisham, Stratford, the fields of Hacchesham, Camberwell and Southwark.

Sum 460*l.* 11*s.* 4*d.*

Increment of Rents :— The same render an account of 57*s.* 9*d.* from the increment of the rents of divers tenements.

The same render account of 20*s.* from the farm of the fishery under London Bridge.

The same render account of 136*l.* 11*s.* 6*d.* from the fishmongers and butchers standing at lez stockes, for the passage of ships under the bridge, and from carts passing over it.

For 32*l.* 18*s.* 8*d.* from thirty-eight cupboards for the drapers standing over lez stocks, and the sale of cloth.

Sum of the receipts 755*l.* 19*s.* 6*d.*

Whereof the same pray allowance of 48*l.* 15*d.* on account of divers tenements vacant, and of 18*l.* 8*s.* 4½*d.* for rents resolute payable from certain tenements, of 20*l.* for the stipends of the Wardens, and 10*l.* for a man collecting the rents belonging to the bridge, and of 50*l.* 9*s.* 8½*d.* for divers expenses.

Sum total of allowances 699*l.* 19*s.* 2¼*d.*, and so they owe upon the account 56*l.* 3¼*d.*

After this follows an account in detail of the receipts week by week, of rents, tolls, etc., payable to the Wardens ; occasionally an item appears for some extra receipt, such as 6*s.* 8*d.*

received from a Flemish mariner for damage done by his boat to the Bridge House ; 6s. from the sale of 1,000 Flaundrish tyle ; 3s. 4d. from Gilbert Beuchamp, fishmonger, for a gersum of certain shops in Bridge Street which James Rameseye, fishmonger, held ; 3s. 2d. received from the collection upon the bridge on Easter Day, and various legacies.

The weekly expenses then follow, which include 11s. 5½d. a week for the wages of five chaplains celebrating in the Chapel upon the bridge ; 3d. for bread and wine, 15d. for the clerk of the Chapel, 20d. for the clerk of the drawbridge, 22s. for the wages of six carpenters, 14s. 3d. for the wages of four masons, 7s. for the wages of two sawyers, 2s. 6 l. for the wages of a mariner, 2s. 6d. for the wages of the cook and [keeper] of the dogs, 22d. for the wages of the carter, 15d. for provender for the horses, 2s. for the wages of a boy, 2s. 4d. for the wages of a paviour, 4s. 6d. the wages of one plasterer and his servant, 12s. for the wages of twenty-one tidemen working at the ram for six hours : besides these there occasionally occur the expenses of the repair of the house and tenements belonging to the Wardens, for paving, a new boat, incense, surplices and other vestments for the Chapel, one " polyne de laton " weighing 55lbs, for a certain " portcodys " in the stone gate upon the bridge.

A quarterly account of the tenements vacant, in which there are mentioned the weigh house and counting house upon the bridge, and a mansion in the stone gate upon the bridge.

4. Grant by Michael Tovy and the Brethren of the Bridge to Roger Alabaster and Emma his wife.   Sealed with the Common Seal of the Bridge.

(See illustration on p. 41.)

[Translation.]

To all seeing or hearing the present writing, Michael Tovy, Proctor of the Bridge of London, greeting know all ye that I with the common assent, consent, and will of the brethren of the bridge aforesaid have granted, given, demised, and by the present writing have confirmed to Roger Alehast and Emma, his wife, a certain house with its appurtenances in Suwerk, in the parish of St. Olave, which house is situate upon a certain place of land lying between the land of the lord Archbishop of Canterbury on the one side and the land of Ralph de Hybernia on the other ; and the said place extends from the King's highway in front to the land of Margaret de Bodeleye behind. To have and to hold to the said Roger and Emma, his wife, freely, quietly, wholly, well, and in peace all the days of their lives, and whichever should survive the other may have and hold the aforesaid place with the house aforesaid and all its appurtenances all the days of his [or her] life as freely and wholly as they both held and had it. Rendering therefore, by the year, 6s. 8d. at the four terms of the years, to wit, at the Feast of St. Michael 20d., at the Nativity of Our Lord 20d., and at Easter 20d., and at the Feast of St. John the Baptist 20d. for all services, exactions, suits and demands. So, nevertheless, that the said place with the house and all its appurtenances after the decease of the longer liver may revert, quit and free, to the said bridge without any contradiction, impediment, and further delay. And I, Michael, and the brothers of the bridge aforesaid will warrant, defend, and acquit the aforesaid place with the house and all its appurtenances to the said Roger and Emma, his wife, while they live, against all men and women during the aforesaid term at our own costs, charges, and expenses. And that this our grant, gift, demise, warranty, defence, and acquittance and confirmation of our present charter may remain ratified and confirmed during the aforesaid term, we have made them the present charter, sealed with the common seal of the bridge aforesaid. These being witnesses: Sir J., at that time Dean of Suwerk, Ralph de Hybernia, William the vintner, Sir Henry the chaplain, Reginald de Helte . . . , Godwin the serjeant, Ralph le Chaloner, and many others.

5. Rents of Houses on the Bridge, 1358.

This following rental was made by Richard Baconn and John de Hatfeld, "chandelre," Wardens of the bridge, and written by John de Canefeld, chaplain controller, in the 32nd year (1358) of the reign of King Edward the Third after the Conquest.

Rental of the tenements belonging to the Bridge of London, in London, Southwerk, Hacchesham, Camerwelle, Lewesham, and Stratford, as they lie in divers parishes.

UPON LE CAWE.

Towards Bermundesseye are two shops with a garden, which are situate between the Hospital of St. Thomas of Southwerk on the west and a tenement, formerly of Walter de Mourdon, on the north side, and the causeway (cawe') which leads towards Bermundesseye on the east, and is worth by the year to the bridge 10s.

BEHIND THE GARDEN OF THE BRIDGE HOUSE.

In the parish of St. Olave of Southwerk is a shop with a garden, situate between the garden of the Bridge House on the north side and the highway on the south, and the ditch called "La Goter" on the east, and worth by the year to the bridge 10s.

Twenty-seven other shops, one inn and one brew-house.

BETWEEN THE STAPLES OF THE BRIDGE AND THE STONE GATE ON THE EAST SIDE.

TEN SHOPS.

In the aforesaid gate is a certain house which is delivered to John Bedell for keeping the gate.

Sum 11*l*. 9s. 4*d*.

ON THE WEST SIDE.

Ten shops and a mansion (mansio) in the Stone Gate.

Sum 8*l*. 2s. 4*d*.

BETWEEN THE STONE GATE AND THE DRAWBRIDGE ON THE EAST SIDE.

Seven shops (three with *hautepas*).

Sum 8*l*. 6s. 8*d*.

ON THE WEST SIDE.

Seven shops (three with *hautepas*).

Sum 8*l*.

BETWEEN THE DRAWBRIDGE AND THE CHAPEL ON THE EAST SIDE.

Seventeen shops (five with *hautepas*).

Sum 14*l*. 6s. 8*d*.

ON THE WEST SIDE.

Twenty shops (four with *hautepas*).

Sum 16*l*. 2s. 8*d*.

BETWEEN THE CHAPEL AND THE STAPLES OF THE BRIDGE TOWARDS LONDON ON THE
EAST SIDE.
Thirty-five shops (nine with *hautepas*).
Sum 50*l.*

ON THE WEST SIDE A NEW SHOP NEXT THE COUNTER.
Thirty two shops (10 with *hautepas*).
Sum 42*l.* 16*s.* 4*d.*

6. Inventory of Stores at the Bridge House, 1350.

Reprinted from Riley's "Memorials of London," 1868, pp. 261-2. The notes are Mr. Riley's.

Inventory and valuation of stores belonging to the works at London
Bridge, delivered to the Wardens thereof by the outgoing Wardens.

24 Edward III. A.D. 1350   Letter Book F, fol. cxv.   (*Norman French.*)

"This is an indenture, made on the Thursday next after the Feast of All Hallows
[1 November], in the 24th year of the reign of King Edward, after the Conquest, the Third,
between Aleyn Gille and John de Hardingham, late Wardens of London Bridge, upon their
surrender of such Wardenship, of the one part, and John Litle and James Andrew, now
Wardens of the same bridge, upon their entry on the same Wardenship, of the other part;
that is to say, as to the goods and chattels found in the court of the house[1] belonging to the
said bridge in Suthwerk and elsewhere, which have been appraised and delivered by this
indenture unto the aforesaid John and James, to answer for the same to the Mayor and to
the Commonalty of the said City at the fitting time, that is to say:

"400 great pieces of oak timber, value 40*d.* by the piece, making 100 marks. Also a
pile of timber, lying in the garden close adjoining to the water of Thames, valued at
20 marks. Also, timber for 14 shops, fully wrought and framed for immediate building,
36*l.* Also, divers pieces of timber, lying in various places in the said court, valued at
19*l.* 6*s.* 8*d.* Also, 120 pieces of elm for piles at 2*s.* the piece, 12*l.* Also, in the grange 125
rakes,[2] at 5*d.* each, 52*s.* 1*d.* Also divers boards of oak and of *estrichebordes*[3] value
6*l.* 12*s.* 4*d.* Also, 57,000 *hertlathes*,[4] value 4*s.* per thousand, 11*l.* 8*s.* Also, 30,000 *saplathes*,[5]
value 2*s.* per thousand, 3*l.* The total of the items before mentioned being 166*l.* 10*s.* 1*d.*
Also, 690 feet of stone of Porteland, hand worked and squared, as also, 1044 feet of stone of
Porteland, not wrought, the total being 1734 pieces, value 5*d.* per piece, 36*l.* 3*s.* 11*d.* Also,
600 feet of *Corsbon*,[6] value 5*s.* per hundred, 40*s.*[7] Also, 18 great stones of Bere,[8] weighing

---

[1] The old Bridge House.
[2] For catching refuse carried down by the stream.
[3] Deal boards from the eastern countries, probably the Baltic.
[4] Superior laths, made of the heart of wood.   [5] Laths, with the sap in the wood.
[6] Correctly, 2*s.* 6*d.*   [7] Corner-stone.   [8] Correctly, 30*s.*   [9] Perhaps stone from Bere Regis, in Dorset.

18 tons, value 6s. 8d. per ton, 6l. Also, a heap of mixed mortar, value 4l. 8s. Also, 12,000 tiles, value 8s. per thousand, 4l. 16s. Also, cement for the bridge, 3l. Also, 7 barrels of pitch, value 4s. per barrel, 28s. Also two boatloads of *ragston*, value 23s. Also, one boatload of chalk, value 7s. 6d. The total of the stone and other items being 59l. 6s. 8d.

"Also, in the *werkhous*, 7½ weys of old lead, value 6s. 8d. per wey, 50s. Also 12,000 of *plaunchenail*[1] in the same house, value 4s. per thousand, 48s. Also, 3,000 of *dornail*,[2] at 2s. 6d. per thousand, 7s. 6d. Also 400 large nails for the drawbridge, at 12d. per hundred, 4s. The total thereof being 3l. 9s. Also, one mazer, with a silver foot, value 10s. Also, 3,000 great plaunchenail and 7,200 dornail, the total whereof is 10,200, at 4s. the thousand, 40s. 10d. Also, 2,400 of *wyndnail*,[3] at 2s. 6d. the thousand, 6s. 6d. Also, 23,000 of *rofnail*,[4] at 12d. the thousand, 23s. Also 9,000 of *traversnails*,[5] at 8d. the thousand, 6s. Also, in the chapel there, in a *pokete*,[6] 2,500 of wyndnail, at 2s. 6d. the thousand, 6s. 6d.[7] Also, 500 *grapes* of iron, at one penny each, 41s. 8d. Also, 18 pieces of new cord, weighing 1,640 lb., at 8s. per hundred, 6l. 11s. Also 110 irons for piles, value 4d. per iron, 36s. 8d. The total of which amounts to 16l. 2s. 2d.; the whole of the sums aforesaid being 220l. 18s. 2d.

"There were also delivered unto the aforesaid John le Litle and James Andrew, Wardens of the bridge, the articles underwritten, but not valued, belonging to the said bridge, that is to say: one great boat, and one small boat, and one *shoute*[8]; also, two engines with three *rammes*, for ramming the piles of the said bridge; two cauldrons for melting pitch for cement; one presser for fixing; five pots of brass; and four posnets, old and worn out."

7. Inventory of Ornaments and Goods in the Chapel, 1350.

Reprinted from Riley's "Memorials of London," 1868, pp. 263-4. The notes are Mr. Riley's.

Inventory of Articles in the Chapel on London Bridge, delivered to the Wardens thereof by the out-going Wardens.

24 Edward III, A.D. 1350.   Letter Book F, fol. cxvi.   (*Latin.*)

This is an indenture made between Aleyn Gille and John de Hardyngham, late Wardens of London Bridge, of the one part, and John Litle and James Andrew, the present Wardens of the bridge aforesaid, of the other part; that is to say, as to the books, vestments and other ornaments and goods in the Chapel thereof found, and to the same belonging to the aforesaid present Wardens by this indenture delivered, namely:—

---

[1] Plank-nails.
[2] Door-nails.
[3] Window nails.
[4] Roof-nails.
[5] Tree-nails.
[6] Pocket, poke, or bag.
[7] The value of the *pokete*, or bag, must be included here.
[8] Prongs.
[9] Or schuyt: a large for timber is probably meant here, similar to vessels from the Low Countries, so called.

In the first place 3 Portifories[1] with notation,[2] two of which are covered with white and one with red leather ; also, 3 Legends of Saints, 4 Psalters, 3 Gradals[3] with notation, and 1 Tropary[4] with the Sequence[5] and other chaunts ; Also 2 Antiphonars,[6] of which one is in notation, without the Psalter ; 1 quire filled with Hymns and Meritatories[7] ; 1 Ordinal[8] with a Martyrology of the Saints ; 2 Missals, one of which is in notation, and the other without notation ; 1 book, which is called an " Epistolar " ; also 1 Missal, well set to notation, with large letters, well gilt.

Also one veil[9] for lent ; also, 2 linen cloths for covering the cross, and the image of St. Thomas[10] before the altar ; also, one towel[11] with an edging of samite,[12] with heads of the apostles thereon ; also, 7 towels of the said cloth, for covering the altar ; also, 3 napkins,[13] and 4 sets of vestments for week-days, with the chasubles, amices, and other things pertaining thereto ; also, one set of vestments for Sundays, with all the appurtenances thereof ; one set of vestments for festivals, with the chasuble and other appurtenances ; also, 9 surplices ; also, 3 chalices with patens, one chalice of which is well gilt ; also, one silver cup for the body of Christ ; also, 5 choir cops, and 4 tunicles of silk and other materials, in divers colours ; and one silver thurible,[14] with one silver boat for holding incense ; also, one *paxbred*,[15] covered with a silver plate, with a gilded image on it of the Holy Trinity. One cross of latten ; 5 candlesticks, three of which are *peautre*, and two of latten ; 2 corporals,[16] with their cases ; also 5 phials of *peautre*, and one silk cloth for the altar ; also divers relics of Saints, with two silver phials, which are shut up in a certain chest with an iron lock, the key of which is now in the custody of the aforesaid John and James, the present wardens ; also, a cross, in which is set a portion of the Cross of Christ ; and a vessel of crystal with a silver foot, and a ring with a tooth of St. Richard, as it is said ; together with divers relics within the said crystal ; and with a purse, in like manner, with divers relics in it, which always stand upon the altar of St. Thomas, for pilgrims who resort thereto ; also a small enamelled table, which stands upon the altar.

Given in the aforesaid Chapel of St. Thomas, on the Thursday next after the Feast of All Hallows (1 November), in the 24th year of the reign of King Edward, after the Conquest the Third.

[1] Or Breviaries, containing the daily service of the Romish Church.
[2] Musical notes.
[3] Or *gradiles*, books containing the responses sung by the choir.
[4] A book of Tropes or verses preceding the Introit on Festivals.
[5] Or Prose, a song of Exultation.
[6] Books of Antiphons or Anthems.
[7] Probably lists of *Merita*, or relics of Saints.
[8] A book of the Ritual.
[9] For covering the altar.
[10] A'Becket, to whom the Chapel was dedicated.
[12] *Pailleu.*
[11] A rich texture of silk.
[13] *Manutergia.*
[14] Or censer.
[15] Or *pax lords*, a tablet of wood or metal, ornamented with some sacred device, and used in the service of the mass.
[16] Cloths for covering the consecrated elements.

8. Account of Bastard Falconbridge's attack upon the Bridge, 1471.

From the Wardens' Accounts, Mich. 10 Ed. IV to Mich. 11 Ed. IV.

Allowance of the rent of 14 tenements situate upon the bridge, in the parish of St. Olave, between the drawbridge and the stone gate, newly constructed, burnt by the most wicked rebels and traitors of the King. Thomas Facomberge, lately named Bastard Facomberge, Nicholas Gascoyne, John Bromley, and John Benstede, Knights, and very many other rebels adhering to them, to the number of 20,000 persons, arrayed and armed in warlike manner, imagining among them to depose the King, coming to the City of London on Saturday, 11 May, in this year, with banners and pennons displayed with "gonnes" and other habiliments of war, and falsely and traitorously beseiged the same City as if they were in a land of war, and burnt a certain gate of the City, situate upon the said bridge, on Sunday, 12 May, and the said 14 tenements on Tuesday next following, and feloniously killed and murdered Richard Gamell, citizen and bowyer of the same City with other faithful leiges of the King, and wounded other faithful leiges of the King, keeping the City against the same rebels, 8 li. (6s. 8d.).

Foreign expenses: paid to John Miles and William Pye, watching and attending upon George Ireland and Thomas Stalbrooke keeping the gate upon the bridge in the month of October, at the entry of divers Knights, Esquires, and other persons coming to the City of London attending upon George, Duke of Clarence; Richard, Earl of Warwick; George, Archbishop of York, and other Lords then congregated and delivering the Lord Henry the Sixth, late (in deed, but not of right) King of England from the Tower of London there a long time detained, the same John Miles and William Pye watching 4 days and 4 nights, 6s. 8d., and to Roger Payne and William Pykerell watching and attending there for 3 days and 3 nights, 6s. For the expenses of the said Aldermen and others with them there at the time aforesaid beyond 66s, allowed for the same expenses last year, 24s. To —— Chamberlain for the wages of 4 men called "gunners," there attending for the defence of the City for 3 days and 4 nights, 18s. 8d. To the same for carriage of guns and other habiliments of war to the bridge, 18d. To the same for 12 bows, 20s. To the same for 12 sheaves of arrows, 18s. To the same for 6 lb of "gunne poudre," price of a lb. 12d., 6s.

In money paid for divers expenses in the defence of the City of London, at the bridge aforesaid, in the month of May, against the traitors and rebels, Thomas Facomberge, lately called Bastard Facomberge, and Nicholas Gascoyne, and many other rebels of the King adhering to them, to wit, the carriage of guns and other ordnance from Guyhalda of London to the bridge 2s., and for 38 lb. of gunpowder 38s. To William Takley, Thomas Baker and John Clement for 3 days and 3 nights, and to John Davy for 6 days and 6 nights watching and attending the guns, each of them taking by day and night 20d., 25s.; and for 12 bows bought, price of each of them 20d., 20s.; and for 11 sheaves of arrows 76s. 6d. Money paid to men, for their labour and horse hire for them, called "spies," to inquire and view the same rebels coming and returning 13s. 4d. For the carriage and re-carriage of 12 "sakkes" of stone and wood from Leadenhalle to the bridge and placed there for defence from the guns fired at the bridge by the same rebels 2*s.* 2*d.*, and for 41 yards of canvas bought and put in vineger and hung over the drawbridge for defence from fire called " wildefire " fired by the same rebels at the said drawbridge 17*s.* 1*d.* For 6 barrels of vineger bought for the said canvas 27*s.* For one cable for binding and fixing the said drawbridge 22*s.* 6*d.* For cord for hanging the sacks of wool at the drawbridge 2*s.* 6*d.* To 2 carpenters for making 3 holes in the drawbridge for firing "gunneshotte" there 12*d.* For 10 lb. of candles expended in the towers next the said drawbridge 12½*d.* For 12 lendes of the livery of the City expended among the men keeping the said tower 12*d.* For 6 buckets bound with iron for removing and throwing " robissh " coming from the houses upon the bridge burnt into the River Thames 2*s.* For 7 "payles" and 4 "bolles" for throwing and sprinkling water upon the timber sinders and " le robissh " burning upon the bridge 2*s.* 2*d.* To Hugh Smert for carrying to the said bridge 62 loads of water to throw upon the fire 2*s.* 7*d.* To divers labourers removing and throwing " le robissh " into the River Thames and extinguishing the fire and in keeping the ironwork and other utensils which could be found after extinguishing the fire 13*s.* 6*d.* In bread and ale expended there among the labourers 4*s.* 4*d.* Paid to George Irelond and Thomas Stalbroke, aldermen, being there for the safe keeping and defence of the City and other good men of the City, attending upon them from Saturday, 11 May, to Wednesday following 44*s.* 10*d.* For 6 men watching in the Tower aforesaid, as well by day as night for drawing the said drawbridge from the same Saturday to Thursday following 30*s.* To John Parker, scrivener, for composing and writing a letter acquainting the King with the injuries to and burning of the new tower and 14 tenements upon the bridge by the aforesaid rebels and for providing a remedy therefor by his abundant grace 6*s.* 8*d.* For 6 empty pipes for defence between the staples of the bridge towards Southwark 2*s.* For horse hire for a messenger sent by the Mayor and Aldermen to the King from London to Coventry 4*s.* Sum 23*l.* 4*s.* 8*d.*

9. List of Principal Benefactors.

12th century. Henry Fitz Ailwyn, first Mayor of London. A quit-rent out of lands in the parish of St. Swithin.

1214 Elicia, daughter of Rose Prudence, of Southwark. Land in the parish of St. Olave, Southwark.

Temp. Henry III. Alan, son of Ralph de Hibernia. Land in the parish of St. Olave, Southwark.

1220 *circa.* Richard Renger, afterwards Mayor of London. Seynemill at Stratford.

1221 Walter, son of Maud. Land in the parish of St. Olave, Southwark.

1225 *circa.* Warin de Wadessele. Rent for land had of him.

1228 Peter de Hereford. The patronage of the church of Stanham.

1232 *circa.* Richard Tapmel. A shop in St. Leonard, Eastcheap.

1236 Roger le Duk. Bequest of a rent from houses on London Bridge.

1239 Sir Ralph de Raleg', Knt. Release of houses in the parish of St. Dunstan-in-the-East.

1240 *circa.* John Everard, senior. 2*s.* rent from a house on the bridge.

1243 *circa.* Robert de Suthwerk, cobbler. A messuage on the bridge.

1248 *circa.* Eufemia, daughter of Andrew le Ferun. A tenement adjoining the stone gate of London Bridge.

1249 Margery, daughter of Reginald de Beceles. Houses in the parish of All Hallows, London Wall.

1251　William Bernard. Rent in East Greenwich.

1257　William Ricolf. Release of a rent paid by the bridge for a curtilage called "Tussees Side."

1263　Meysenca de Solio, of Lewisham, widow. House in East Greenwich.

1268　John de Lanfare, of London. Release to the bridge of rent.

1272　Isabella la Juvene. Bequest of 5s. to the fabric of London Bridge and 2d. to the house of the same bridge.

1279　John, son of Adrian Aswi. The rent annually paid to him by the bridge for a tenement at La Lock.

1280　William, son and heir of Alex. de Lewisham. A curtilage in Lewisham called Suthaghe.

1287　William, son of Henry Boydin, William Boydin, and Thomas and Adam, sons of Richard Boydin. A rent in Lewisham.

1298　Brother John de Brockley, brother of the Bridge House. Release of all his right in the Manor of Lewisham.

13th century. Adam, son of Alexander (*temp.* Thos. de Chalk, Warden of the bridge). A house and mill in Lewisham.

13th century. Martin, son of Robert Dun. A yearly rent of 10d.

13th century. Bequest by Thomas Juvenis of half a mark towards the structure of the bridge.

13th century. Roger Walensis and Hagenilda his wife, land and tenements in the parish of St. Swithin.

1300　Gregory de Rokeslee, citizen of London, bequest of rent in the parishes of SS. Magnus and Botolph Bishopsgate.

1304　Mathew le Chaundler, citizen of London. An annual quit-rent of 1 mark in the parish of St. Leonard, Eastcheap.

1312　Richard de Halliford. A tenement in St. Denis Backchurch.

1320　Adam Besevyle. A piece of land called Hachchelond, at Brockley, in the parish of Lewisham.

1320　John de Gubbleford, cook, and Alice his wife. A tenement in the parish of St. Leonard, Eastcheap.

1322　Richard de Beusted, citizen of London, and Margaret his wife. A rent of 3s. 9d. a year in Bridge Street (Bregge Strete).

1327　Roger le Palmere. Land in the village of Lewisham.

1332 *circa.* Roger Hosebond, citizen and tallow chandler. The "Cock" in Ivy Lane.

1342　William, son of William le Wyle. Release of rent paid by bridge for Bakeresfeld, in Lewisham.

1343　Nicholas de Gloucester. A yearly rent of 10s. on a tenement in Friday Street.

1350　Richard Vincent, clerk. 5s. rent paid by the bridge for a meadow, etc., near La Lock, in Southwark.

1350　Bequest by Ralph de Lenne. Tenements in the parish of St. Mary Magdalene, Old Fish Street.

1353　Bequest by Roger de Essex. Shops in the parish of Honeyland.

1358 *circa.* Richard le Keu. A tenement in Colechurch Street.

1362　John de Hatfelde. Land in the parish of St. George's, Southwark.

1363　Bequest by Nicholas Runge, citizen and vintner. A tavern in the ward of Bishopsgate.

1369 John Malberthorp, Warden of the Friars Minors, London, and his convent. A rent charge on land in Newgate Street.

1375 William, son of Henry Elliot, called Will. de Kingston. Bequest of tenements in the parishes of St. Peter, Cornhill, and St. Magnus, Bridge Street.

1385 John Morden, called Rothing. Bequest of a tenement in the parish of St. Edmund, Lombard Street.

1386 Joan, wife of John Makyn. Bequest of land in All Hallows Barking, St. Olave, and St. Mary-at-Hill.

1386 John Coggeshale. All his land in the parish of St. Margaret Bridge Street, St. Botolph, and St. Andrew Hubberd.

1421 William East. Conditional bequest of divers tenements in the parish of St. Denis Backchurch.

1425 Richard Malt, citizen and stock fishmonger. Tenements and a wharf in the parish of St. Magnus.

1430 Christina Mallyng. Bequest of tenements in the parish of St. Mary Woolchurch.

1436 John Feckenham, citizen and brazier. Bequest of tenements in the parish of St. Augustine Papay. He directs his anniversary to be celebrated by, *inter alia*, a repast.

1440 John Edwards, citizen and butcher. Bequest of a tenement and garden in the parish of St. Botolph.

1456 John Lyttleton, citizen and mercer. Bequest of tenements in the parish of St. Mary Abbchurch.

1545 Sir William Forman. The rent from Battlebridge Mills in the parish of St. Olave Southwark, for the repair and support of London Bridge.

1545 Robert Draper, citizen and goldsmith. Meadow and pasture in Rotherhithe for the support of the bridge.

1673 Roger Gooday, of "All Hallows-in-the-Wall." 20s. yearly to be paid out of the "Bull," in Thames Street, towards the repair of London Bridge for ever.

10. Ceremonial to be observed at the Opening of the Tower Bridge

BY HIS ROYAL HIGHNESS THE PRINCE OF WALES, K.G.,

Accompanied by Her Royal Highness The PRINCESS OF WALES, on behalf of Her Most Gracious Majesty The QUEEN,

On Saturday, the 30th day of June, 1894, at Twelve o'clock.

The Prince of Wales, accompanied by The Princess of Wales and the Princesses Victoria and Maud of Wales, and by The Duke of York, will leave Marlborough House at 11.15 o'clock, attended by the Great Officers of Her Majesty's Household and the Household in Waiting.

The Carriage Procession will be formed in the following Order :—

FIRST CARRIAGE.

The Equerry in Waiting to	The Equerry in Waiting to
His Royal Highness The Duke of York.	His Royal Highness The Prince of Wales.

The Equerry in Waiting to the Queen.

SECOND CARRIAGE.

The Groom in Waiting to	The Lord in Waiting to
His Royal Highness The Prince of Wales.	His Royal Highness The Prince of Wales.

THIRD CARRIAGE.

The Comptroller to	The Chamberlain to
His Royal Highness The Prince of Wales.	Her Royal Highness The Princess of Wales.
The Lord Chamberlain.	The Lord Steward.

FOURTH CARRIAGE.

The Woman of the Bedchamber to	The Lady of the Bedchamber to
Her Royal Highness The Princess of Wales.	Her Royal Highness The Princess of Wales.
The Master of the Horse.	Her Royal Highness The Princess Maud of Wales.

FIFTH CARRIAGE.

Her Royal Highness	His Royal Highness
The Princess Victoria of Wales.	The Duke of York, K.G.
Her Royal Highness The Princess of Wales.	His Royal Highness The Prince of Wales, K.G.

A Captain's Escort of the Life Guards will accompany His Royal Highness, who will proceed by Pall Mall, Duncannon Street, the Strand, Fleet Street, Ludgate Hill, St. Paul's Churchyard, Cheapside, the Poultry to the Mansion House, and thence by King William Street, Eastcheap, Trinity Square, Tower Hill to the Tower Bridge.

The Lord Mayor, the Lady Mayoress, the Sheriffs and their Ladies, and others who are to take part in the Procession will await the arrival of the Royal Procession at the Mansion House, where the Lord Mayor will address to Their Royal Highnesses a few words of welcome.

The Procession will then proceed from the Mansion House to the Bridge in the following order :

Mounted Police.

The Engineer, John Wolfe Barry, Esq.

Albert Joseph Altman, Esq., The Chairman of the Bridge House Estates Committee.

The Under Sheriffs.

The City Surveyor.	The Secondary.
The City Solicitor.	The Remembrancer.
The Comptroller.	The Common Serjeant.
The Town Clerk.	The Chamberlain.

The Sheriffs of London.

The Recorder.

The City Marshal.

The Right Honourable The Lord Mayor.   The Lady Mayoress.

Attended by the Sword Bearer and the Mace Bearer.

The Royal Procession as above mentioned.

The following Members of the Royal Family, who will have previously arrived separately at the Northern Approach to the Bridge, where they will be received by a

Deputation of the Bridge House Estates Committee, will here join in the rear of the Procession and drive over the Bridge :—

Their Royal Highnesses The Duke and Duchess of Saxe-Coburg and Gotha.
Their Royal Highnesses The Duke and Duchess of Connaught and Strathearne.
Their Royal Highnesses The Prince and Princess Henry of Battenberg.
Her Royal Highness The Duchess of Albany.
His Royal Highness The Duke of Cambridge, K.G.
Her Royal Highness The Duchess of Teck and His Highness The Duke of Teck, G.C.B.

The Procession will pass over the Bridge, accompanied by the Escort, into Queen Elizabeth Street, turn westward round the vacant piece of land into Tooley Street, then by the Approach therefrom to the Southern abutment of the Bridge, and will then proceed to the Pavilion erected on the North Approach of the Bridge, where The Prince and Princess of Wales, the Royal Family, the Lord Mayor and Lady Mayoress, and others taking part in the Procession will alight, and Their Royal Highnesses will be conducted to the Dais.

On the Dais will be :—

Their Royal Highnesses The Prince and Princess of Wales.
The Members of the Royal Family.
The Secretary of State for the Home Department (on the Right of the Dais).
The Bishop of London and the Bishop of Rochester (on the Left).
The Lord Mayor and Lady Mayoress.
The Sheriffs and their Ladies.

The Recorder will be at the foot of the Dais on the right-hand side ; the Chairman of the Bridge House Committee at the foot of the Dais on the left-hand side, and the Engineer will be at the foot of the Dais on the right-hand side.

The following persons will be at the side of the Dais :—

LEFT SIDE.
The Members of the Bridge House Estates Committee.

RIGHT SIDE.
The before-mentioned Corporation Officers.
The Under Sheriffs.

The late Chairmen of the Bridge House Estates Committee: T. Beard, Esq., Edward Atkinson, Esq., George Shaw, Esq., Thomas Loveridge, Esq., Alfred Pursell, Esq., and Arthur Byrne Hudson, Esq., F.S.I.

The Contractors: Mr. John Jackson, Mr. William Webster, Mr. H. H. Bartlett, Sir William Arrol, and Lord Armstrong.

When Their Royal Highnesses The Prince and Princess of Wales and the other Members of the Royal Family have been seated, the Recorder will read an Address on the part of the Corporation, to which His Royal Highness will make a reply.

His Royal Highness will then, in the name of the Queen, declare the Bridge " Open for land traffic," after which His Royal Highness will turn the lever of a valve communicating with the hydraulic machinery, and when the leaves of the Bridge have been raised will declare the Bridge "Open for river traffic."

The Declaration having been made, will be announced by a Flourish of Trumpets.

A Benediction will be pronounced by the Bishop of London, The Bishop of Rochester being also present.

Upon a signal being given from the Bridge by the hoisting of a flag a Royal Salute will be fired from the Tower guns.

The firing of the Tower guns will be a signal for a procession of ships to steam up the river. The vessels will be dressed, and will consist of the following ships, viz.:—

The Harbour Master's vessel "Daisy."

The "Conservator" steamer.

The Trinity yacht "Irene."

H.M.S. "Landrail."

The President of the Local Government Board's vessel "Bismark."

The Corporation of London's steamer "Clacton Belle."

The Vintners' Company's steamer "Empress Frederick."

The London County Council's launch "Beatrice."

The General Steam Navigation Company's steam ship "Lapwing."

Messrs. Leach & Co.'s steam ship "Sea Belle."

The General Steam Navigation Company's steam ship "Oriole."

The London Shipping Exchange's launch "Orchid."

The Victoria Steam Boat Association's steamer "The Shah."

The Watermen and Lightermen's Company's vessel "The Snowdrop."

The Band on Board the "Landrail" will play "God save the Queen" as she passes through the Bascule Bridge.

The Band on board the "Clacton Belle" will play "God bless the Prince of Wales."

The following gentlemen will be presented to His Royal Highness by the Lord Mayor:—

The Sheriffs of London, Mr. Alderman Moore and Mr. Alderman Dimsdale.

Albert Joseph Altman, Esq., Chairman of the Bridge House Estates Committee and Mover of the Address.

Mr. Alderman Frank Green, Seconder of the Address.

Arthur Byrne Hudson, Esq., F.S.I., Immediate Past Chairman.

John Wolfe Barry, Esq., the Engineer.

After the Ceremony Their Royal Highnesses The Prince and Princess of Wales, and other Members of the Royal Family, will take leave of the Lord Mayor and Sheriffs, and having re-entered their carriages, will proceed along the Northern Approach, down Little Tower Hill under the Archway, and through the gate leading to the Tower Wharf, where a tent will be prepared for their reception.

Here they will be received by the Constable of the Tower and other authorities of the Tower, and will embark in the Victoria Steam Boat Association's vessel, the "Palm," placed at their disposal by the Bridge House Committee.

The following gentlemen will, on behalf of the Committee, here take leave of Their Royal Highnesses:—

The Chairman of the Bridge House Committee,

Mr. Alderman Green,

Mr. A. Byrne Hudson, and

Mr. J. Wolfe Barry, the Engineer.

Their Royal Highnesses will return privately by water to the landing stage at the Palace of Westminster, where private carriages will await them.

The Ladies and Gentlemen in attendance on Their Royal Highnesses will accompany them in the steam boat.

The Warders of the Tower will be on duty on the Tower Wharf.

The Queen's Watermen will be on duty at the stairs leading to the steamer.

The streets will be lined by troops from Temple Bar to the Tower Bridge.

A Guard of Honour of the Royal Navy will be mounted on the North span of the Bridge (West side).

A Guard of Honour of the Guards will be mounted near the Dais on the North span of the Bridge (East side).

A Guard of Honour of the Honourable Artillery Company will be mounted at the Northern Approach to the Bridge on the West side, and

A Guard of Honour of the London Rifle Brigade will be mounted on the East side. Detachments will be formed up as follows:—

The 15th Middlesex V.R.C. and the 1st London V.R.C. on the Western side of the South span of the Bridge.

The 3rd Middlesex Volunteer Artillery and the 2nd London V.R.C. and the 1st Tower Hamlets on the Eastern side of the South span.

The 1st Cadet Battalion Royal West Surrey Regiment and the 1st Surrey V.R.C. on the Western side of the Southern Approach.

The 2nd Cadet Battalion Royal West Surrey Regiment and the 3rd Battalion Royal West Surrey Regiment on the Eastern Side.

The Members of the Bridge House Estates Committee will leave Guildhall at 10 o'clock and proceed to the Northern Approach to the Bridge, where they will be set down and proceed to their places in the Pavilion.

The Chairman of the Committee, the Engineer, and the before-mentioned Corporation Officers will leave Guildhall for the Mansion House at 11.

The Lord Mayor and the Lady Mayoress, accompanied by the Sheriffs, the Under Sheriffs, the Corporation Officers, and the Chairman and Engineer, will leave the Mansion House upon the arrival of Their Royal Highnesses The Prince and Princess of Wales, and proceed to and drive over the Bridge as before mentioned.

The holders of Tickets for Seats will be admitted from 9.30 to 11 a.m., but no one will be admitted after 11 a.m.

All persons in the Procession to wear Levée or Official Dress or Uniform.

Members of the Court of Common Council to wear their Mazarine Gowns and Morning Dress.

Ladies in Morning Dress.

www.ingramcontent.com/pod-product-compliance
Lightning Source LLC
Chambersburg PA
CBHW020926120726
47905CB00008B/2400